To Colin
From Paul
with love,
and apologies
11/11/03

errata: 118, 127, ~~v~~, ix, xi

The USA in the Making of the USSR

The USA's contribution to the making of the USSR was accidental. In the belief that the Russian Socialist Federative Soviet Republic could not survive, American statesmen strove to keep the former Tsarist empire intact for a non-communist successor regime in the face of attempts by other powers to carve out spheres of influence in both European and Asiatic Russia. In this manner, they unwittingly facilitated the formation of the Union of Soviet Socialist Republics.

At the Washington Conference on the Limitation of Armament and on Pacific and Far Eastern Questions of 1921–1922, hosted by President Harding, the USA established predominance over Britain and its empire, France and Japan in a series of treaties limiting the size of the world's major navies and aiming at stability throughout the Pacific as well as on the Asiatic mainland. Meanwhile, 'Uninvited Russia' was attempting to establish its hold on the former Tsarist lands, partly through the stratagem of the Far East Republic used against Japanese intervention. In 1922, Soviet power was consolidated in the creation of the USSR.

The USA in the Making of the USSR will show the importance of the 'Russian question' at the Washington Conference and throw light on the emergence of the 'Versailles–Washington' system of international relations.

Paul Dukes is Emeritus Professor at the University of Aberdeen where he has worked since 1964. He has published widely on Russian, European and comparative history.

RoutledgeCurzon Studies on the History of Russia and Eastern Europe

1 **Modernizing Muscovy**
  Reform and social change in seventeenth-century Russia
  Edited by Jarmo Kotilaine and Marshall Poe

2 **The USA in the Making of the USSR**
  The Washington Conference, 1921–1922, and 'Uninvited Russia'
  Paul Dukes

The USA in the Making of the USSR

The Washington Conference, 1921–1922, and 'Uninvited Russia'

Paul Dukes

Taylor & Francis Group
LONDON AND NEW YORK

First published 2004
by RoutledgeCurzon
2 Park Square, Milton Park, Abingdon,
Oxon OX14 4RN

Simultaneously published in the USA and Canada
by RoutledgeCurzon
270 Madison Ave, New York, NY 10016

RoutledgeCurzon is an imprint of the Taylor & Francis Group

© 2004 Paul Dukes

Typeset in Times New Roman by
Newgen Imaging Systems (P) Ltd, Chennai, India
Printed and bound in Great Britain by
TJ International Ltd, Padstow, Cornwall

All rights reserved. No part of this book may be reprinted or
reproduced or utilized in any form or by any electronic,
mechanical, or other means, now known or hereafter
invented, including photocopying and recording, or in any
information storage or retrieval system, without permission in
writing from the publishers.

British Library Cataloguing in Publication Data
A catalogue record for this book is available from the British Library

Library of Congress Cataloging in Publication Data
A catalog record for this book has been requested

ISBN 0–415–32930–2

Contents

Preface vii
Synchronic table, 1921–1922 x
Map xi

1 Introduction: before the Washington Conference 1

The calling of the conference: 'Uninvited Russia' 3
Intervention in Russia, 1918–1920 6
Open Doors and Monroe Doctrines 13
The conference agenda 20
Perspectives 21

2 The Washington Conference: armaments and the Far East 25

Naval and land armaments 26
The Five-Power and Four-Power Treaties:
  armaments limitation 30
Siberia and the FER 34
The Nine-Power Treaty and China 38
Evaluations 43

3 Soviet Russia and the USA: the new diplomacy 48

The new diplomacy 49
The Third International and world revolution 52
The First Congress of the Toilers of the Far East 57
Soviet foreign policy and the struggle for recognition 61
US attitudes towards Soviet Russia 64
Herbert Hoover and US aid to Russia 68

4 The Far Eastern Republic: a Trojan Horse? 74

The Japanese intervention 75
The formation of the FER 79
The FER's constituent assembly 83
The continuation of the Japanese intervention 85
The Dairen Conference: 26 August 1921 to
 20 February 1922 90
The Washington Conference 93

5 After the Washington Conference: conclusion 100

Ratification of the treaties and
 the FER delegation 101
The Dairen Conference: 20 March to
 16 April 1922 106
The Genoa Conference: 10 April to
 19 May 1922 110
The Changchun Conference:
 4–28 September 1922 115
The end of the FER: the formation of
 the Soviet Union – Soviet relations with
 Japan and China 121
Conclusion 125

Notes 129
Bibliography 145
Index 151

Preface

More than thirty years ago, two books presented a re-interpretation of the Peace Conference following the First World War. A. J. Mayer, *Politics and Diplomacy of Peacemaking: Containment and Counter-Revolution at Versailles, 1918–1919*, New York, 1967, and J. M. Thompson, *Russia, Bolshevism and the Versailles Peace*, Princeton, 1966 argued the case for considering the problem of Soviet Russia as one of the major influences on Woodrow Wilson and the other statesmen in Paris, even though it was not represented there.

The present project aims at a comparable approach to the Washington Conference on the Limitation of Armaments of 1921–2, hosted by Woodrow Wilson's successor, Warren G. Harding, advocate of a return to 'normalcy'. In the authoritative assessment of Walter LaFeber, this was 'one of the most significant, and overlooked, diplomatic meetings in American history'. (Walter LaFeber, *The Clash: US–Japanese Relations throughout History*, New York, 1997, p. xix.) Much the same could be said of the Conference as far as the history of Soviet Russia is concerned. Although one official aim was to establish limits on the size of the naval and other armaments of the USA, the UK, France, Italy and Japan, as well as of other countries, there was another such aim, too, to bring stability to the Pacific and the Far East, where Soviet Russia was attempting to establish its hold on the lands of the former Tsarist empire through the stratagem of the Far Eastern Republic (FER). The book will seek to show the importance of the Russian question at the Washington Conference, even though Soviet Russia was not invited to it and has been neglected in the historiography on the subject since.

Through an emphasis on the relations between the USA and Soviet Russia, both formal and informal, in the context of the realignment of great power relations in general, it will come to the conclusion that, through its policy of the Open Door and belief that Soviet Russia could not survive, the USA strove to keep the former empire intact for a non-communist successor regime and thus facilitated the formation of the Soviet Union. Thus, fresh perspectives will be gained on the nature and significance of the 'Versailles–Washington system' of the 1920s and of international relations in later periods. Moreover, new light will be thrown on the transition of Soviet Russia from revolutionary regime to established state trying to gain recognition and take its place on the international scene, as well as on a significant point in the emergence of the superpowers, the move towards US 'isolationism' and Soviet 'Socialism in One Country'.

The exposition of the argument is part chronological part thematic. This approach has been adopted in the belief that it makes for the clearest possible exposition of a complex subject. The first of five chapters sets the global scene. While the USA vied with the other great powers for supremacy, it joined their intervention into Soviet Russia – the RSFSR or Russian Socialist Federative Soviet Republic. In the Far East, it clashed with Japan especially regarding influence in China and Siberia. Chapter 2 describes the manner in which such great power rivalry developed at the Washington Conference, while Soviet Russia protested at its exclusion at the same time as attempting to exert influence through the agency of the FER's Trade Delegation. The third chapter examines the new diplomacy of the USA and the RSFSR, with considerable attention being given to the Third International or Comintern and US famine relief as well as diplomacy itself. Chapter 4 takes a closer look at the FER, its formation, its opposition to the continued Japanese intervention and the activities of its trade delegation during the Washington Conference. The fifth and final chapter focuses on the further activities of the trade delegation as the US Senate was ratifying the Washington treaties; successive conferences in Dairen, Genoa and Changchun; and the merger of the FER with the RSFSR just after the end of Japanese intervention and just before the formation of the USSR – the Union of Soviet Socialist Republics. A conclusion evaluates the implications of the years 1921–2 and after for the Far East and the world.

People and places are given major focus where most appropriate. Thus, for example, while the US Secretary of State Charles Evans Hughes and the Soviet People's Commissar for Foreign Affairs Georgii Vasilevich Chicherin make frequent appearances in the first two chapters, Chapter 3 on American–Soviet relations has been deemed the most appropriate place for assessments of these two leading players in the drama. Chapters 1 and 2 make extended use of two perceptive contemporary commentators, the American Raymond Leslie Buell and the Russian L. E. Berlin. The FER, while receiving earlier mention, is not fully described before Chapter 4 which is devoted to it. A synchronic table for the years 1921–2 and a map of the Far East from 1922 aim at further clarification.

Preface ix

Acknowledgements go to Cathryn Brennan, Alexander O. Chubarian, Owen Dudley Edwards, Robert W. Foglesong, Clifford Foust, John Kent, L. N. Nezhinskii, Edward Ranson, Jon Smele, Joyce Walker, Wang Li and Natalia I. Yegorova; associates of the Queen Mother Library in Aberdeen, the British Library in London and the Boldleian Library in Oxford, of the Library of Congress in Washington, DC, of the Arkhiv vneshnei politiki russkoi federatsii and History Library in Moscow. While I am grateful for all these sources of help, I must single out for special gratitude Owen Dudley Edwards, Robert W. Foglesong and Jon Smele, all three of whom have read versions of the whole work and made most useful comments. Of course, I accept full responsibility for the final version. Warm thanks are due also to Cathryn Brennan for her research assistance as well as her expert advice and constant companionship. The dedication is to Walter LaFeber, whose publications have influenced me greatly and whose friendship, guidance and support have helped me more than I can easily say.

Paul Dukes
King's College, Old Aberdeen
10 December 2003

Synchronic table, 1921–1922

USA	UK and EUROPE	RSFSR	Far East
4 March Harding's Inaugural	16 March Anglo-Russian Trade Agreement	15 March New Economic Policy announced	12 February–26 April Constituent Assembly of FER
8 July Washington Conference invitations	21–29 June British Imperial Conference	22 June–12 July Third Comintern Congress	26 August–20 February Dairen Conference
12 November 1921–6 February 1922 Washington Conference	6–12 January Cannes Conference	21 January–2 February First Congress of the Toilers of the Far East	18 March FER–RSFR economic union
9 February Foreign Debt Funding Act	10 April–19 May Genoa Conference	16 April Rapallo Treaty with Germany	20 March–16 April Dairen Conference
28 July Recognition of Estonia, Latvia and Lithuania			
			4–28 September Changchun Conference
21 September Fordney–McCumber Tariff Act		5 November Treaty with Mongolia	15 November FER–RSFSR political union
	20 November–24 July Lausanne Conference	30 December Creation of USSR	

Source: Drawn by James M. Darley. J. B. Wood, 'The Far Eastern Republic', *National Geographic Magazine*, XLI, 6, p. 567. Used with permission of the National Geographic Society.

1 Introduction
Before the Washington Conference

In his inaugural address of 4 March 1921, President Warren G. Harding declared that 'we must strive for normalcy' in order to reach stability. As far as international relations were concerned, he rejected the Versailles peace so passionately defended by his predecessor Woodrow Wilson, asserting that 'a world supergovernment is contrary to everything we cherish' (although during the campaign he had talked of an 'association of nations'). In particular, Harding stated that 'the League Covenant can have no sanction by us'. In general, he stressed that to retain American sovereignty inviolate was not selfishness, but sanctity: neither aloofness nor suspicion of others, it was 'patriotic adherence to the things which made us what we are'. On the other hand, under his leadership, the government of the USA would confer and take counsel with other nations in order 'to recommend a way to approximate disarmament and relieve the crushing burdens of military and naval establishments'.[1]

Meanwhile, other nations were also attempting to adhere patriotically to the things that had made them what they were. Both in Europe and Asia, however, there could be even less return to 'normalcy' than in the USA. For the First World War had brought vast changes to virtually every quarter of the globe. On the continent of Europe, three empires – the Austrian, the German and the Russian – had fallen (not to mention the partly European Ottoman), while the French had lost much of its strength. And if the sun was not yet setting on the most powerful of all empires – the British, it had certainly passed its zenith. In Asia, the sun was rising on Japan, seeking to assert its power throughout the Pacific region, at sea and on land, especially in China, which still awaited a new dawn.

By 1921, the USA was becoming the world's strongest power, taking over from Great Britain. The new order was made brutally clear by Warren G. Harding's Secretary of State Charles Evans Hughes at a meeting with the British Ambassador Sir Auckland Geddes in mid-April. Hughes had earlier sent Geddes a note requesting British support versus Japan on a minor matter concerning the small Pacific island of Yap which was a significant communications centre. Geddes observed that his government's reply would no doubt make some mention of His Majesty's obligations as set out in the Anglo-Japanese alliance of 1902. According to the Ambassador, the Secretary of State stood up as if stabbed with his face turning the colour of 'the light rings in boiled beet-root', and began a lengthy invective charged with high emotion

> You would not be here to speak for Britain! You would not be speaking anywhere! England would not be able to speak at all it is the Kaiser (all this in a grand crescendo moving to a shouted climax) – the Kaiser who would be heard, if America seeking nothing for herself, but to save England, had not plunged into the war and (screamed) won it!! And you speak of obligations to Japan.

Hughes, somewhat inconsistently since his own government had rejected it, declared that the Versailles Treaty had removed all previous obligations.[2]

The Anglo-Japanese alliance of 1902 had recognised the interests of both powers in China and provided for the defence of those interests. Renewed in 1905 and 1911, it was due to expire in 1921, and therefore constituted one of the most important subjects for discussion at the British Imperial Conference in the summer of that year. In his opening address on 21 June, Prime Minister Lloyd George declared that 'Friendly co-operation with the United States is for us a cardinal principle, dictated by what seems to us the proper nature of things, dictated by instinct quite as much as by reason and common sense.' At the second meeting, the South African premier Jan Smuts observed that the British Empire 'emerged from the war quite the greatest Power in the world, and it is only unwisdom or unsound policy that could rob her of that great position'. To his mind, it seemed clear 'that the only path of safety for the British Empire is a path on which she can walk together with America... The most fateful mistake of all... would be a race of armaments against America'. Smuts was conceding, then that the world's 'greatest power' was sufficiently in decline to need the support of her transatlantic partner.[3] There was much talk at about this time of the necessity for close English-speaking relations, led by Great Britain and the USA. In the view of one commentator, they inhibited the long drift 'into a long series of wars which will sap the vitality of the white races and expose the civilised world, as we know it, to incursions from the barbarians of our epoch'. However, as the historian Denna Frank Fleming observed later: 'It was true that Great Britain was so impoverished by the war that she could ill afford to undertake a new rivalry, yet she could hardly be expected to relinquish without a struggle her century-old control of the seas.'[4]

The calling of the conference: 'Uninvited Russia'

On 29 June 1921, the US House of Representatives followed the Senate to pass a resolution that had first been introduced the previous December by Senator William E. Borah, one of the most implacable foes of the League of Nations and a sceptic concerning one of President Wilson's later policies, expansion of the navy. Borah proposed that the USA should collaborate with Japan as well as the British Empire to reduce naval building for the next five years by as much as a half. A congruence of interest was leading towards the realisation of the idea put forward by President Harding in his Inaugural. On 2 July, the British Imperial Conference formally called for a conference specifically concerned with the Pacific and the Far East. On 8 July, US Secretary Hughes sent cables to the American ambassadors in the UK, Japan, France and Italy instructing them to find out more generally if the governments would participate 'in a conference on limitation of armament... to be held in Washington at a mutually convenient time'.[5] Through all the diplomatic interchanges, the new realities of international power politics shone through, with the American, not the British, capital at the centre.

On 21 July 1921, the US Minister at Stockholm was handed a note composed by the Soviet Russian 'Commissar of the People for Foreign Affairs' Georgii V. Chicherin and dated 19 July, Moscow. Addressed to the governments of Great Britain, France, Italy, the USA, China and Japan, it began with the observation that the news had come to the Russian Government through the medium of the organs of the foreign press that a conference of the sovereign powers of the Pacific or possessing interests there would be convoked immediately at Washington. In its capacity as one such sovereign power, the Government of the Russian Socialist Federal Soviet Republic could not conceal its surprise on learning that the intention existed of assembling a conference of that character without its participation. Both the Russian Republic and the Democratic Republic of the Far East should have been invited. Instead, however

> the powers in question declare that they themselves will take in consideration the interests of Russia, without the presence of this latter, reserving to themselves to invite eventually a new Russian Government replacing the present government to accede to the resolutions and agreements which will be adopted there.

The Russian Government could not consent to the other powers arrogating to themselves the right of speaking for it, the more so as there was no intention of subjecting the counter-revolutionary government which might replace it to the ostracism aimed at the Russian Government. Such an attitude could be

4   *Introduction*

interpreted only as a new manifestation of the interventionist system as well as clearly favourable to the counter-revolution. The Russian Government formally declared that it would not recognise any decision, which might be taken by the Conference in question as long as this assemblage took place without its participation.

While on the one hand, 'The Russian Government would greet only with joy all disarmament or diminution of the military burdens which crush the workmen of all countries', on the other hand

> A policy aiming to leave Russia out of the collective resolutions of the different Powers upon questions which concern her, far from favoring the removal of the rivalries which trouble the world at the present time, will only aggravate them and increase them with new complications.[6]

In his note of 19 July, Chicherin claimed that the right of Soviet Russia to participate in a conference concerned with the Pacific had been plainly recognised in an exchange of views on the subject which had been communicated to the press. In a leader of 23 July entitled 'Uninvited Russia', *The New York Times* begged to differ, arguing that the note was 'probably intended for home consumption', to show how the 'Bolshevist Government' stood up to America. Erroneously, the leader said that the note had not mentioned Soviet exclusion from the disarmament part of the conference, adding 'There must not be admitted even a suggestion that the Red Army might be disbanded; for that would be fatal to the Soviet régime.'

As far as omission of the Soviet government by the USA was concerned, 'Germany might as well make a sour face over the fact that she was not invited to the Washington conference.' Several other states had not been invited – 'Not even Belgium[7] or Brazil was included.' While considering it only natural that China should be asked to send delegates, the leader went on to declare that

> No such footing as hers could possibly be asserted for Russia. The fact is that the dictatorship of the proletariat in Moscow is imitating the imperialistic tone of Czarist Russia in the days when Dalny and Port Arthur were taken from China without so much as saying by your leave.

The Soviet government had never lacked assurance, even impudence, in dealing with foreign affairs, *The New York Times* considered. Just the previous month, Chicherin had sent the British government 'a most offensive communication' in connection with a disturbance in Vladivostok, asserting that it was a proof of 'hostile activity' on the part of Great Britain.

But Lord Curzon, the British Foreign Secretary, had returned the note as 'unacceptable', pointing out that it was 'neither customary nor good manners' for one government to address 'baseless charges' to another. Curzon concluded by curtly declining to enter 'into any correspondence with you on the matter'. Should Secretary Hughes decide to give Chicherin's note any consideration, Curzon's response would doubtless be a 'model' for him.

If the new world's leading newspaper was calling in the old world to redress a perceived balance of diplomatic expertise, it could not have lighted on a better individual choice than Lord Curzon. The British Foreign Secretary combined evident self-assurance with the strong belief that... 'The British Empire is a saving fact in a very distracted world. It is the most hopeful experiment in human organisation which the world has yet seen.'[8] While Curzon conceded that the British policy of 'splendid isolation' was no longer possible, he might have had some inkling that here, too, might be a legacy for the USA. Moreover, while Curzon was a great advocate of the British Empire's moral superiority, he also shared with *The New York Times* a much dimmer view of the Tsarist Russian Empire as well as of its Soviet successor.

In a press release dated 19 September, the State Department put forward the principle that until a single recognised Russian Government was in existence, the vast territory formerly constituting the Russian Empire except for that portion conceded to the new Polish nation should remain under 'a moral trusteeship' of the powers which were to participate in the international conference in Washington in November. Secretary of State Hughes made clear the US Government's strict adherence to the position maintained under both Wilson and Harding administrations that the break-up of Russia and Siberia into a number of independent states would be a calamity. For this reason, the Far Eastern Republic (FER) centred on Chita could no more be admitted to the conference than Soviet Russia with its capital in Moscow. While the communication acknowledged the FER's concern about decisions which might be made at the conference concerning the Chinese Eastern Railway (CER), it insisted that in every respect other than the territorial inviolability of Siberia 'the principle of the open door and equal opportunity be observed'.[9]

A somewhat different reception was given two days later to the news that a special mission to the forthcoming conference in Washington was to be sent by the Russian Constituent Assembly representing virtually all the anti-Bolshevik groups and led by Nikolai Avksent'ev, the Socialist–Revolutionary, and Pavel Miliukov, the liberal Constitutional Democrat. In a leader of 27 October entitled 'Russian Relief', *The New York Times* welcomed Avksent'ev and Miliukov on their arrival in the USA as 'the representatives of sane and moderate democratic ideas which, some time or other, being those of the majority of the Russian people, must get the better of the fanatical and cruel absolutism that has brought a mighty country to ruin'. These visitors would be heard with respect when they explained Russian democratic views on the problems to be discussed at Washington. Meanwhile, 'The friendship of Americans for the Russian people, outside of the few hundred thousands of Soviet masters of the nation, is sufficiently manifested by what the two Russian statesmen call "the marvellous American Relief Administration, led by the untiring energy of Herbert Hoover"'. Miliukov was also soon to voice his satisfaction at 'the tradition of American diplomacy to defend Russia's unity from all attempts at dismembering and weakening Russia'.[10] The arrival of anti-Bolsheviks would be welcomed by the still recognised Ambassador from the Provisional Government overthrown in November 1917, Boris A. Bakhmetev, who himself had come round to the view that economic, rather than political aid to the anti-Bolsheviks in any part of Russia 'might so undermine the Soviet power as to nullify it and cause it to lose its hold and collapse'.[11] Meanwhile, the unofficial spokesman for the Soviet government, Ludwig C. A. K. Martens, had been expelled from the USA in January 1921.

At the time of the arrival of Avksent'ev and Miliukov, the FER government was asking for visas to send representatives to the USA. Although insisting that these representatives would have no official status, the State Department was understood to favour granting these visas. The anti-FER government in Vladivostok was also asking for permission to send observers to the conference, although no action had been taken in this case. Meanwhile, the White General Horvath, previously administrator of the CER, had also expressed a desire to come to Washington.[12] Amid all the conflicting claims to speak on behalf of the country, one voice was for certain not to be heard, the voice of Moscow, which remained 'Uninvited Russia'.

Intervention in Russia, 1918–1920

The lack of an invitation to Soviet Russia to attend the Washington Conference in November 1921 must be viewed in the context of American and Allied policy towards the Russian Revolution. In particular, it is necessary to consider the problem of intervention.

When tsarism fell in March 1917, the USA and the Allies were quick to recognise the new Provisional Government. The American elder statesman Elihu Root, formerly a leading business lawyer and secretary of war, was sent in the summer on a Special Mission that came to bear his name. Its avowed intent was 'to convey to the Russian democracy the good will of America, her sister democracy; to seek to establish closer cooperation and friendship between the two nations, and to learn what the needs of Russia are and to assist her in every way possible'. Although Root returned believing that his mission had been accomplished,[13] the Russian government was to be taken over in the name of the socialist Soviets by Lenin and the Bolsheviks in November 1917. Now, both the USA and the Allies held back from recognition. Understandably enough, they were reluctant to have dealings with extremists dedicated to the overthrow of world capitalism who soon demonstrated that they meant anti-business by repudiating Tsarist foreign loans and nationalising foreign assets. And how could there be relations with a regime which was quick to issue a Decree on Peace abolishing secret diplomacy, annulling annexations, declaring an armistice and calling on workers involved in the war to support the movement for peace? If anything, the policy of the first People's Commissar for Foreign Affairs was even more radical. Describing his approach as 'active internationalism', Leon Trotsky announced: 'I will issue a few revolutionary proclamations to the people of the world and then shut up shop.'[14] With the Central Powers bearing down on Soviet Russia, however, business had to be done. After lengthy negotiations necessarily quelling the appetite of some of Lenin's colleagues for revolutionary war, the Treaty of Brest–Litovsk making vast territorial concessions to the enemy, was finally signed on 3 March 1918.

Meanwhile, the USA had joined in the war in on 6 April 1917. Some months later, President Woodrow Wilson had issued his Fourteen Points for peace on 7 January 1918, acknowledging that the Russian representatives at Brest–Litovsk were 'sincere and earnest' while a voice calling for definitions of principle and purpose 'more thrilling than any of the many moving voices with which the troubled air of the world is filled' was that of the Russian people. Wilson called for the evacuation of all Russian territory pending 'an unhampered and unembarrassed opportunity for the independent determination of her own political development and national policy' as well as for other readjustments capped by a 'general association of nations... formed under specific covenants for the purpose of affording mutual guarantees of political independence and national integrity to great and small states alike'.[15]

On 20 January 1918, a telegram was sent from Acting Secretary of State Polk in Washington to the US Ambassador in Japan, with copies to his counterparts in Britain, France and China declaring that 'any movement towards the occupation of Russian territory would at once be construed as one hostile to Russia' and opposing the occupation of Vladivostok in particular. On 8 February, a fuller State Department memorandum was sent to those same representatives as well as to their colleagues in Belgium and Italy, speaking out against a British proposal to encourage and assist certain local organisations in south and southeast Russia and to allow the Japanese army to take over the Trans-Siberian Railway. On 5 March, Polk asked the

US Ambassador in Japan to advise the Japanese government against intervention. Otherwise, 'the Central Powers could and would make it appear that Japan was doing in the East exactly what Germany is doing in the West'. Moreover, the US government considered

> that a hot resentment would be generated in Russia itself, and that the whole action might play into the hands of the enemies of Russia, and particularly of the enemies of the Russian Revolution, for which the Government of the United States entertains the greatest sympathy, in spite of all the unhappiness and misfortune which has for the time being sprung out of it.[16]

Following Japanese and British landings in Vladivostok in early April, 1918, Trotsky's replacement as Commissar for Foreign Affairs G. V. Chicherin sent the first of many notes of protest to the US and the other Allied Governments. However, partly no doubt under the influence of David R. Francis, the US Ambassador to Russia[17] situated in Vologda, and other advocates of intervention, the US Government decided to send troops to Murmansk in Northern Russia in June ostensibly as part of the war against Germany. In July, following pressure from the Supreme War Council in Paris, the US Government agreed to join in the Far Eastern intervention in Vladivostok ostensibly for the protection of Czecho-Slovak troops formerly prisoners of the Central Powers and now located at different points along the Trans-Siberian Railway.[18]

On 17 July 1918, US Secretary of State Robert Lansing sent a lengthy aide-memoire composed by President Woodrow Wilson to the ambassadors of the Allied powers explaining his government's position on intervention. 'The United States is at a great distance from the field of action on the western front', he observed, but went on to add that 'it is at a much greater distance from any other field of action'. All its efforts had been put into its contribution in France, and dissipation of its force was inadvisable elsewhere, except perhaps in Italy. Furthermore, the US Government firmly believed that military intervention in Russia would add to 'the present sad confusion in Russia' rather than relieve it as well as being of no advantage in securing the USA's main aim, victory over Germany. The only possible deviations from this course would be support for the Czecho-Slovaks in the Far East and protection of military stores in the North. At the same time, the US Government did not wish to criticise in the least the policies of its Allies: for example, it would cooperate with 'a small military force like its own from Japan and if necessary from the other Allies'. However, it proposed that all those involved in Siberia or in the North should unite in publicly and solemnly assuring the people of Russia that none of them contemplated 'any interference of any kind with the political sovereignty of Russia, any intervention in her internal affairs, or any impairment of her territorial integrity either now or hereafter'. A small US commission of merchants, experts and advisers, Red Cross and YMCA representatives would be sent to Siberia for educational and humanitarian purposes only. In fact, US troops landed in Vladivostok on 5 August 1918 to fulfil the other avowed objective of prosecuting the war effort through cooperation with the Japanese to protect the Czecho-Slovaks and to guard military stores.[19]

While David Francis, the US Ambassador now in Archangel, and the Consul in Moscow, DeWitt C. Poole,[20] continued an acrimonious debate with Chicherin, Wilson and Lansing adhered to their avowed limited aims throughout the summer of 1918. On 24 October, Chicherin sent a long note to Wilson accusing the USA of complicity in a Czecho-Slovak conspiracy (financed by France to control the Trans-Siberian Railway and cut off supplies to the peasants along the Volga and in Siberia) as well as participation in an invasion of the North. While pressing for the independence of European nations under the aegis of the League of Nations, the US President had said nothing about the liberation of Ireland, Egypt or India, or even of the Philippines. The League of Nations should annul war loans and expropriate the capitalists of all countries. Only thus could peace be guaranteed and the exploitation of workers everywhere be curtailed. In the light of these latter demands, the negative response to an offer of 8 November from Chicherin to negotiate with the USA and the other Allies for the end of intervention was hardly surprising. On 2 December, Chicherin made an even more vigorous protest against Allied intervention in support of the counter-revolution being waged by the Czecho-Slovaks and White Guards.[21]

By this time, of course, the Armistice had been signed on 11 November 1918, the war was over and the stated aim of intervening to support the struggle against Germany no longer valid. On 27 November, Wilson's Secretary of War Newton D. Baker urged the President to 'simply order our forces home by the first boat', primarily because he feared that otherwise the USA might be 'rudely awakened some day to a realization that Japan has gone in under our wing and so completely mastered the country that she cannot be either induced out or forced out by any action either of the Russians or of the Allies'.[22] Despite Baker's exhortation, however, the USA became more deeply embroiled in the Russian Civil War. Moreover, in the face of warnings from General William S. Graves, the commander of the US expeditionary force in Vladivostok, about the reactionary nature of the Siberian regime led by Admiral Kolchak, the US government joined with the British, French and Japanese in lending him support. Little if any attention was paid to the observation by Graves that the peasant choice would be for a more responsible and representative government, which, in the circumstances, would appear unattainable anyway.[23]

In January 1919, the Peace Conference opened in Paris, with Wilson keen to push his Fourteen Points in the face of the scepticism of British Prime Minister Lloyd George and French Premier Clemenceau. On 22 January, the Big Three adopted a proposal for every 'organised group that is now exercising...political authority or military control anywhere in Siberia, or within the boundaries of European Russia as they stood before the war just concluded (except in Finland)' to send representatives to Prinkipo Island off the coast of Turkey for discussions with representatives of the Allies about achieving 'happy co-operative relations' between the Russian people and other peoples of the world. Chicherin, who had been continuing his denunciations of intervention and appeals for peace, gave a positive response to the invitation on 4 February. In spite of the fact that the Soviet government had not received an invitation directly, but learned about the Prinkipo Proposal from a radio review of the press, it was anxious to enter into immediate negotiations with the Allied powers wherever, and prepared to make concessions on the Russian Empire's debts and other problems. The French and White representatives in Paris were particularly passionate in their opposition to the Proposal, as was Poole in Moscow and other Americans in Paris, while Wilson was soon to point out that what he was looking for 'was not a rapprochement with the Bolsheviks'.[24] Prinkipo came to nothing.

Nevertheless, later in February 1919, Wilson sent William C. Bullitt from the State Department as head of an unofficial mission to Moscow to explore possibilities of peace with the Soviet government. After conversations with Lenin, Chicherin and his assistant Litvinov, Bullitt was able by 16 March to send Wilson the draft of a provisional agreement with the Soviet leaders pending a conference to take place as soon as possible after the beginning of an armistice, with the following terms: provisional recognition of de facto governments on the territory of the former Russian Empire; cessation of the economic blockade on Soviet Russia and restoration of fair trade relations; establishment of freedom of transport for goods and passengers along with the right of official (but specifically not diplomatic) representation for all Allied countries and Soviet republics; introduction of a general amnesty along with the conclusion of intervention; and confirmation of the acknowledgement given by the Soviet republics on 4 February of the foreign debts of the Russian Empire. With 'regard being had to the present financial position of Russia', the Russian gold seized by the Czecho-Slovaks or taken from Germany by the Allies would be regarded as part payment.[25]

Disappointed by the negative response given by Wilson to such a climbdown by the Soviet side, as well as later reports and suggestions, Bullitt resigned from the State Department on 17 May 1919. Referring to the President's own phrase from the Fourteen Points, Bullitt asserted that 'Russia, "the acid test of good will", for me as for you, has not even been understood.' A number of unjust decisions had been made, and the principle of the Freedom of the Seas abandoned, while the League of Nations appeared powerless to prevent ensuing wars. Although Bullitt conceded that Wilson had accepted most of the settlements only under great pressure, he was nevertheless convinced that 'if you had made your fight in the open, instead of behind closed doors, you would have carried with you the public opinion of the world'.[26] In spite of Bullitt's observations, and further reservations from General Graves concerning the Siberian people's support for Kolchak, Wilson joined the Allies in an invitation of 26 May to the Admiral 'to form a single government and army command as soon as the military situation makes it possible' provided that he proceeded towards the introduction of democratic government. Kolchak's reply was accommodating, but his subsequent behaviour as 'Supreme Ruler' throughout 1919 was far from democratic.[27]

Meanwhile, the US President was contemplating the shattering of his earlier great dreams. What has been called 'a Paris-chastened Wilsonian credo' had come from one of his advisers Herbert Hoover in a letter dated 11 April 1919

> I have the feeling that the revolution in Europe is by no means over. The social wrongs in these countries are far from solution and the tempest must blow itself out, probably with enormous violence... I have no doubt that if we could undertake to police the world and had the wisdom of statesmanship to see its gradual social evolution, we would be making a great contribution to civilization, but I am certain that the American people are not prepared for such a measure and I am also sure that if we remain in Europe with military force, tied in an alliance which we have never undertaken, we should be forced in under terms of co-ordination with other people that would make our independence of action wholly impossible.[28]

As finally signed by Germany on 28 June 1919, but never ratified by the USA, the Treaty of Versailles formally abrogated Brest–Litovsk. However, the territories ceded to Imperial Germany in 1918 were not now automatically returned to the 'Maximalist' or Bolshevik government of Soviet Russia.[29] Poland, to take the most important example, had been reborn from the ruins of the Russian, Austrian and German Empires. The Baltic states were also asserting their independence, as were Finland, Ukraine, Bessarabia and the Transcaucasian states – Armenia, Azerbaijan and Georgia.

As he took up the cause of ratification of the Treaty by the US Senate, Wilson also had to give attention to a request from that body dated 23 June for a justification of the reasons for sending American soldiers to Siberia and keeping them there. The President's response on 22 July was that, after they had made a great contribution to the war effort, they could now

> keep open a necessary artery of trade and extend to the vast population of Siberia the economic aid essential to it in peace time, but indispensable under the conditions which have followed the prolonged and exhausting participation by Russia in the war against the Central Powers.

In particular, the Trans-Siberian and Chinese Eastern Railways had to be kept open since the population of Western Siberia and the forces of Admiral Kolchak were entirely dependent on them. The fact that Woodrow Wilson made no mention at all of the Soviet government strongly implied that he had given a full measure of de facto recognition to that of Kolchak.[30]

For their part, Lenin and his associates continued to support the Bullitt peace plan while encouraging the idea of economic relations with the USA. In his report on the international relations of the year to the Seventh All-Russian Congress of Soviets at the end of December 1919, Chicherin mentioned several possibilities of peace including the Prinkipo Proposal and the Bullitt 'agreement'. But, of course, they had all come to naught. Through January 1920, the Soviet government kept up its offer of peace, not least through an appearance before the US Senate Subcommittee on Foreign Relations by Martens, the Soviet representative in the USA, arguing in favour of 'no forcible annexations' and 'self-determination for all nations', while expressly insisting that Soviet Russia had no intention to interfere with the establishment and development as independent states of Finland, Poland, Estonia, Latvia, Lithuania, Ukraine and 'Caucasus'.[31]

Although the offer was not accepted, there were nevertheless significant developments early in 1920. In a letter of 9 January, the State Department informed the Japanese Ambassador Shidehara that the Czecho-Slovak forces whose welfare had been one of the original reasons for intervention were about to be evacuated from Vladivostok while the situation in Siberia was so unstable and uncertain that the other purposes of intervention (to promote Russian self-government and self-defence and to protect the Trans-Siberian and Chinese Railways) could not be continued. On 30 January, however, the State Department accepted Japan's decision to continue intervention, asserting that the US Government had no desire to impede 'such measures as the Japanese Government may find necessary to the achievement of the announced purposes which induced the cooperation of the American and Japanese Governments in Siberia'.[32]

Meanwhile, in Siberia itself, there were attempts to make the situation more stable and certain, not least the first steps towards the foundation of the Far East Republic which we will examine more closely in Chapter 4. These were considerably facilitated by the execution on 7 February after capture by the Bolsheviks of Admiral Kolchak, the 'Supreme Ruler' and great White hope. Together with the impending departure from Vladivostok of the American Expeditionary Force, these events make early 1920 an appropriate moment to bring our account of intervention, if not to a conclusion, at least to a temporary halt.

The US historian David S. Foglesong argues that the Red Scare of 1919 'did not lead to greater public support for military intervention, as it was counterbalanced by a rise in isolationist sentiment'. But he also makes clear that the nature of the intervention cannot be established by diplomatic correspondence alone. He points out that action might have been taken further in the North had more Russian oppositionists rallied round the interventionist nucleus. The USA's 'secret war' against Bolshevism involved clandestine support for British activity in South Russia and intelligence activity in many areas. The search for a 'strong man', after several failures elsewhere, led the Wilson administration to back Kolchak in Siberia more than he deserved. From the point of view of Lenin and his associates, the post-Soviet historian V. I. Goldin emphasises that intervention has to be considered in the context not only of the Russian Civil War but also of the aspiration for world revolution.[33]

Undoubtedly, intervention cannot be adequately assessed as a preliminary to the Washington Conference without appropriate attention to the global circumstances in which it took place. These may appropriately be considered under the heading of 'Open Doors and Monroe Doctrines'.

Open Doors and Monroe Doctrines

Secretary of State John Hay is often credited for the enunciation of the Open Door policy. In 1899, he wrote to the other powers, with Russia and Germany most in mind, asking them to charge foreigners no more than they asked of their own citizens for privileges by sea and on land within their respective spheres of interest in China. He also requested that all powers should allow the Chinese to collect a general tariff while respecting the territorial integrity of China. Hay reiterated and reinforced such views in 1900 during the 'Boxer Rebellion'. However, while Hay may have given the two little words their capital letters, the Open Door had been the policy of the USA in China from way back in the nineteenth century, while something like it was to be directed towards other parts of the world, notably Latin America.

But a different label was applied nearer home, the Monroe Doctrine of 1823, which kept the door of the Western Hemisphere more open for the USA than for other powers. The Doctrine was originally provoked by what appeared to be Russian intervention on the west coast of North America, but France and Spain also seemed like interlopers further south. The possibility of a joint declaration with Great Britain was discussed, but President Monroe came round to accepting that to announce the policy unilaterally would be more candid and dignified 'than to come in as a cock-boat in the wake of the British man-of-war'. Moreover, Monroe and his advisers had Great Britain as well as the other powers in mind when declaring that the American continents were not to be considered as subjects for future colonisation by them and that the Old and New Worlds should keep apart as much as possible.[34]

Nevertheless, throughout the nineteenth century, as long as Great Britain ruled the waves, an important part was played by its navy in maintaining order on both sides of the Atlantic, and in the Pacific, too. For Great Britain was a senior member of the global imperial society, a circumstance which had to be kept in mind by its near equals, its juniors and by candidates for membership. Position and time, as everywhere and always in history, were of cardinal importance in addition to national characteristics in the imperialist process when it confronted its great crisis in the early twentieth century. Germany was especially determined to search widely for the consolidation of its appropriate place in the sun, which Japan saw rising to its own expansionist advantage in Asia, in particular. The First World War inflicted a great blow to the ambitions of Germany, Austria and Russia while weakening the other European powers. The major gains were made by the USA and Japan, even more on a collision course now than before.

By 1921, Japan held not only Korea which it had annexed in 1910 but also former acquisitions of Germany and Russia in China. It had a virtual protectorate over Manchuria and a foothold in Shantung province with access to coal mines as well as a military presence scattered between Port Arthur and Harbin. Raymond Leslie Buell, whose early work on the Washington Conference and its context has received positive appraisal in more recent times, commented: 'As a result of acquiring the Asiatic possessions of two European powers, Japan held the capital of China in a pair of tongs.'[35] Moreover, it also controlled three entries into Siberia: the mouth of the River Amur; the port of Vladivostok; and the port of Dairen situated in Manchuria. Japan's cruisers patrolled off Kamchatka, while her troops occupied northern Sakhalin. Such was the situation as the representatives of the invited powers convened in Washington for their conference.

Of the Japanese ideology, Buell wrote

> In the hope of misleading the world by a liberal phraseology, they have dubbed their ambitions with the high-sounding title, 'An Asiatic

Monroe Doctrine'. They blandly assert that Japan wishes to do for Asia what the United States has done for the Americas: both have undertaken a mission of mercy. But in view of the past intrigues of this military clique, the Asiatic Monroe Doctrine is obviously no Monroe Doctrine at all. Politically, the real Monroe Doctrine means that the independence of the South American nations is guaranteed by the United States against the encroachments of the world. This has been a real guarantee. The United States has never attempted to establish a political hegemony over Canada and South America. Economically, the real Monroe Doctrine means a free field for all. It has never been used to the profit of American trade and investments. In fact, the majority of foreign investments in South America before the war were held by Europeans, and the greater part of South America's foreign trade went to Germany and England. The real Monroe Doctrine means political independence and equality of commercial opportunity. The Asiatic Monroe Doctrine means political domination and the Closed Door.[36]

Buell indicated that even the US Open Door was not fully ajar, noting that 'European debts owing to this country can be paid only in goods, but goods cannot come into this country if we impose a high tariff barrier to shut them out'. Moreover, he pointed out, 'If supertariffs become general, the foreign markets of Japan will be killed; factories will close down; the Japanese people will be obliged to rely on their own soil for food, and when this becomes impossible, to seek exclusive monopolies in Asia.'[37] In the view of Asada Sadao forty years later, it was important 'to bear in mind always that Japan colored her interpretation of the Open Door by the light of the Rising Sun, that is, through the prisms of Nippon's "economic existence" and "national defense"'. Many Japanese understood this term 'in the tangible and material sense of throwing open China's resources for their exploitation rather than in the sense of equality of commercial opportunity for the citizens and subjects of all nations in China'.[38]

In a note on 'political hegemony', Buell conceded that there should be 'due regard for our occasional departures from the policy of non-intervention, as in Cuba and Santo Domingo'. He could have added Mexico, Panama and enough other examples to make these departures from the Monroe Doctrine more than occasional. As Walter LaFeber has observed

> The Japanese, resembling every other nation except the United States, viewed the doctrine as a convenient rationale for controlling neighboring territory. After all, that was how Americans long treated neighbors in Latin America. Tokyo officials had become transfixed with the idea of the doctrine because they believed they had a right to employ a similar doctrine in their region...Japan wanted not only

16 *Introduction*

to join the imperialists but obtain all the rights and privileges of the club.[39]

But that was not how it appeared to most US observers in the early 1920s, including Buell, in whose estimation Japan used three different means to carry its policy into effect: force; divide and rule; persuasion. Although the first of these was amply applied in Korea and China, even the militarists realised that it was not enough. And so, allegedly, 'to weaken Russia's position in the Orient', Japan subsidised the revolutionary movement in Finland, and then, in an agreement made at Geneva, agreed to deposit $23,000,000 in London to the credit of the Russian revolutionaries of 1905. It was also said that she had financed destabilising intrigues in Korea in order to justify her annexation, and stirred up revolts in Abyssinia and India. As well as supporting the Chinese Revolution of 1911, the militarists gave financial backing to Sun Yat-sen in 1913 and again in 1915, although the Chinese Revolution of 1917 was actually caused by China's declaration of war against Germany. Earlier in the First World War, Japan signed a secret treaty with Russia providing for 'the safeguarding of China from the political domination of any third power whatsoever'. Later, taking advantage of rumours quite possibly fomented by Japan itself that the US delegation intended to advocate international control over China at the Washington Conference, in the months leading up to it Japan took the opportunity to cry 'hands off' China and to pose as her sole defender against 'Nordic imperialism'.[40]

Further impetus for the Japanese Monroe Doctrine came from the Japanese acquisition of post-war League of Nations Mandates over the former German islands north of the equator, principally the Caroline and Marshall islands. These were less important for commerce than for communications and strategy. However, the Mandates forbade the application of conscription laws and the erection of fortifications and naval bases.[41]

Buell illustrated the workings of the Japanese Monroe Doctrine with two examples taken from the Russian Far East. On 8 January 1921, Warren H. Langdon, an American naval officer, was without any provocation on his part shot and killed by a Japanese sentry in the streets of Vladivostok. The USA's note of protest was reported to have raised the whole question of the right of Japan to occupy Vladivostok and to maintain its military authority there.[42] Although the Japanese authorities offered their regrets and condolences, they neither punished the sentry for his offence nor even discussed their rights of intervention. The second example followed the announcement in October 1920 of a lease by the Soviet government for a period of seventy years of 400,000 square miles of Far Eastern territory including Kamchatka to an American consortium represented by an adventurer named Washington Vanderlip. The lease was to include the exclusive right to exploit all oil, coal and fishing resources. According to *The New York Times* of 29 November 1920, Lenin admitted that the lease had been granted to foment dissension between the USA and Japan,[43] which already possessed some of the same concessions, especially in fishing, and had been seeking the others. Representatives of Japan pressed the Far Eastern Republic's government in Chita to extend its fishing rights and used 'Russian dummies' to acquire timber concessions. Thus, they clashed directly with the Vanderlip consortium. Here, Buell made a second exceptional admission

> As a matter of fact, it was just as reprehensible for Americans to obtain exclusive concessions in Siberia or in China as for Japanese. So far as morals were concerned, the Japanese had a better right to the exclusive exploitation of the resources than the United States, already wealthy and many thousand miles away. If the American government should recognize concessions based on the monopolistic principle, in direct contravention with the Open Door, the conflict between it and Japan would become more acute than ever. And Japan's attempt to fasten an economic monopoly on Asia would be stimulated by the bad example of this country.[44]

Buell also found examples of the workings of Japanese militarism in the Russian Far East. When the civilian members of the government became persuaded that the troops should be withdrawn because of the pressure of world opinion and the financial expense, the military party remained opposed, still wedded to their cherished dream, that of Japanese hegemony over Asia. General Tachibana, the commander of the interventionist forces, gave an interview to the Tokyo *Asahi* in which he declared that the growing opinion in favour of evacuation was unwise, adding: 'It is strange that the false impression should now prevail among some Japanese that the Empire's diplomacy has been transferred to the military from the Foreign Office authorities.' He continued: 'If the military men ever played the part of diplomats in Siberia, certainly that was only because the Foreign Office failed to take the necessary steps for the maintenance of the national prestige as well as of interest.' Buell comments that thus Tachibana proved what he had just denied: 'According to this astounding admission, the War Office interferes with Japanese diplomacy only when the latter is bold enough to run counter to the military party's designs!'[45]

General Sato had put forward the views of many of his brother officers and fellow-countrymen in his book *If Japan and America Fight*, published in 1920. He declared that Japan had been faced in her history by two great threats: the Mongolian invasion of the thirteenth century; and the Asiatic expansion of Russia, culminating in the Russo-Japanese War of 1904–5. On each occasion, victory had ensued because 'the Japanese in those days were not weak-kneed men such as the present day Japanese are!' Another threat was now posed: 'America's insolence is far worse than Russia's before the Russo-Japanese War.' Enriched by the First World War, its people were now 'drunk with gold', and its businessmen intent on carrying out 'a gigantic economic development in the east Asiatic continent and to fulfill her capitalistic imperialism on a large scale in China and Siberia'.[46]

Japanese feelings of animosity towards the USA were exacerbated by the race issue. Count Okuma had given strong voice to deeply felt sensitivities in his observation that 'the white races regard the world as their property and all other races are greatly their inferiors...The whites were defying destiny, and woe to them'.[47] Commenting on such signs in California as 'No Japanese trade wanted' and 'Shave – Japanese $10, Whites 25 Cents' as well as incidence there of violent 'deportation', *The New York Times* of 23 July 1921 remarked that such demonstrations of racial antagonism were particularly embarrassing to the Federal Government at a time when Japan was being invited to a conference to discuss not only limitation of armaments but also questions connected with the Pacific, of which she might consider treatment of her subjects to be one.

About two months earlier, at a Colonial Conference held in Tokyo in May 1921, the decision was taken to evacuate Siberia, but with severe conditions as described previously. The Japanese military were so angered that they resolved to make sure that the conditions would never be carried out. Soon, revolts broke out in Vladivostok and Nikol'sk driving the local 'independent' governments out of power. These were facilitated by the Japanese army which had neutralised the FER forces at the same time as encouraging the Kappelite counter-revolutionaries, who were among the offshoots from the forces of Admiral Kolchak. Buell remarked

> This constant intriguing of the Japanese military with the Russian *émigrés* was not so much inspired by a fear of Bolshevism, as by the desire to keep Siberia seething with disorder. If the Colonial Conference had not determined to evacuate Siberia as soon as order was assured, the Vladivostok Revolution would quite probably never have occurred. The General Staff will not be balked.[48]

Generally speaking, in Buell's view, the 'combination of big business and the military party' had given to Japan 'one of the most powerful political machines' the world had ever seen, while the 'autocratic control of the Japanese Government' was an important factor accounting for Japanese imperialism.[49] An important factor here was the Anglo-Japanese Alliance which, as originally negotiated in 1902, was brought into existence for five years. While Article I of the Alliance stated that the parties were 'entirely uninfluenced by any aggressive tendencies in either country', each party was to take such measures as were 'indispensable' for its 'special interests' when 'threatened by the aggressive action of any other Power, or by disturbances arising in China or Korea, and necessitating the intervention of either of the High Contracting Parties'. If either became involved in a war to defend these interests, the other would remain strictly neutral, unless a third party became involved, when the second ally would join in.[50]

The major first aim of the Anglo-Japanese Alliance was to oppose the designs of two other imperialisms – of Russia and Germany. If Russia had realised the aims of the pro-German and Asiatic party led by Baron Rosen, fervently believing that 'the great autocrat of Russia was divinely appointed to become the benevolent master of Asia' while giving a free hand to Germany in the Balkans, 'Pan-Germanism and Pan-Slavism would have appropriated to themselves about three-quarters of the world'.[51] The signing of the Anglo-French *Entente Cordiale* in 1904 reduced another imperial rivalry, while the Russo-Japanese War of 1904–5 not only checked the threat to Asia but if anything reversed it, at the same time as strengthening the Anglo-Japanese Alliance. Now, if either party became involved in a war to defend its territorial rights or special interests, the other would immediately join in. Moreover, with Russia switching its attention from the Far East to Central Asia, where it had earlier tried to include Tibet in its sphere of influence, the area of coverage of the Alliance was extended to include 'the consolidation and maintenance of the general peace in the region of eastern Asia and India'.[52] By 1911, when the Alliance was renewed for a further ten years, stability had been achieved in Central Asia, Great Britain having reached an advantageous agreement about spheres of influence with Russia in 1907, and so specific reference to India was dropped. Specific reference was also dropped to Korea, deemed to be firmly within the Japanese sphere of influence since the annexation of 1910. A further significant insertion was an article removing the obligation to go to war against a party with which the ally in question had a general arbitration treaty. An arbitration treaty had been agreed between Great Britain and the USA in 1908 and another was about to be agreed in 1911. And so, Japanese newspapers declared that the Alliance was 'unilateral' and that 'Japan is now America's slave'.[53]

During the First World War and after, nevertheless, in Buell's view the existence of the Anglo-Japanese Alliance continued to promote Japanese imperialism. As it became due for expiry on 13 July 1921, the Japanese military pressed for renewal, warning of the danger of a Bolshevised Asia, or suggesting the alternative of a Russo-German-Japanese alliance. But there was strong pressure against renewal, especially from the USA which saw the Alliance as an obstruction to its restraint of Japan. After much debate, the Anglo-Japanese Alliance was provisionally renewed, but the military obligations were removed as inconsistent with the procedure prescribed by the Covenant of the League of Nations. To some extent, perhaps, the pride of British politicians had been temporarily protected, but the Japanese press was not alone in looking upon the Alliance as a 'ghost' and 'dead letter'.[54]

The Washington Conference was to bring about a complete end to the Anglo-Japanese Alliance, and to reveal further reasons for it doing so, including an enormous shift of strength and potential from Europe to the USA. Less apparent in Europe itself at the time of the Versailles Conference, this sea change became more marked during the Washington Conference on the other side of the Atlantic Ocean.

The conference agenda

After some preliminary discussion of the matter at home and abroad, the State Department announced an agenda for the forthcoming conference on 10 September 1921. As previously foreseen, there were to be two major areas of settlement: armament; Pacific and Far Eastern questions. Limitation of naval armament, divided into basis, extent and fulfilment, came first, followed by rules for control of new agencies of warfare, then limitation of land armament. Questions relating to China were given pride of place under the second heading, with principles to be applied and their application directed at the following subjects: territorial integrity; administrative integrity; open door – equality of commercial and industrial opportunity; concessions, monopolies or preferential economic privileges; development of railways, including plans relating to CER; preferential railroad rates; status of existing commitments. After China, came two more Pacific and Far Eastern questions – Siberia (with similar subjects) and mandated islands (unless settled earlier).[55]

The Chinese wanted the subject of tariff autonomy to be included, and Hughes agreed. The French and British enquired about new agencies of warfare, and Hughes proposed gas, submarines and aircraft. In general if privately, the British Foreign Office was dismissive of the agenda, which it considered 'better calculated to make the Japanese Government withdraw from the conference than to produce any result'. Moreover, for the Foreign Office, the items in the agenda suggested 'such a complete lack of grasp of the situation on the part of the United States government that nothing short of a regular course of education seems to offer the slightest chance of the matter being put on anything like a rational basis'.[56]

On 2 November 1921, the Soviet People's Commissar for Foreign Affairs Georgii V. Chicherin issued a second note of protest to the governments of

Great Britain, France, Italy, Japan and the USA about the exclusion of Soviet Russia from the Washington Conference. This complained that his first such note of 19 July 1921 had been disregarded, and that therefore Soviet Russia wished to reiterate that it would reserve for itself all questions to be discussed at the conference. Struggling towards economic reconstruction in the face of the famine brought about by the allied blockade and severe drought, the Russian people could only be indignant about statements that the great powers were assuming for themselves the safeguard of Russia's interests. Such 'solicitude' was now to be shown again by the same governments 'that have been bleeding her, sending the Tsar's generals against her, trying to strangle her by a ruthless blockade'. The labouring masses understood full well in advance that any further agreement of the powers would turn out to be of the same order as the Versailles and Sèvres treaties

> No matter what are the public agreements that will be concluded in Washington, there will always remain the suspicion, almost the certainty, that secret agreements have also been made, directed against Russia, and as a result an additional element of mistrust, suspicion, and complications of all kinds will be introduced into international relations. Under such circumstances the decisions of the Washington Conference will inevitably become merely the sources of new conflicts, new entanglements, and new catastrophes. No peace, but discord and strife and hatred will be brought into international relations, surely to become the cause of new disasters for the entire world.[57]

Chicherin's second note of protest was ignored more than his first had been, as the great powers prepared for participation in the Washington Conference. While their silence did not mean indifference, they nevertheless had other priorities, which had changed little since Versailles.

Perspectives

In his book on containment and counter-revolution at Versailles published in 1968, Arno J. Mayer argued that 'As compared to France, and even as compared to Britain, the USA had a markedly limited stake in Russia.' From the point of view of security, there could be little concern while the USA remained essentially a naval power and Russia – a land power. Therefore, the objective was to remove Japanese influence from the Russian Far East rather than to extend American influence in that region. Diplomatically, whereas France and Britain sought a return to their pre-war relations with Russia, the USA 'was ready to settle for a Russia hostile to new violations of the Open Door in China'. By no means indifferent to the fate of the new states of Eastern and East Central Europe, the USA tended to concentrate on Russia in the Far East at the same time as France – in Europe and Britain – in the Middle East. Economically, future trade and investment opportunities for American business were by no means discounted, but there was no Russian trade lobby of any consequence and much more excitement about China.[58]

Like Versailles and any other subject of historical enquiry involving Soviet Russia, the Washington Conference has been viewed from shifting perspectives, before, during and since the Cold War.

In a survey of successive lessons on disarmament drawn from the Washington Conference published in 1994, Ernest R. May began by noting that, throughout the 1920s, the agreements made in Washington – most famously on the 5–5–3 ratio for the American, British and Japanese navies – were taken to be examples of how the cause of peace could be advanced by 'bold risk-taking'. In the 1930s and 1940s, however, arms experts moved towards recommendation of the calibration of force levels to potential threats, now looking upon the decisions taken in 1921–2 as 'exemplifying wishful thinking'. In the early Cold War period, emphasis was given to 'the need to nail down details, to police performance, and to depend as little as possible on simple good will'. Later during that conflict, as tension between the superpowers lessened somewhat, American and Soviet statesmen took up arms limitation negotiation as a means of averting the final showdown. However, the political scientist Hedley Bull pointed out how the Washington treaties on the limitation of capital warships had encouraged the development of alternative armaments such as aircraft carriers and submarines. Comparable consequences might ensue if the American and Soviet negotiators concentrated exclusively on intercontinental nuclear weapons. Then, with the emergence of *détente* in the 1970s, other political scientists made use of further historical studies of the Washington Conference to argue for the advisability of sustainable public support for arms limitation agreements in the USA. They also warned against agreements making the assumption of 'a constraint like public opinion on the Soviet side'.

May rightly observed that, while most of the academic discussion of the Washington Conference had concerned arms control, the agenda in 1921–2 was in fact much larger, including Pacific and Far Eastern questions as well. In post-Cold War retrospect, he noted, we can also more clearly perceive its broader setting in a series of attempts to create a post-First World War new international order following the failure of the 'comprehensive effort' at Paris in 1919. But the interconnected systems emerging from these attempts turned out to be fragile owing to their dependence on 'the great storage battery of the North American economy', which ran dry at the end of the

1920s. Nevertheless, May asserted, the short life of this new order should not lessen its interest or relevance

> Like those who convened in Washington in November 1921, we who live in the 1990s face a future more full of uncertainty than the futures faced by our immediate forebears. We have no clear sense of what would be the sides or stakes in the future.

There was even some doubt that future competition would concern nations rather than civilisations, added May following Huntington. Nevertheless, the study of 'the specifics of past attempts to construct new systems of relationships crossing national and cultural boundaries...ought to help the thinking of those who were trying to see their way into a post-Cold War world'.[59]

In agreement with May on this last point, we also insist that more must be done to remove one of the main barriers to such comprehension – historiographical unilateralism.[60] As we turn to attempt to take our own advice, however, we have to accept that there are certain difficulties in turning to the other side, Soviet historians possessing their own preconceptions and their own restraints. With that reservation, let us turn to E. I. Popova's study of the Washington Conference in the evaluation of Soviet historians published in 1971.[61] From that vantage point, she suggested division of Soviet historiography on the Conference into three phases: from 1922 to the mid-1930s; from the mid-1930s to the mid-1950s; and from the mid-1950s to the early 1970s. (In parentheses, perhaps, we should note that 'mid-1950s' could be a euphemism for the death of Stalin, while the early 1970s were part of another although not so deep 'freeze'.) The first phase was characterised by illumination of the Washington system, with special emphasis on the role of Soviet diplomacy and the importance of the Chinese revolution. However, under the influence of the dominant Soviet historian M. N. Pokrovsky, there was too much emphasis on commerce, and under the influence of American historiography, too much concentration on Japan. Moreover, the new role of the USA was imperfectly understood. The second phase was marked by the comparative neglect of the Conference, although a considerable amount of attention was paid to the triangular relationship of the USA, Great Britain and Japan. The third phase strongly reflected the influence of the Cold War, with an exaggeration of the part played by the USA in the Allied intervention in Soviet Russia. Following Soviet practice, Popova asserted that great progress was being made at the time of writing.

In a work published in 1997, A. Iu. Sidorov emphasised the inadequacies of Soviet historiography, which he found not to be not so much quantitative as qualitative. That is to say, ideological preconceptions warped the conclusions of even the most serious scholars including Popova. However, Sidorov also noted the absence of any overall study of the Washington Conference, Soviet or post-Soviet, even though there had been many references to the 'Washington System'. In his own excellent work on the foreign policy of Soviet Russia in the Far East, 1917–22, however, he himself devoted little more than ten pages to the Conference.[62]

We will discuss the evaluations of Sidorov and other scholars within Cold War and post-Cold War perspectives at the end of Chapter 2. In conclusion to this chapter, let us reiterate our own basic purpose – to examine the Washington Conference and the relations of the great powers with 'Uninvited Russia' in their context, concentrating on the years 1921 to 1922 and making appropriate use of primary and secondary sources, principally but by no means exclusively of American and Russian provenance. We will then be in a position to estimate the part played by the USA in the making of the USSR as it resisted attempts made by other great powers to oppose such consolidation. Having put earlier perspectives in their place, however, we need to strive to recognise the limitations of our own.

2 The Washington Conference
Armaments and the Far East

As the Washington Conference approached, the Carnegie Endowment for International Peace was among those institutions attempting to make a contribution to the great cause. Expressing the belief that the dissemination of information regarding the status of armaments and the situation in the Pacific, together with other relevant material, would be of service to the public and perhaps even to the delegates, the endowment undertook the publication of a series of pamphlets. One of them was *The Limitation of Armaments* by Dr Hans Wehberg, the translation of a work originally published in French in 1914 by the Interparliamentary Union. In the historical introduction to his Eurocentric work, Dr Wehberg argued that there could be no discussion of the reduction of armaments before the beginning of the eighteenth century because alliances before then normally envisaged 'an aggressive alliance against the Turks, and a suppression of the armies could naturally, at that time, not figure in the program…' Wehberg brought in the USA with a description of the Rush–Bagot Agreement of 1817 concerning the limitation of British and American warships on the Great Lakes. However, he also noted that Pan-American conferences had not examined the problem of disarmament, adding that 'the reason for this silence lies in the fact that in America the system of permanent armies is not as far developed as with us in Europe'.[1]

Wehberg's main focus was on the Hague Peace Conferences first proposed by Tsar Nicholas II of Russia for 1899 and then reconvened in 1907. He also mentioned subsequent negotiations between Great Britain and Germany on the limitation of naval armaments. Although he noted the presence of the USA and Japan at The Hague, Wehberg's emphasis remained Eurocentric. Pertinent illustrations may be drawn from his description of a number of projects put forward for peace in the years leading up to the First World War. For example, in 1913, Pastor Otto Umfrid put forward a plan entitled 'Protection of European Culture'. Certainly, there were references to the USA. For example, a retired German naval captain L. Persius noted in March 1913 that in the US House of Representatives, Speaker

26 *The Washington Conference*

Champ Clark had characterised as the 'height of idiocy' the international rivalry in the building of fleets. However, in February 1914 Persius observed: 'Doubtless the Americans like everything which is "big", and even today they are constructing the largest vessels of the line.' In a prescient manner, he went on to remark: 'But the United States would at the present time be inclined to adopt a reduction of displacement tonnage.'[2]

Except for the USA, Latin America and Japan, most of the rest of the world was subsumed in Dr Wehberg's pamphlet under the heading of Europe and its colonies. It included a pertinent point made by a Monsieur Toinet in 1912: 'Should we distinguish between colonizing nations and others? Doubtless the former need larger armies and particularly larger navies with more stations.'[3] Undoubtedly, the Great War that broke out in the year of its original publication began as European. Before it ended, however, with the entry of the USA, the activities of Japan in China and the Russian Revolution aspiring to a global impact, the conflict had widened enough for it fully to deserve the label of First World War. The Versailles and Washington Conferences gave emphasis to the global nature of the conflict, even if the approach of President Wilson differed from that of his successor.

With the authorisation of the Senate, President Harding proclaimed 11 November 1921, Armistice Day, a national holiday. Standing in Arlington Cemetery before the newly consecrated Tomb of the Unknown Soldier, he gave an earnest address asserting that there must be no more war. In the preceding period and on the day itself, there were many ballots, petitions and demonstrations in support of this great idea. Among the more noteworthy statements on the subject was that of Charles M. Schwab of the Bethlehem Steel Company: 'I am at the head of the largest war materials manufacturing works in the world, but, gladly would I see the war-making machinery of the Bethlehem Steel Company sunk to the bottom of the ocean...' Judge Gary from the United States Steel Corporation concurred, declaring that disarmament would be good for all businesses.[4]

Naval and land armaments

But hardly anybody knew what was to come on the opening day of the Washington Conference on the Limitation of Armament and on Pacific and Far Eastern Questions on 12 November 1921. After some more well received unexceptionable words from the President, the delegates and other members of the audience no doubt expected more of the same from the elected chairman US Secretary of State Charles Evan Hughes. However, they were stunned when he proceeded from some preliminary remarks about the Hague Conference first promoted by the Tsar of Russia at the end of the nineteenth century to propose a concentration on 'a practical program' for the solution to the limitation of armament question, leaving other questions to committees. Hughes stated that rivalry on the high seas had created a hopeless situation and that it must be stopped. For this sacrifices would have to be made by the sea powers. With the President's authorisation, Hughes proposed the cessation of construction of all capital ships for a period of not less than ten years, and the destruction by the USA, Great Britain and Japan of enough battleships to establish a ratio of 5–5–3. In the words of historian John Vinson

> His auditors felt that Hughes in less than thirty minutes had sunk sixty-six battleships, thereby transposing disarmament from idealistic theory to practical reality. They were engulfed by the assurance that the millenium was not simply to be planned, but was to be ushered in immediately.[5]

Not everybody joined with equal fervour in the prolonged applause, however. The US Assistant Secretary of the Navy, Theodore Roosevelt Jr, one of the few in the know before the speech itself, recorded the reactions of the British delegation in his diary in the following manner

> Lord Lee, the First Lord of the British Admiralty turned the several colors of the rainbow, and behaved as if he were sitting on hot coals. He threw notes to [Admiral] Beatty...He half rose and whispered to Balfour. Beatty, after the first step, sat with eyes fixed on the ceiling. Admiral Chatfield...turned red and then white, and sat immovable...[6]

Another observer of the scene, Mark Sullivan, wrote

> When Hughes began to enumerate British ships to be sunk – ships whose very names are milestones in the history of British sea-power – Lord Beatty came forward in his chair with the manner of a bulldog sleeping on a sunny doorstep who had been poked in the stomach by the impudent foot of an itinerant soap-canvasser seriously lacking in any sense of the most ordinary proprieties or considerations of personal safety.[7]

The leader of the British delegation, Arthur Balfour, remained impassive, according to Roosevelt. Erik Goldstein suggests 'Perhaps the difficulty that now faced Britain at Washington was that Balfour, when faced with a public forum, instinctively treated the situation as a simulacrum of Westminster.'[8] An additional interpretation could be that Balfour was among the first to realise that Westminster had been overtaken by Washington as a centre of global influence.

During discussions at the Washington Conference on the limitation of surface navies, there was no mention of Soviet Russia, and very little when the focus shifted to armies, submarines and aircraft. Even if Foreign Commissar Chicherin's complaints had been answered by an invitation to him to participate, he could not have said much on the major subject, since there was virtually no Soviet Russian navy to limit, especially in the Far East. At the time of the Conference, there were no more than 35,000 Red sailors in total. On 28 October 1920, Lenin had doubted the use of warships, saying that it was better to concentrate on industrial production. On 30 July 1921, he had recommended the immediate liquidation of the Naval Department. And on 29 November 1922, he was to observe that the Red fleet was still too big for the economic and political circumstances in which Soviet Russia found itself. Such resources as there were should be devoted to the development of aviation and to the naval defence of the Far East after its liberation.[9] In his own way, then, Lenin was reflecting some of the priorities of the Washington Conference. Moreover, as he and his fellow commissars kept an eye on the proceedings, they were aware of the signficance of the priorities of the delegates who were in attendance as an integral part of global international relations in 1921 and 1922.

An early Soviet Russian critic, L. E. Berlin, was soon to point out that the US proposal meant that, with a minimum of sacrifice, the USA would become almost as powerful at sea as Great Britain. But apart from this, he suggested that the USA had a number of special considerations. The locks of Panama Canal were too narrow for the gigantic naval vessels projected for construction. If limits were not placed on such capital ships, then, in order to allow the possibility of new ships crossing from the Atlantic Ocean to the Pacific and back, huge works in the Panama isthmus or in Nicaragua would be necessary. Moreover, for the defence of its possessions in the Pacific Ocean or for the commencement of action against Japan, the USA would have to carry on operations at a distance of 6,000 miles distance from its mainland bases, relying exclusively on its distant, poorly equipped bases of Guam and others while needing an incredible amount of fuel and other material.[10]

The USA proposed equal tonnage for Great Britain and the USA, 60 per cent of this for Japan. France demanded the same tonnage as Japan. In its turn, Italy observed that France was not a country of the Pacific Ocean but of the Mediterranean Sea, and demanded for itself the same allotment as France. Great Britain, which had considered itself mistress of the seas before the World War, and did not think then that Germany should have a fleet equal to 60 per cent of her own, was now obliged not to object to parity with the USA. The British renunciation of the principle that her fleet must always be equal to the combined fleets of the next two greatest naval powers in the world was brought about for the most part by the fact that Great Britain had lost its financial power and become a debtor of the USA. The interest paid by Great Britain to the USA alone would have allowed the construction over several years a whole squadron of super-dreadnoughts. However, Berlin considered, Great Britain was also motivated by her desire not to push the USA too close to France, which appeared to want to aggravate Anglo-American relations.[11]

Apart from this, world stability would be difficult to achieve without a reduction of land armaments. To the extent that Great Britain would reduce its naval forces it would become weaker in comparison with its neighbour, France, which possessed a powerful army superior to the British, in spite of the insignificance of its navy compared to the British. Naturally, Great Britain would be reconciled to the reduction of its sea forces only if France would carry out a reduction of its land forces. Equally, the USA was interested in the reduction of the powerful army of Japan, looking with a wary eye upon its activities in China and the Soviet Far East.

The European theatre was to the fore in the Third Plenary Session of the conference on 15 November 1921. France, in the person of its delegate to Washington, Aristide Briand, argued that Germany always had two aims, trade and war. Her industry had been developing since the Armistice, and everything was ready for a new conflict on land. 'In Europe, where, so they say, there is peace', he exclaimed, 'one need only to scan the horizon to see many wisps of smoke which indicate that all the volcanic fires are not extinguished. Since peace has been signed, war would already have broken out had not France been strongly armed.' Russia, which was boiling over with anarchy, had an army of 1,500,000 men of whom 600,000 were fully equipped. Briand asked what might Germany do in order to equip Russia and exploit her? If other powers intended to keep their navies to the extent necessary to defend their liberty and insure their life, what should France do when the danger was there at her very doors?[12]

On behalf of Great Britain, Arthur Balfour asserted with sadness that Briand's speech did not give hope for the limitation of land forces. Carlo Schanzer spoke up for Italy and the preservation of its 200,000 strong army, because of the post-war situation in which new states had appeared with the collapse of old empires and some former states grown in size. Admiral Kato, for Japan, demanded an army corresponding in numbers to the seriousness of the position in the Far East.

In reply to Briand, Hughes said that the USA could never forget the sacrifices of France and that it was taking into account the difficulties experienced by France.[13]

In its own way, the Soviet critic L. E. Berlin argued, France posed the question of the guarantee of the Versailles peace. The allies could not give France what it demanded: the USA wanted to have its hands free for the solution to problems linked with the security of its Pacific shores, while Great Britain did not want to allow the complete disarmament of Germany, which it saw as a seller's market. Apart from this, it did not like the idea of complete French hegemony in Europe. Proceeding from the position taken by France, Lord Curzon in a speech before the representatives of the City had said that naval disarmament could not be realised while land armaments were strengthened, and that Great Britain could not make sacrifices while other powers not only refused to do so, but even had the possibility of creating new weapons for attack from the air or under the sea.[14]

At the conference, it was generally agreed that the question of land armament should be referred to the Committee on Limitation of Armament, where it was passed on to subcommittees,[15] only to fade away. Without the participation of Germany and Soviet Russia, the problem could not be conclusively discussed as far as Europe was concerned, and Europe was not the prime concern of the Washington Conference.

The Five-Power and Four-Power Treaties: armaments limitation

On 6 February 1922, after long and sharp disagreements concerning the limitation of naval armaments, the so-called Five-Power Treaty was signed. The ratio suggested by the USA for naval forces was accepted: for the USA, Great Britain and Japan – 5–5–3; and extended to France and Italy, 1.75–1.75. The powers committed themselves not to acquire and not to build capital ships of more than 35,000 tons (35,560 metric tonnes) water displacement, while gun calibre was not to exceed 16 inches.[16] Thus, although a total tonnage was placed on aircraft carriers, too, the shipbuilding yards of the five great powers could still build huge new fleets, excluding capital ships alone. As far as the USA, UK and Japan were concerned, agreement on the 5–5–3 ratio was readily enough accepted since it was approximately equal to that which would inevitably have taken place at the time of the completion of shipbuilding programmes in 1924. France and Italy, which kept their fleets as they were and received the right to strengthen and renovate them up to the end of the decade of breathing space, lost nothing from the limitation.

The achievement of agreement about the limitation of the tonnage of aircraft carriers was inspired, evidently, by some uncertainty about their tactical significance, but when the question was posed at the conference about the reduction of the auxiliary surface fleet, cruisers and minesweepers, the powers participating in the conference all put forward inordinate demands, and the question remained open, and the general tonnage of military auxiliary ships was not limited.

Even sharper contradictions at the conference were aroused by the question of the limitation of the submarine fleet. In the Pacific Ocean theatre of any Second World War, with the participants scattered around the surface of the whole world, the submarine with a wide radius of action would probably play as important a part as had the German U-boats in the Atlantic Ocean during the first such global encounter. When the USA proposed a limitation of the tonnage of submarines, Great Britain at first put forward the question of the eradication of submarines and the complete cessation of their construction, insisting that they constituted almost exclusively a weapon of ruin and destruction, and not of defence. Balfour argued that the construction by France of a colossal submarine fleet was nothing else than a threat exclusively against Great Britain. Sarraut, speaking for France after Briand's departure, insisted that submarines constituted the sole means of defence of small or economically weak powers unable to build super-dreadnoughts.[17] According to L. E. Berlin, Briand had pointed out that when Great Britain arrogated to itself the right to maintain a vast surface fleet, he did not say that this was directed against France. He added that if, in all probability, Great Britain kept its ships of the line to catch sardines, surely it could allow France to build submarines for the botanical investigation of the deep sea.[18]

After a futile discussion the question of the submarine fleet remained undecided. Finally, at the suggestion of Hughes, a treaty was signed on 6 February 1922 by the five powers 'in relation to the use of submarines and noxious gases in warfare.' According to Article I of this treaty, a merchant ship would have to submit to visit and search to determine the nature of its cargo before it could be seized. It could be attacked only if it refused to submit to inspection or to proceed as ordered after seizure. However, it could not be destroyed, if the passengers and the crew were not protected from danger. The powers recognised 'the practical impossibility of using submarines as commerce destroyers without violating, as they were violated in the recent war of 1914–18, the requirements universally accepted by civilized nations for the protection of the lives of neutrals and noncombatants.' Therefore, the prohibition of the use of submarines as commerce destroyers should be universally accepted as 'a part of the law of nations', just as much as the prohibition of the use of noxious gases.[19]

On 30 December 1921, a report of a Committee on Aircraft on Limitation of Aircraft as to Numbers, Character and Use was adopted, expressing the view that it was not easy to foresee what consequences would come in the future from 'the development of aeronautics in all its branches' and coming to the conclusion that it was not practicable to impose any effective limitations upon the numbers or characteristics of aircraft, either commercial or military. A resolution accepting this conclusion was adopted on 9 January 1922.

Then, on 4 February 1922, the five powers accepted two insignificant resolutions. The first concerned the institution of a commission for the study of the laws of war and the composition of a report about them. The second resolution removed from this commission the power to examine the question of submarines and that of the use of poison gases and chemical compounds.[20]

Thus, the Soviet critic Berlin argued, the Washington Conference could not resolve the problems of actual disarmament nor of the reduction of the armaments of the surface or submarine fleets, nor of land armies and air forces. There could only be attempts to establish a relationship between the powers, which would give no advantage to any one of them and would oblige them all to reach an understanding on disputed questions. Moreover, whatever agreements were concluded and whatever the value of the peace-loving speeches of the diplomats, the stocks and shares of war industry did not fall in the slightest during the whole period of the conference.

The partial disarmament achieved at the conference certainly lessened to some extent the unbroken naval rivalry between the USA, Great Britain and Japan and also meant some economy in expenditure, but it still left colossal naval forces at the disposition of these three great powers. As a result of the Washington Treaty, the British fleet of the line turned out to be weaker than the combined fleets of the USA and Japan, the USA and France, and even of the USA and Italy. At the same time, the USA became the possessor of a fleet just a little weaker than the British and exceeding the Japanese fleet by 200,000 tons. Nevertheless, Great Britain preserved her leading significance as a sea power while relieved of the burden of colossal and endless expenditure. The parity of its fleet of the line with that of the USA was compensated by the superiority of the number of its cruisers and of the fast ships of its merchant fleet, which could be used in wartime as cruisers. Apart from this, the possession of huge telegraph cables and ubiquitous naval bases gave Great Britain freedom of operations in any part of the world.

As far as Japan was concerned, it had agreed to the reduction of its fleet of the line to ten ships only after the recognition by Great Britain and the USA of the status quo in the Pacific Ocean. In this way, it had averted the danger brewing in connection with the strengthening by the USA of the Philippine and Mariana Islands. As for its financial situation, the cessation of construction of ships of the line worked out well for Japan since it could find complete compensation in the increase of the number of its cruisers and submarines. The numerous naval bases of Japan along with the presence within her waters of a great auxiliary navy gave her the possibility of being scarcely vulnerable.

France could not rival Great Britain with a capital fleet, but the tonnage of her auxiliary surface and submarine fleet – appropriate for her means in the case of a struggle with Great Britain – and her army both remained unlimited. In this way, France could consider that she had defended her interests at Washington. On the other hand, however, France found unsatisfactory the treaty's condition that her fleet should have parity with the Italian, which weakened the possibility of her predominance in the Mediterranean Sea that she considered necessary for her African policies. By the same condition, Italy found her position on the Mediterranean Sea more advantageous.[21]

Back over the Atlantic Ocean, the USA maintained the strategic significance of the Panama Canal through the limitation of the water displacement of a ship of the line to 35,000 tons, while postponing an untimely and dangerous war for dominance in the Pacific Ocean. The status quo was to be preserved regarding naval bases, shore defences and facilities for the refitting and the support of naval forces on the Pacific Ocean. But exceptions were made for the shores of the USA, the Alaska Territory apart from the Aleutian Islands, the Panama Canal zone, and the Hawaiian Islands. For the British Empire, exceptions were made for the shores of Canada, Australia and New Zealand. All the island possessions of Japan, the Kuriles, the Bonins, Amami-Oshima, the Loo Choos, Formosa and the Pescadores, along with others to be obtained by Japan in the Pacific Ocean, were also made exceptions.[22]

The British Empire compensated for the maintenance of the status quo in Hong Kong through construction of a powerful naval base at Singapore, where the British Pacific Fleet could be concentrated. The main argument in favour of this measure was that the security of British possessions in the Far East and the Pacific Ocean during the existence of the Anglo-Japanese alliance depended on Japan and that a self-respecting people could not depend for an uncertain period on the goodwill of another country. Moreover, in the context of the extension of the 'Open Door', the question of British renunciation of the alliance with Japan was put forward by the USA at the very beginning of the Washington Conference. The British Imperial Conference which preceded it revealed some difference of opinion concerning this alliance in the dominions of Canada, Australia and New Zealand. With the transfer by the Versailles Treaty of the German colonies in Micronesia to Japan, the latter came very close to Australia, which grew alarmed about the possibility of Japanese forces on its territory, an apprehension shared to some extent by New Zealand. Canada was more Atlanticist in outlook, but on the Pacific side fully shared the negative point of view of California concerning Japanese immigration. For its part, Great Britain had to take into serious consideration the wishes of the dominions, since in any aggravation of Anglo-American antagonism or war between the USA and Japan, she could be confronted by the collapse of her empire. Meanwhile, as a creditor of Great Britain, the USA could apply the necessary economic pressure. Therefore, Great Britain was obliged to abrogate its alliance with Japan, and the significance of Singapore was enhanced.[23]

On 13 December 1921, a Four-Power Treaty was signed by the USA, France, Japan and the British Empire regarding their insular possessions and insular dominions in the Pacific Ocean. Its chief significance was to be found in its last clause, formally bringing to an end the Anglo-Japanese Agreement of 1911.[24] One observer described Balfour's reaction thus

> As the last sentences sounded and the Anglo-Japanese Alliance publicly perished, his head fell forward on his chest exactly as if the spinal chord had been severed. It was an amazing revelation of what the Japanese Treaty had meant to the men of a vanished age.[25]

Nevertheless, L. E. Berlin asserted, the British government was determined to preserve the close link with Japan and to patronise Japanese interests in order not to lose the possibility of using Japan against the USA if and when necessary. And because of this France was invited into the alliance by the USA, although French interests in the Far East were no greater than those of the Netherlands, the possessions of which were under threat from Japan and which nevertheless did not participate in the quadruple treaty. For its own part, France saw in its position a way of exerting pressure on Great Britain in Near-Eastern and Central-European questions.

Thus, through the route of compromise agreement the clash expected in the Far East was put off at the risk of a sharp aggravation of US–Japanese contradictions and continued Anglo-American rivalry. No more than a temporary alliance balance was achieved.[26]

Siberia and the FER

On 20 December 1921, an appeal of the National Assembly of the FER to the peoples and governments of the world was sent to US Secretary of State Hughes as Chairman of the Conference. The appeal concluded with the observation that the great powers were silently sanctioning Japanese violence in the Russian Far East, and deciding the fate of the FER without any consultation with it. Hughes replied that the USA knew about the difficult state of affairs in the Far East and was taking steps to regularise the position by all peaceful means. On 28 December, Iazikov as head of the FER delegation sent a note to Hughes expressing similar sentiments.

However, the attempts of the delegation of the FER to gain the right of participation in the conference resulted in failure. While the British said that the Siberian question could not be considered in the same way as the Chinese question, the Japanese and French simply refused to discuss it at all. In order to encourage the conference to enter into such a discussion, on 2 and 5 January 1922, the delegation of the FER released for publication what it claimed to be a series of secret diplomatic documents. Among them was a protocol, signed on 14 January 1921 in Paris, and a similar protocol of 12 March 1921, signed by French, Japanese and Russian White Guard representatives, bearing witness to the agreement of France to the temporary occupation of Siberia by the Japanese, the transport of White troops to Vladivostok, and the establishment of a special Russian government under the control of the Japanese, with France taking upon itself the responsibility of bringing these arrangements to the attention of Great Britain. In an alleged secret diplomatic meeting in Tokyo, the Japanese government expressed its recognition of France's help on the Siberian question. In an alleged agreement between Japan and the followers of the White Guard Cossack leader Grigorii M. Semenov, Japan was obliged to provide finance and arms in pursuit of the struggle against the FER.

The publication of the documents had the effect of a bomb thrown into the conference. The head of the French delegation said in an official letter to Hughes that the documents were forgeries, and that the aim of the delegation of the FER was the creation through their publication of an atmosphere of distrust. The French Ministry of Foreign Affairs sent a categorical denial, calling the documents 'pure fabrication'. In response to this French communication, the delegation of the FER publicly asserted that it expected not formal declarations proving nothing but assurances that France was not linked to the aggressive actions of the Japanese in the Russian Far East. On 4 January the delegation released further documents concerning relations between Japan and the followers of Semenov, contrasting them with the statement of the Japanese representatives in Washington that their country was interested only in the security of Japanese subjects on the territory of the FER and that it was determined to take its forces out of the Maritime Province as soon as stable order and government were created there.

To the communication of the chairman of the French delegation Albert Sarraut, Hughes replied that

> he is very pleased to learn that the French government *formally* denies that it has reached any agreement or carried on any discussions whatsoever concerning the situation in Siberia, and is pleased to accept the statement that the above documents are not genuine.

However, as a result of the publication of the documents, the Siberian question was brought up in an active manner, and the French and the Japanese were put into the position in which they had to exercise maximum care.

On 23 January 1922, the Siberian question was at last put forward at the conference at a meeting of the Committee on Pacific and Far Eastern Affairs. The leader of the Japanese delegation, Baron Shidehara, began by reminding his listeners that the Japanese military expedition was originally undertaken in collaboration with the USA. But the withdrawal of troops from Siberia was not as easy for Japan as it was for other Allied powers. Not only did nearly 10,000 Japanese citizens lawfully resident in Siberia 'long before the Bolshevik eruption' need to be protected, districts near the frontier with Korea had for many years been 'the base of Korean conspiracies against Japan'. In 1920, for example, together with 'lawless elements' from Russia, hostile Koreans had attempted an invasion via the Chinese territory of Chientao, set fire to the Japanese Consulate at Hunchun, and committed 'indiscriminate acts of murder and pillage'. The Japanese government was anxious 'to see an orderly and stable authority speedily re-established in the Far Eastern possessions of Russia'. In that spirit, it had shown 'a keen interest in the patriotic but ill-fated struggle of Admiral Kolchak'. Support had been given to Ataman Semenov as he organised a movement to check Bolshevik activities and 'to preserve order and stability'. Although the Japanese had been reluctant to abandon their friend, they had severed all relations with him 'when it was found that the assistance rendered to the Ataman was likely to complicate the internal situation in Siberia'. Negotiations for an orderly withdrawal of Japanese troops were being carried on at Dairen with the representatives of the FER. However, certain parts of the Russian province of Sakhalin would remain occupied temporarily in reprisal for the massacre of more than 700 Japanese citizens including women and children at Nikolaevsk on 13 March 1920.[27]

On 24 January 1922 Hughes gave his response to Shidehara's statement, indicating some difference of views concerning intervention. While not unmindful of 'the direct exposure of Japan to Bolshevism in Siberia and the special problems' that conditions existing there had produced, the USA had been strongly disposed to 'the belief that the public assurances given by the two Governments at the inception of the joint expedition nevertheless required the complete withdrawal of Japanese troops from all Russian territory...' While not unimpressed by the seriousness of the 'catastrophe' at Nikolaevsk, the USA nevertheless regretted that Japan should consider necessary 'the occupation of Russian territory as a means of assuring a suitable adjustment with a future Russian government'. Hughes recalled some of the contents of a communication to Japan from the USA on 31 May 1921, including the expression of the US conviction that

> in the present time of disorder in Russia, it is more than ever the duty of those who look forward to the tranquillisation of the Russian people, and a restoration of normal conditions among them, to avoid all action which might keep alive their distrust and antagonism towards outside political agencies.

The Japanese government had replied in July 1921 along the lines of Shidehara's statement of yesterday. With the greatest friendliness, the American delegation reiterated the hope of their government that Japan would find it possible in the near future to terminate the Siberian expedition and to restore Sakhalin to the Russian people.[28]

On 28 January 1922, the delegation of the FER sent a note to Hughes expressing confidence that the USA would not tolerate 'the oppression of a kindred-spirited, democratic people by a military absolutism'. The delegation was assured that the US administration would make certain that Japan would keep to its gentleman's agreement.

Regarding the question of the CER, on 8 December 1921 Soviet Commissar for Foreign Affairs Chicherin sent US Secretary of State Hughes a note of protest. This question, he asserted, concerned Russia and China alone, and should not therefore be discussed at the Washington Conference. The Soviet government would protest against any decision which would be taken by the conference to the detriment of Russian rights and would not recognise any infraction of the rights of the workers whom it represented. The Soviet government had declared itself ready to return the CER to China with the proviso of certain indispensable guarantees. Until they were given, Russian rights on the railway would remain intact.[29]

On 23 January 1922 the committee on Far Eastern questions was given a report on the CER by the technical sub-committee, which began with the observation that the railway was indispensable for the economic development of Siberia as well as of Northern Manchuria and that it must be preserved as an essential link in a trans-continental railway system. The report recalled that the CER's status was determined by the contracts concluded in 1896 and later years between China and the railway itself whose construction was funded and supervised by the Russian government. No Russian government had been recognised since 1917. Nevertheless, 'as a consequence of assistance which had been given to Russia, at her request, in the operation of the entire Trans-Siberian system, including the Chinese Eastern Railway', 'certain powers' now represented at the Conference committed themselves to continue such assistance upon definite terms. The US and Japan made an agreement in January 1919, and were soon joined by China, France, Great Britain and Italy. However, the trusteeship needed readjustments in three areas:

1 *Finance*: A special financial committee should be set up in Harbin staffed by one member from each of the powers participating in the Washington Conference which chose to participate. This new body would replace the previous inter-allied committee in Vladivostok and the technical board at Harbin. It should exercise general financial control and trusteeship until the general recognition of a Russian government.

2   *Operation*: The technical operation of the CER should be left in the hands of its company without interference, although the Harbin committee could intervene for financial reasons.
3   *Police*: To guarantee the defence of railway property and maintenance of public order within the railway zone, an effective and reliable police or gendarmerie consisting of Chinese should China so desire but paid and controlled by the financial committee should be created.

The suggested plan for changes in the CER could not be introduced since the Chinese delegation alone was decisively against them. On 4 February, however, the conference accepted a resolution concerning the CER which was accepted also by China. It concerned the more careful selection of the railway's personnel with the aim of achieving better protection, an efficient service and a more economical expenditure of resources as well as the prompt discussion of these questions by the proper diplomatic channels. On the same date the powers excluding China accepted a resolution insisting on the responsibility of China for the execution of its obligations to the foreign holders of shares and bonds and the creditors of the CER company.[30]

As a consequence the question of the CER remained in much the same situation as before, according to our Soviet critic L. E. Berlin, who went on to insist that, without the participation of Soviet Russia, discussion of the problems of the CER would be condemned to failure. In his view, the same failure was exacerbated by the contradictory interests concerning the CER of the USA and Japan. The CER, as the sole route open for the trade of transoceanic countries with Siberia and the Far East while the Trans-Siberian Railway could not get through to Vladivostok, had a colossal significance. If the repeated efforts from 1918 of Japan to seize the CER with the collaboration of the counter-revolutionary administration were to meet with success, the possibility would open up to Japan of control over the trade relations of the USA with Siberia and the Far East. Neither the USA nor Great Britain could allow such exclusive Japanese control over very rich markets. Moreover, in case of the seizure of the CER, Japan would have acquired an extraordinarily important strategic position, thanks to which it would in fact gain possession of all Manchuria, and be poised to seize Mongolia as well.[31]

The Nine-Power Treaty and China

Westel W. Willoughby, formerly legal adviser to the Chinese Republic and technical expert of the Chinese delegation at the Conference, commented soon afterwards how remarkable it was that, except for a part of one session concerned with Siberia, the consideration of political questions connected with the Pacific and Far East exclusively centred on China.[32] For his part, the Soviet critic L. E. Berlin considered that 'The most important question brought before at the Washington Conference was China.' However, far from satisfying the aspirations of the Chinese people, the idealistic assertions of the imperialist powers were nothing more than a cover for their predatory interests, in Berlin's view. Of course, there was no single voice to express Chinese views. Before the opening of the conference, the government of Southern China centred on Canton refused to recognise the future decisions of the conference, since it was not represented there. The interests of China were represented solely by the government of Northern China with its capital at Peking. Apart from the five great powers, the examination of Chinese affairs was joined also by Belgium, the Netherlands and Portugal. The participation of Belgium, Berlin asserted, confirmed that the conference was called together by the USA not only for the discussion of the question of the limitation of naval armaments but even more for the exploitation of China, since Belgium possessed railways in Peking and Hangkow, but had no possessions in the Pacific Ocean and only an insignificant amount of armament.[33]

At the First Meeting of the Committee on Pacific and Far Eastern Questions on 1 February 1922, the representative of China Sao-ke Sze proposed the following general principles to the 'Powers': to respect the territorial integrity and administrative independence of China; not to conclude any agreements about it without preliminary notice to China; to annul all special rights and advantages of every power, as well as limitations on Chinese political, jurisdictional and administrative freedom of action; to establish exact terms for present limitless obligations; to respect neutral rights in any war in which China was not involved; to take measures for the peaceful resolution of conflicts in the Pacific Ocean and in the Far East; and in future to call periodic conferences for the discussion of international questions concerning the Pacific Ocean and the Far East. For its part, China would not in future transfer any of its territory to any power, and would respect the Open Door.[34]

In particular, the Chinese delegation sought the abolition of the '21 Demands' imposed by Japan in 1915 and concerning occupation of Shantung, influence in Manchuria and Inner Mongolia, and a range of further concessions. The Chinese largely followed the promptings of Westel W. Willoughby and their other US advisers. Nevertheless, making use of such Western concepts as sovereignty, the Chinese delegation attempted to do away with the privileges and interference in the internal affairs of China not only by Japan but also by other powers, of which Great Britain possessed Wei-hai-Wei, France – possessions in South China, and so on.[35]

A central question at the conference, therefore, was that of the reconciliation of the US principle of the Open Door with the demand of

40 *The Washington Conference*

Japan for the acquisition of further possibilities for expansion in the Far East and the desire of China to assert its independence. In an attempt to promote US interests without ignoring other pressures, Elihu Root suggested to the conference the acceptance of four principles constituting the 'firm intention' of the powers as a basis for the solution of the Chinese question: the respect of the sovereignty, independence and territorial and administrative integrity of China; the provision of the fullest and most unembarrassed opportunity to China to develop and maintain for herself an effective and stable government; the greatest possible safeguard of the principle of equal opportunity for the commerce and industry of all nations throughout the territory of China; and restraint from seeking special rights or privileges which would abridge the rights of the subjects or citizens of friendly states, and from countenancing action inimical to the security of such states.[36]

In the session of the Committee on Pacific and Far Eastern questions on 2 and 3 February 1922, statements were made on behalf of the Japanese, Chinese and American delegations regarding the '21 Demands'. Baron Shidehara said that Japan could not agree to the request of China concerning the revision and the annulment of the Sino-Japanese treaty and other 'agreements' of 1915, since in these acts China took upon itself the obligation 'as a free sovereign nation'. It was inaccurate and grossly misleading to refer to 'agreements' as 'demands'. Having referred, however, to the changes in the general situation of things taking place after the conclusion of the acts of 1915, Shidehara spoke of Japanese readiness to transfer to the International Financial Consortium set up in 1920 the right of option which Japanese capital had obtained in relation to loans for the construction of railways in Southern Manchuria and Eastern Inner Mongolia, and also in relation to the loans to be secured on taxes gathered in these regions. As Walter LaFeber aptly comments, 'The success of the Washington Conference ultimately was to rest not on the ability of the diplomats to manipulate the treaties' terms, but on the talents of the private bankers...to maintain an international flow of dollars.'[37] Apart from this, Shidehara noted that Japan did not have the intention to insist on other concessions, including a preferential right to send to China advisers and instructors on questions of the political, financial, military and police matters in Southern Manchuria.

Chief Justice Wang Chonghui stated that the Chinese delegation had learned with satisfaction of the decisions taken by the Japanese delegation, but deeply regretted that the Japanese government had not renounced other claims made in the 'agreements' of 1915. The Chinese delegation suggested that the conference should consider the question of their equity and justice. An impartial consideration of this question could not help but lead to the abolition of all the 'agreements' of 1915, in view of the following facts: that

Japan had given China no compensation for the huge one-sided concessions demanded from it; that these 'agreements' broke treaties made earlier by China with other powers; that they were incompatible with the principles accepted by the conference on the Chinese question; and that they had created, finally, ceaseless misunderstandings between China and Japan, and in the future could lead only to the destruction of friendly relations between the two countries and to the difficulty of achieving the aims of the Conference.

Secretary of State Hughes referred to the American note of 1915 to Japan and China to the effect that the USA could not recognise the 'agreements' being made then. He was gratified to learn from Baron Shidehara of the renunciation of many of the 'agreements' prejudicing the principles of the integrity of China and the Open Door. Nevertheless, Hughes stated that the USA would claim from the Chinese government the benefits for its citizens accruing from the most-favoured nation clauses in treaties between the USA and China, while also observing that these should be kept separate from the question of the validity of treaties between Japan and China. Hughes also reiterated 'the traditional policy of the American Government to insist upon the doctrine of equality for the nationals of all countries'.[38]

On 4 February 1922, Baron Shidehara made a statement at the Plenary Session of the Conference about the special interests of Japan in China. Sources of raw materials and markets for manufactures both had to be found on the Asiatic mainland, where a good and stable Chinese government was a further necessity. With hundreds of thousands of its nationals resident in China, and vast amounts of its capital invested there, Japan largely depended on its neighbour for its national existence, and was 'naturally interested in that country to a greater extent than any of the countries remotely situated'. To say, then, that Japan had special interests in China was simply 'to state a plain and actual fact'. Nevertheless, she did not ask for preferential or exclusive economic rights, and was not afraid of foreign competition, but sought 'a field of economic activity beneficial as much to China as to Japan, based always on the principle of the open door and equal opportunity'.[39]

On 4 February 1922, too, with the active mediation of the USA, China and Japan signed a treaty on unresolved questions concerning Shantung, including the return to China of the territory of Kiaochow formerly leased by Germany. On 21 June 1922 in Peking an exchange of ratifications was carried out, and the treaty went into effect, completing the most complete victory of the USA over Japan in the struggle for China, in the view of L. E. Berlin who commented: 'Under the pressure of an advancing USA Japan gave up its vast conquests and privileges in China.'[40]

Back in early February, the British Empire was obliged to embark on negotiations with China concerning the return of Wei-hai-Wei, Japan having advanced this as a condition of the return of Shantung. Balfour made a statement at the conference intimating that since Wei-hai-Wei had been leased for the purpose of defence against Russia and Germany and for the maintenance in the Far East of the status quo, the reasons for continuing the arrangement had now disappeared and so Great Britain agreed to return Wei-hai-Wei to China, although wishing to make arrangements for 'the innocent and healthful purpose' of maintaining there a sanatorium or summer resort.[41] (In a letter to Curzon of 20 January, Balfour had talked of 'leasing from the Chinese owners on a commercial basis of such things as a cricket club...and golf links....'[42] Probably, he had in mind, too, the continuation of exercises for the navy of a more professional nature.)

On 6 February 1922, the powers participating in the conference concluded a treaty on principles and policies regarding China. With this Nine-Power Treaty the powers recognised the sovereignty, the independence and the territorial and administrative integrity of China. In addition the powers bound themselves to refrain from receiving special rights and privileges in China. With a view to the more effective application of the 'Open Door or equality in China for the trade and industry of all nations', the powers agreed that both they themselves and their citizens would not seek agreements giving them superiority in the field of commercial or economic development, and China agreed to be guided by these principles.[43]

Particularly significant for China was the revision of its customs tariff, on which the nine powers signed a treaty on 6 February, annulling all previous agreements between China and the powers which were incompatible with it.[44] Among other questions concerning China reviewed at the conference was that of its armed forces. On 20 January 1922, the former Canadian Prime Minister Sir Robert Borden gave a report about the necessity of freeing China from inordinate militarism, calculating that not less than one million men were under arms there, maintained mostly for the purpose of civil war. Having behind them centuries of splendid tradition, the Chinese people were passing through 'a period of transition from the autocratic rule of an ancient dynasty to the development of advanced democratic institutions.' Although the establishment of a permanent system of stable government must be the work of the Chinese people themselves, those of other nations had a duty to lend a helping hand. To this end, on 1 February 1922, the conference passed a resolution instituting an enquiry into the presence in China of the armed forces of other powers. On the same day, the conference passed another resolution expressing the serious hope that the Chinese government would take immediate and effective steps to reduce armed forces and expenditure.[45]

In consonance with the principle of the Open Door and equal possibilities put forward by the USA at the conference, with the aim of liquidating in China the exclusive influence and privileges of individual powers, especially of Japan, resolutions were passed about post offices, radio stations and railways.[46]

Evaluations

However, in the estimate of the Soviet critic L. E. Berlin in 1924, the powers that made agreements in Washington showed no immediate serious readiness to take measures for the practical implementation of many of the treaties signed and resolutions taken, including those on China and the Far East. On the contrary, openly supporting the generals and governors fighting among themselves in China with arms and money, individual powers including the USA aimed to strengthen and extend their own spheres of influence by impeding the unification of the various parts of China and the establishment of peace in the Far East.

Moreover, as a result of the Washington conference, Berlin observed, feverish armaments of the 'great powers' occurred, while huge appropriations were made for new naval bases by Great Britain in Singapore, by the Netherlands in their East Indies and by the USA in Alaska and the Hawaiian Islands and elsewhere. New imperialist groups were constituted for new wars. Thus, the Washington Conference did not free the world from the danger of armed conflicts even more terrible than the War of 1914–18. Indeed, it could only put off for a short period the squabbling between the great powers on the basis of the contradictions existing and arising between the powers in the Far East and Pacific Ocean. While the Japanese earthquake of 1923 significantly weakened Japan, it strengthened the positions of the USA and Great Britain in the Pacific Ocean and China, and thus, instead of reducing the activity of the Japanese militarists, encouraged them to press their government for more armaments.

And so, in Berlin's view, the Washington Conference was no more than part of a series of conferences of the imperialist states which, in spite of many discussions and agreements, could not bring to tortured mankind anything but further disappointment and grief.[47]

More than forty years on, the Soviet historian E. I. Popova noted that Berlin wrote his essay on the Conference under the influence of two pressing questions of the year 1924, disarmament and the Chinese revolution. He also overestimated the extent of Japanese aggression and underestimated the military and political elements in American imperialism. He should have given more emphasis to the anti-Soviet as well as the anti-Chinese aspects of the Washington treaties, the lack of an invitation to Soviet Russia as well as the activity of the FER delegation. However, some of these faults would be found in any short treatment of the subject while reflecting the preoccupations of the time and place in which Berlin wrote. Moreover, in Popova's estimation, Berlin's essay deserved the consideration due to the first general Soviet overview of the Conference. She also noted that it received a full amount of attention in later Soviet analysis, partly because it constituted an introduction to a complete translation of the Washington treaties, about which Berlin himself wrote that they gave a particularly striking and instructive picture of the aggressive imperialism of the great powers of their time.[48]

The nearest American counterpart to Berlin, Raymond Leslie Buell, came to a somewhat more optimistic if guarded conclusion in what has been called the 'standard work on the whole conference'[49] of 1922. For him, the Washington Conference did not fail. It made war between Great Britain and the USA impossible, while postponing ('let us hope indefinitely') war between Japan and the USA. Three years before, Woodrow Wilson had been prepared to purchase the League of Nations with the Treaty of Versailles. Peace at Washington was bought with the sacrifice of the Open Door. The price in both cases was too much, in Buell's view, in spite of compensations. That is to say, the onerous terms of the Paris treaties could be changed. As for the Washington Treaties, they might not have succeeded in establishing the equality of commercial opportunity in China, but they did exclude the Oriental problem from the Pacific, from the Western coast of the USA, in fact, from the Western world. The Conference 'prevented it from becoming a world problem – at least for a quarter of a century'.

However, Buell commented, instead of easing the Far Eastern situation, the Conference strengthened the position of Japan and increased the hostility of the Chinese and Siberians towards the Japanese. The Conference was unable, due to no fault of its own, to alter Japanese imperialism and the military machine responsible for its existence. Only one force, that of world opinion, could be brought to bear upon Japanese imperialism, the force of world opinion. 'Such indeed is the theory', Buell concluded in 1922. 'But at the present time, the moral opinion of the Western world has little influence on the peoples of the Orient...'[50]

Eighty years afterwards, the shortcomings of Buell's evaluation of the Conference are all too clear. Twenty-five years later, the 'Oriental problem' had been exacerbated in a Second World War pitting the USA against Japan, while belief in 'world opinion' such as recommended by Elihu Root had not been justified.[51] Moreover, while Buell's own forecasts were patently inaccurate, some of his observations about the world around him also appear now to fall short of objectivity. The USA did not 'sacrifice' the Open Door at the Conference. Japan was not the only imperialist power seeking self-aggrandisement. However, for the moment, let us leave provisional verdicts to these Soviet and American contemporaries of the Conference, and consider later evaluations.

In 1970, Thomas H. Buckley wrote

> The Washington Conference on the Limitation of Armaments, which met in 1921–1922, seemed at the time to be one of the most important diplomatic assemblages in all history, and yet today its significance has slipped into oblivion. Most Americans of the 1970s probably are unaware that the conference ever met, and many of those who do remember it recall a meeting in which the government of the United States foolishly, so they believe, undertook to limit its weapons at a time when if anything there should have been more weapons. The conference, however, deserves remembrance because it was the only successful arms limitation conference in modern history.[52]

Even before Buckley wrote, there was little that could be called scholarly. The first comprehensive survey after Buell was by Yamato Ichihashi in 1928.[53] In 1955, John Chalmers Vinson produced his monograph on the Senate and the Conference.[54] There were some significant articles, too, notably by Asada Sadao on Japan's 'Special Interests'.[55] Since Buckley, there has been the collection of articles with a foreword by Ernest R. May that we looked at in Chapter 1.[56] Among other references to the subject, there is a perspicacious chapter in Lloyd C. Gardner's work on the Anglo-American response to revolution, 1913–23.[57] The other items cited here say very little about Soviet Russia, and virtually nothing about the FER.[58]

In 1971, the year after the publication of Buckley's book, E. I. Popova made seven general observations from the Soviet point of view:

1. Plutarch had aptly observed that the most important aspect of a subject appears last. Not until the Conference was all over did the realisation fully dawn that it marked the emergence of the USA as a leading world power with an emphasis on American national security rather than the security of Asia and the Pacific.
2. Similarly, under the guise of the limitation of armaments, the USA aimed at establishing naval predominance at the same time as arranging an informal 'association of nations' as prefigured in the Conference treaties.
3. The debate between isolationism and globalism concurrent with the Conference reflected internal US circumstances, including close relations between the government and monopolies.

4 The Conference indicated imperialist contradictions, especially between the USA and two other powers, Japan and Great Britain. Emphasis was given throughout the 1920s to agreement with Japan in order to defend Asia from revolutionary and independence movements.

5 Giving up the alliance with Japan at the Conference, Great Britain began to cultivate the 'special relationship' with the USA which, in spite of ups and downs, continued throughout the 1920s and beyond. The study of the beginning of this relationship threw light on its nature.

6 The Conference also marked a significant moment in the USA's 'special relationship' with China, the nature of which had been indicated by the earlier enunciation of the concept of the 'Open Door'. Top priority had to be maintenance of enough stability to keep the door open.

7 The Conference reflected the clash of interests between the imperialist powers and Soviet Russia, which spoke out against unequal treaties and expansionist intervention. Nevertheless, the USA came near to the recognition that was finally accorded in 1933.[59]

An excellent post-Soviet analysis of the subject is A. Iu. Sidorov's book on the foreign policy of Soviet Russia in the Far East, 1917–22.[60] In his conclusion, Sidorov underlines the importance of the FER as a 'buffer' during the period of the Washington Conference, a role enhanced by its 'bourgeois' democratic nature. The FER assisted Soviet Russia to achieve its basic aims in the Far East, the restoration of territorial integrity and resumption of influence in Mongolia, without war against Japan. Meanwhile, 'Uninvited Russia' maintained a useful dialogue with both Japan and China. Although the Soviet régime did not welcome the new world order established by the Washington Conference, 'the key Russian interests were completely taken into account'. By the end of 1922 on the eve of the formation of the Soviet Union, Soviet Russia had achieved the status of a leading power in the Far East.[61]

Two perceptive post-Soviet articles by Marina Fuchs also merit attention, the first analysing the role of the regions in the foreign policy of Soviet Russia in the Far East in the first half of the 1920s, the second scrutinising characteristics of the development of US–Soviet relations in the context of the strengthening of US–Japanese military–political rivalry, 1917–23.[62] Like Sidorov, Fuchs underlines the importance of the FER as a 'buffer', pointing out the significance of networks of communication developed across vast distances by Chicherin, Trotsky and other individuals at a time when Soviet Russia as a whole was far from constituting a unitarian state. She looks at not only the official diplomatic links between the powers concerned with the Far East in the years following the Russian Revolution but also the activities of secret agents – a corrective to any unreserved acceptance of the higher motives of the powers involved.

Of course, the great hopes held out for the Washington Conference went unrealised. It did not so much promote arms limitation as clear the decks, so to speak, for rearmament. Nevertheless, if the cause of peace was promoted to a restricted extent and for a limited time, it helped to promote a postwar system of international relations reflected in, at the same time as obscured by, the 'new diplomacy'. We must now turn to the exposition and analysis of this paradoxical process, keeping in mind the perspective in which we make our own evaluation.

3 Soviet Russia and the USA
The new diplomacy

From the sixteenth century onwards, Tsarist Russia and colonial America developed as transcontinental and transoceanic frontiers of Europe. In America from almost the beginning, there was an intimation of 'Manifest Destiny'. Later, in 1776, the Declaration of Independence at the beginning of the American Revolution marked a conscious attempt to break away from Europe, amplified in the debates leading to the framing of the Constitution in 1787. Alexander Hamilton put the argument forcefully

> The world may politically, as well as geographically, be divided into four parts, each having a distinct set of interests. Unhappily for the other three, Europe, by her arms and by her negotiations, by force and fraud, has, in different degrees, extended her dominion over them all. Africa, Asia, and America, have successively felt her domination. The superiority she has long maintained has tempted her to plume herself as Mistress of the World, and to consider the rest of mankind as created for her benefit... It belongs to us to vindicate the honor of the human race, and to teach that assuming brother, moderation. Union will enable us to do it. Disunion will add another victim to his triumphs. Let Americans disdain to be the instruments of European greatness! Let the thirteen States, bound together in a strict and indissoluble Union, concur in erecting one great American system, superior to the control of all transatlantic force or influence, and able to dictate the terms of the connection between the old and the new world![1]

Already, the cast of mind was apparent that would lead through the enunciation of the Monroe Doctrine to some of the views expressed at the time of the Washington Conference. Then indeed, as we have seen, the USA was able 'to dictate the terms of the connection between the old and the new world'.

Continuity of world outlook in the Russian case is less easily established, since the Revolution of 1917 appeared at the time to be a bigger discontinuity than 1776. The debate about the nature of Soviet as opposed to Tsarist Russia was still going on at the time of the Washington Conference, and therefore forms an integral part of this book as a whole. However, the collapse of the end product of that Revolution, the Soviet Union, in 1991 put new life into the search for lines of filiation and the essence of the Russian spirit. To cut a very long story extremely short, we may resort to three triads. The first is Tsarist, explicitly set out in the reign of Nicholas I by his minister Count Uvarov: Orthodoxy, Autocracy, Nationality: that is to say Russian Christianity, separate from the Western since the middle ages; the unlimited power of the tsar; and the distinctive character of the people. The second, Soviet version – never of course actually set out – could be defined as Marxism-Leninism; the Communist Party of the Soviet Union; and Nationality. Allowance has to be made here for the dominance of Stalin and other leaders. Thirdly, as yet in process of formation in the post-Soviet period, we might suggest Orthodoxy; Democracy; Nationality, although Orthodoxy is far from the force it once was and the 'democratic' nature of the Russian polity is at least as subject to reservations as that of most of its peers elsewhere. Each of these triads, needless to say, could be discussed at far greater length. Moreover, comparisons suggest themselves, not least with successive stages of American 'Manifest Destiny'.[2]

Throughout the nineteenth century, Russo-American relations were mostly but by no means exclusively via Europe.[3] An exception was Tsarist infiltration down the west coast of North America helping to bring about the enunciation of the Monroe Doctrine. At the end of that century, however, relations were more explicitly carried on via Asia, too, when John Hay directed his Open Door policy largely at Russian activities in China. Still transcontinental and transoceanic, Russian and American empires were now clashing more on the Pacific than on the Atlantic.[4]

The new diplomacy

The manner in which the First World War began, created, after it was all over, a widespread revulsion against diplomats. The historian Walter Alison Phillips wrote that they were widely looked upon

> as representing not peoples but a class, as in league with capitalists and munition manufacturers to stir up the war, as fraudulent trustees of the nations' welfare, who in their pitiful game of international chicanery habitually used language 'false-friendly, circumlocutory, and non-committal, full of duplicity and secret reserves'.[5]

Phillips' quotation is from *Towards International Government* by J. A. Hobson, who had been an influence on both Lenin and Wilson, each of whom wanted to make his own version of international government a reality. Lenin had been directly influenced by Hobson as he wrote his *Imperialism: The Highest Stage of Capitalism* in 1916, arguing that by 1900 'when the whole world was divided up, there was inevitably ushered in the era of monopolistic possessions of colonies and, consequently, of particularly intense struggle for the division and redivision of the world'. Less directly, the ideas of Hobson percolated through to Wilson as he developed his own ideology during the First World War. In November 1914, the British radical Union of Democratic Control put forward a programme asking for, among other things, self-determination and the open forum of an international council. In May 1916, it added another point to its programme drafted by Hobson himself concerning the promotion of 'free commercial intercourse between all nations and the preservation and extension of the principle of the Open Door'. Here would be music to Wilson's ears as he worked towards the third of his Fourteen Points: 'The removal, as far as possible, of all economic barriers and the establishment of an equality of trade conditions among all the nations consenting to the peace and associating themselves for its maintenance.'

Hobson's choice for a new order was in fact far from unique among the many making demands for the guarantee of future peace. But there could be no doubt at all about who made the most challenging responses. Woodrow Wilson was one of them, and V. I. Lenin was the other. Soviet 'new diplomacy' was inaugurated by the government's decree on peace of 8 November 1917 calling for 'peace without annexations' irrespective of whether the nations involved were in Europe 'or in faraway transoceanic countries', as well as the abolition of secret diplomacy and full publication of secret treaties. The first of Wilson's Fourteen Points of 8 January 1918 with its insistence on 'open covenants, openly arrived at' and 'no private international understandings of any kind' was no doubt a response from a faraway transoceanic country to Lenin as well as to 'the voice of the Russian people' more generally.

While enunciating universal principles, then, the 'new diplomacy' was also firmly rooted in two countries, as both its progenitors pointed out. As he struggled to gain acceptance for the Treaty of Versailles and the League of Nations, Wilson insisted in 1919 that 'America...is the only national idealistic force in the world.' And in 1920, he declared: 'Every imperialistic influence in Europe was hostile to the embodiment of Article X in the Covenant of the League of Nations...I hold Article X to be the essence of Americanism.' A few years later, in one of his last writings early in 1923, Lenin criticised Russian reformists for the persistence of their belief that capitalism and the social relations accompanying it were the end of the line of postwar human evolution. For instance, he said

> it does not ever occur to them that because Russia stands on the borderline between the civilised countries and the countries which this war has for the first time definitely brought into the orbit of civilisation – all the Oriental, non-European countries – she could and was, indeed, bound to reveal certain distinguishing features; although these, of course, are in keeping with the general line of world development, they distinguish her revolution from those which took place in the West-European countries and introduce certain partial innovations as the revolution moves on to the countries of the East.

The preaching of the 'presbyterian dominie', as Harold Nicolson called Wilson, differed from the axioms of the 'wooden dogmatist' Lenin, as he was described by Maxim Gorky. The US President's view of democracy followed the British tradition; the Soviet leader's Marxism was more Germanic. But each in his own way was saying that his country had emerged from a provincial or borderline relationship with a European metropolis to a claim for a central role in the world's affairs.[6]

Charles Evans Hughes, Harding's Secretary of State and chairman of the Washington Conference, shared something of Wilson's outlook with a belief in Divine Rule extending throughout the natural and social world in the form of historically revealed reason opposed to the authority of force.[7] However, Hughes' 'liberal isolationism' differed from Wilson's structured internationalism. For Hughes, the behaviour of the great powers should not be regulated by the creation of institutions or mechanisms as at Versailles. Instead, by means of the Washington Conference, he sought to change the way in which the most powerful nations of the world viewed each other as well as effected a limitation of armaments.[8] On Soviet Russia in particular, Hughes observed in 1923: 'We are not concerned with the question of the legitimacy of a government as judged by former European standards. We recognize the right of revolution and we do not attempt to determine the internal concerns of other states.' Yet recognition was an invitation to intercourse accompanied by obligations, which the Soviet government had failed to observe by repudiating the public debt and confiscating the property of American citizens. Moreover, 'What is most serious is that there is conclusive evidence that those in control in Moscow have not given up their original purpose of destroying existing governments wherever they can do so throughout the world.'[9] Therefore, 'The salvation of Russia cannot be contrived outside and injected. Russia's hope lies in Russia's action.'[10]

This negative attitude has to be put in a context admirably set out by Merlo J. Pusey

> Hughes' hatred of imperialism gave him a unique role – protector of Russia – that was almost forgotten in later years. Coming into office at a time when Russian industry and commerce were in a state of collapse and revolution was still rampant, Hughes feared that Russia was slipping into chaos of the sort that made China easy prey for the imperialistic powers a few decades earlier. All the influence that he could muster was used to drive away the vultures while the Russian nation was going through its agony of rebirth.[11]

Thus, as Pusey suggests, Hughes was the foe of Leninism, but the protector of Russia. In such a manner, unwittingly, his own brand of the new diplomacy contributed to the formation of the Soviet Union.

The Third International and world revolution

The Soviet government fought the Russian Civil War against the Whites and other opponents in order to restore the integrity of the maximum possible amount of what had been the Tsarist Empire. The major longer-term losses were Poland, the Baltic States and Bessarabia. Finland was allowed to go without a fight. From 1918 onwards, Reds fought Whites and their interventionist allies from Archangel to Vladivostok as the economy and society disintegrated.

As far as external relations were concerned, Lenin and his supporters attempted to assert their arguments in a new way. Three months after the Peace Conference opened in Paris in January 1919, the First Congress of the Communist International met in Moscow in March. The approach taken in the capital of Soviet Russia was very different to that taken in the capital of France. In 'The Third International and Its Place in History' dated 15 April, Lenin declared

> The imperialists of the Entente countries are blockading Russia in an effort to cut off the Soviet republic, as a seat of infection, from the capitalist world. These people, who boast about their 'democratic' institutions, are so blinded by their hatred of the Soviet republic that they do not see how ridiculous they are making themselves. Just think of it: the advanced, most civilized, and 'democratic' countries, armed to the teeth and enjoying undivided military sway over the whole world, are mortally afraid of the *ideological* infection coming from a ruined, starving, backward, and even, they assert, semisavage country!

This contradiction alone is opening the eyes of the working masses in all countries and helping to expose the hypocrisy of the imperialists Clemenceau, Lloyd George, Wilson, and their governments...

However, as Lenin argued, the Third International was no hastily contrived response to the Paris Peace Conference. As he put it, the First International (1864–72) laid the foundation of the proletarian, international struggle for socialism, while the Second International (1889–1914) marked a period in which the soil was prepared for the broad, mass spread of the movement in a number of countries. The Third International had 'gathered the fruits of the work of the Second International, discarded its opportunist, social-chauvinist, bourgeois, and petty-bourgeois dross and *has begun to implement* the dictatorship of the proletariat'.[12] In 1914, members of the Second International had been transformed into this 'dross' through their support of the individual states going to war rather than adherence to the cause of comradely internationalism.

At the Second Congress of the Comintern in Moscow from July to August 1920, victory for world revolution seemed possible as the Red Army moved towards Warsaw in war with Poland. However, in order to ensure that victory, as well as tightening up the conditions for the admission of parties to Comintern, the Congress also agreed to support national liberation movements of a non-communist character in those parts of the world still under the yoke of colonialism.[13] Then, in September 1920, a Congress of the Peoples of the East in Baku concentrated on Persia, Armenia and Turkey. However, in Moscow almost nothing was said about the Far East, and little more mention was made at Baku, although the leading Soviet Orientalist V. M. Pavlovich (Veltman) argued there that 'This colonial question, the question of the partition of Asia, is the mainspring of this bitter war which the capitalist world has been waging since the first day of the October Revolution against Soviet Russia.' Pavlovich exclaimed that

> The main guarantee of victory for the Eastern peoples in the struggle against the monster of world imperialism, against that fire-breathing dragon compared with which all the fantastic, fabulous creatures of terror created by folk-imagination seem wretched pigmies and dwarfs, is unity of the toiling masses not only of the entire East but also of the West. This war can end successfully only if it be waged on both fronts – against foreign capital and against one's own bourgeoisie.[14]

When the Third Congress of Comintern convened in June 1921, less than a year after its predecessor, peace had been arranged with Poland, and a trade agreement drawn up with Great Britain. Internal crisis had led to the introduction of the New Economic Policy, abandoning the hopes for an immediate new proletarian order in favour of a compromise with the peasant majority. Trotsky declared that the world revolution would take years, not months as previously believed. The changed circumstances in which the Soviet régime would have to deal with the capitalist powers on a less temporary basis rather than following their immediate collapse were reflected by the convocation of the Washington Conference. So, following Chicherin's Note of 21 July protesting against the exclusion of Soviet Russia from the forthcoming conference, on 15 August the Comintern published seven Theses adopted by its Executive Committee on the same subject. These deserve detailed exposition, and for two reasons: first, only in this way can the outlook and language of the Comintern be fully appreciated; second, in spite of their often inflamed rhetoric, the Theses contain some perceptive comments on the relations between the Great Powers and the world situation in general.

(1) The Washington Conference. The conference constituted 'the latest in the series of unsuccessful attempts undertaken by capitalist society in order to find a way out of the insoluble contradictions upon which the imperialist war has thrown a glaring light and which it has proved incapable to solve'. The new arrangement of Central Europe and the institution of the League of Nations had both failed, after British and German capitalism had successively failed to organise the world in a peaceful manner. Now, Europe could be compared 'to a cage wherein wild beasts are fighting for a gnawed-off bone and are taken care of by tamers, who from time to time throw a fresh bone to the beasts or whip them when occasion requires'. And so the USA, having refused to join her own handiwork, the League of Nations, was for the second time taking the initiative. But at best, the conference could end only 'with a regrouping of the various powers and with an intensification of existing differences'.

(2) The return of the USA to Europe. The USA had withdrawn from the League of Nations for three reasons: because Great Britain, with six imperial votes at her disposal, had put her stamp upon the League; because American capitalists did not feel inclined to guarantee the geographical frontiers of a world poorly patched together by the Versailles peace; and

> because the capitalist clique as represented by the Republican party wished to exploit the fact that the petty-bourgeois masses had grown tired of Europe in order to push the capitalist clique as represented by the Democratic party away from the pork barrel.

The USA could not withdraw from world affairs, however, because European capitalists and the Allies owed her $20 billion. Developments in

Europe decided not only whether or not these debts could be repaid but also whether or not American industry could maintain the prosperity brought about by the War. While some American capitalists had been sceptical about the necessity of Europe for their well being, the 'deep crisis'[15] of the years 1920–1 proved to the American farmers in particular that they could not export their products to Europe, if the European economy continued its decline. For this reason, therefore, the USA had already participated in settling the question of the German reparations and taken a stand on the Russian famine. In short, the USA had rejoined 'the true representative of victorious world capitalism, the Supreme Council'[16] and was exploiting the present difficult situation of her principal competitor, Great Britain, to the end.

(3) England's situation. As the dual consequence of her own weakness in the face of her rivals and of the contribution made by her Empire during the War, Great Britain had been replaced by 'a federation of Great Britain and her self-governing capitalist colonies whose foreign interests are not those of their mother country'. British imperialism wanted to continue its alliance with Japan as a counterweight in case of conflict with the USA as a means of arbitration between American and Japanese imperialism, for whose differences it was largely responsible. However, Canada did not want to imperil its relations with its powerful neighbour, Australia would need the USA as an ally in case of conflict with Japan and South Africa did not want to be involved in world political conflicts. Therefore, there was a lack of support from the dominions for continuance of the alliance with Japan, and British imperialism was losing its freedom of movement in regard to the USA in general. In any future conflict with the USA, not only would Great Britain not be able to rely fully on her empire, she would also probably be faced as an enemy by France, whose attempts to dominate Europe while remaining active in the Near East increased their rivalry. Therefore, Great Britain needed an understanding with the USA in order to form 'a capitalist Anglo-Saxon trust'. The Comintern stressed: '*The United States will be the centre of gravity of this trust while Japan is to carry the cost of it.*'

(4) The isolation of Japan. Using the War to her own economic advantage by manufacturing munitions for the Allies and a range of goods for Great Britain's colonies, Japan also increased her influence in China, stirring up troubles and exploiting them in order to establish mastery over this vast empire groping its way from feudal disunity to unity. However, the defeat of Germany and 'the disappearance of Russia as an imperialistic factor which could join Japan in pillaging expeditions' made it necessary for Japan to depend wholly on Great Britain for help versus the USA.

(5) The Plans of the USA in the Far East. In order to satisfy her huge needs for investment and economic expansion, the USA was looking towards China and Russia, especially Siberia. The USA was now powerful

enough to oppose the imperialistic privileges formerly acquired in China and recently in Siberia by France, Great Britain and Japan. Under the slogan of the 'open door in China', the USA was trying to force Japan back while also threatening British interests, though to a lesser degree than the Japanese. For Great Britain was a stronger competitor than Japan for the USA and not so vitally interested as Japan in Far Eastern questions. Moreover, if forced to make a choice, Great Britain would opt for the USA rather than Japan. The Washington Conference therefore represented 'a diplomatic attempt on the part of the United States to snatch the fruits of victory away from Japan'.

(6) Possible results of the Washington Conference. As a consequence of the Washington Conference, Great Britain would attempt to bring about a three-way alliance between herself, Japan and the USA, with Japan receiving privileges in Siberia and the USA being given concessions in China or elsewhere. If this proved impossible, the result would be an economic struggle without limit, the formation of 'an English–American trust' and an unrestricted competition in naval armaments. Japan would be cheated of the fruits of victory in favour of the USA at the further expense of China and, possibly, of Soviet Russia. However, economic conflict between Great Britain and the USA remained the foremost world problem, with the rivalry between Great Britain and France as before. In the background, there was conflict with defeated capitalist powers such as Germany, with the colonial peoples and with Soviet Russia which formed 'a gap in the bulwark of the capitalist states'.

(7) The Washington Conference and the Communist International. The attempt to restrict armaments could not succeed. On land, France was determined to dominate Europe through the exploitation of vassal states created in the Central, Southern and Eastern parts of the continent from the former Austrian Empire, 'inhabited by an alien and hostile population' and 'built upon bayonets'. Meanwhile, France was attempting to limit British influence in the Mediterranean by outflanking the Suez Canal so vital for communications with India and beyond. The two former allies, now rivals, would have to come to terms. However, the capitalist powers in general were already showing how little they believed in the possibility of disarmament: for example, at the same time as accepting Harding's invitation to come to Washington, Great Britain and Japan were both embarking on the construction of new warships. The conference would bring neither disarmament nor universal peace, but, on the contrary, constituted 'only an attempt to settle the disputes of the great Anglo-Saxon imperialist robbers at the expense of the weaker robber, Japan, of China and of Soviet Russia'. Support was lent to this view of the conference by the fact that Russia had not been invited to it 'in order to make it impossible for her to expose the

sinister game played at Washington with the fate of peoples'. Warning all workers and enslaved colonial peoples not to entertain any hopes of liberation from exploitation by way of any diplomatic combination, the Comintern called upon communists and affiliates everywhere to resist imperialist governments whose conflict of interests was certain to bring about a new world-wide clash which could be averted only through a Proletarian Revolution leading towards 'a true world-wide federation of all toiling peoples'. In particular, the Comintern Executive drew the attention of the workers of the world to 'the intrigues that at Washington are being spun against Soviet Russia'. It concluded its theses with a call to

> the toiling masses in China, Korea and Eastern Siberia to ally themselves more closely to Soviet Russia, the only state in the world willing to render assistance upon a mutual and fraternal basis to the peoples of the Near and Far East who are being menaced by the world's imperialists.[17]

The First Congress of the Toilers of the Far East

The most substantial response to this call was the First Congress of the Toilers of the Far East, held in Moscow from 21 January to 1 February 1922 after an earlier preliminary meeting in Irkutsk and before a closing session in Petrograd on 2 February. Representatives attended from China, Japan, Korea, India, the Philippines and Indochina as well as from the Comintern which had convened the congress. Again, the congress provided some significant insights as well as much heated bombast.

The proceedings were opened on 21 January by Zinoviev, the President of the Comintern, observing that 'the Union of the advanced proletariat of Europe and America with the awakening toiling masses of the East is an absolutely necessary fact for our victory'. Meanwhile he also said, 'the question of the attitude towards the colonial nations, far from being disposed of by the Versailles Peace and the Washington Conference, will of course continue to exist even after the forthcoming Genoa Conference'. The next speaker was the Japanese Katayama, also of the Comintern, who asserted the necessity to crush the imperialism of the Western countries which through the Washington Conference were 'trying to find means of exploiting China and Korea, Siberia and the other Far Eastern countries' [sic]. Lozovsky greeted the delegates on behalf of the Red Trade Union International. Then, Yoodzu on behalf of the Japanese delegation observed that after the world war America and Japan remained 'the only big imperialist powers'. A conflict of interests between them was inevitable and the UK and France could not avoid involvement in it, and so a further reason for the convocation of the Washington Conference was avoidance of further armed struggle involving these four powers. Among other speakers at the opening session, Tao expressed the hopes of the communist and revolutionary parties of China, referring to 'a proverb among the European peoples that a revolution is the highest, most harmonious music produced by mankind'. Pak-Kieng spoke for the Korean delegation, and Wong from China on behalf of her sisters throughout the world reminded the Congress that 'Women need their freedom as well as men'. Greetings were given by the People's Revolutionary Party of Mongolia before Simpson on behalf of the 50 million toilers of Java and the Dutch East Indies claimed that their part of the world had been relegated to second place at the Washington Conference because the capitalists of the imperialist countries had long ago decided how to exploit it. Schiller spoke briefly for the Young Communist International and Roy for India. The last speaker at the first session, Carr from the Communist Party of America, also spoke briefly about the solidarity of American workers with the toilers of the Far East, denouncing the Washington Conference for its share in 'the future changing of our labour and sweat into profits' and remarking that the workers of Porto Rico and San Domingo, of Cuba and the Philippines could bear testimony to the fact that 'the imperialism of a reactionary land like Japan and the imperialism of the outpost of democracy – America' were essentially the same.[18]

The longest speech of the Congress, taking up the whole of the second session on 23 January, was given by Zinoviev and concerned the international situation and results of the Washington Conference. Asia was playing a more important part in world politics, he argued, and the Far Eastern question might well assume primacy. The preliminaries to the Genoa Conference demonstrated 'how European disputes are becoming more and more shallow and self-exhausting'. As far as the Washington Conference was concerned, 10[13] December 1921 would remain 'one of the blackest dates in the history of mankind', for it saw the quadruple treaty of the UK, the USA, France and Japan – the 'Alliance of the Four Bloodsuckers', 'the most bloodthirsty imperialist powers'. This would not last, however, nor would any agreement about disarmament while capitalism continued to exist. As far as the problems of the Far East were concerned, neither Korea nor Mongolia was even mentioned at the Conference while the Chinese question was solved 'wholly and entirely in the American spirit' of the so-called 'open door'. Turning to Japan, Zinoviev suggested that the bourgeoisie sought dominance in the Far East and that at least some were proud to be known as 'the Prussians of the East'. Indeed, there was no issue without Japan, but it was the proletariat who held 'the key to the solution of the Far Eastern question,' and would decide the fate of several hundred million people living in China, Korea and Mongolia. While unrest in the USA might lead to a catastrophic civil war, the Soviet Republic had solved the nationalities question with unusual ease even if there were 'still many open wounds causing much suffering'. The Second Congress of the Comintern had addressed the wider problem of national movements, to whose leaders Zinoviev said 'give up your faith in Versailles and Washington'; 'if you will understand that your true leader is the Comintern, then many among you will live to see the real and final victory of the world revolution'.[19]

From the Third to the Sixth Session, the Congress was taken up mostly by reports on the situation in China, Mongolia, Korea and Japan, of considerable intrinsic interest but not directly relevant to theme of the Washington Conference, which arose again substantially in the Seventh Session during a debate on Zinoviev's report. After Yodoshu on behalf of the Chinese delegation suggested acceptance of the report without any discussion or reservations, Katayama from Japan and the Comintern spoke at some length on the Four-Power Treaty and the situation in the Far East. He believed that the USA 'gained her object without giving hardly anything', since the pact 'destroyed the obnoxious Alliance' between Great Britain and Japan while making agreements on Pacific possessions and dominions. Nevertheless, the USA 'joined the pact against her traditional policy of non-interference' in the affairs of foreign countries. And the British and Japanese were still allies under the pact, which was 'nothing but the British proposal of a Triple Alliance presented by Lloyd George to the Washington politicians in a modified form and also disguised as agreements'. If the 'very unpopular British-Japanese Alliance' had been brought to an end, Great Britain still retained Japan as 'her unpaid police for India as before', while the USA had been pacified. But there remained the possibility that Great Britain would attempt 'to involve America and Japan into some trouble with each other and side with one or other of the two Powers'. France could easily be bent to British wishes, and, with British support, could take either side in any conflict between the USA and Japan, confident that her colonial interests in the Far East were not endangered by any of the other three powers.

Japan, in Katayama's view, was also a gainer from the pact, receiving the tacit consent of the other three powers for her activities in the Far Eastern region. Some American capitalists had considered the exploitation of China jointly with Japanese counterparts, while there had been wider American acceptance of the necessity for Japan to expand. For their part, the Japanese militarists had appeared conciliatory in regard to the question of the island of Yap. So, even if the USA made an occasional feeble protest about 'the integrity of the Russian territories', the Washington Conference as a whole gave Japan the power to act freely with the reactionary elements of old Russian Tsarist and capitalist cliques. Of the quadruple pact signatories, the

60 *Soviet Russia and the USA: the new diplomacy*

French government had been 'the most interested in the Siberian invasion and openly or secretly supported the reactionary leaders and Japan as its imperialist representative'. French militarists appeared still 'to have an idea that they are able to crush Soviet Russia by financing Poland and Romania or the Ukraine and by helping the counter-revolutionary leaders in Siberia through the aid of the imperialists of Japan'.[20]

Superficially, the four-power pact assured security in the Far East for ten years, but in reality, the situation was 'much more dangerous and unstable' than before. In such circumstances, it was all the more necessary for the peoples of the Far East to support the Soviet Republic and to follow its example. And so said all the rest of the speakers following Katayama, not forgetting Zinoviev's adjuration to fight against imperialism under the banner of the Third International. Zinoviev himself spoke again to answer some particular points and to ram the general message home, reiterating the necessity for the vanguard of the Western proletariat to aid the foremost ranks of the oppressed workers of the Far East.

At the eighth session of the Congress on 26 January, the Chairman G. Saforov gave a lengthy report on 'The National-Colonial Question and the Communist Attitude thereto'. The focus of attention moved away from the Washington Conference, which received only occasional dismissive mention through several sessions. Then, appended to the eleventh session on 30 January, was a 'Resolution on Comrade Zinoviev's Report' entitled 'The Results of the Washington Conference and the Situation in the Far East', summarising and emphasising the points made by Zinoviev and others

> The Washington Conference, in the name of the Alliance of the Four Blood-suckers, has come out solidly for the predatory policy of Japanese imperialism... The imperialist plot of the four robbers of Washington combines the destinies of all the peoples of the Far East...

Finally, at the twelfth session held jointly with the Petrograd Soviet in the imperial capital, there was more reiteration and reaffirmation, including the observation from Nikolaeva that among the 200 Far Eastern delegates there were only seven women, and Zinoviev's concluding speech declaring that soon Brest–Litovsk, Versailles, Trianon, Washington would be forgotten and even Genoa too 'although there is much talk about it just now'. But Moscow and Petrograd would not be forgotten. An appendix to the proceedings of the Congress contained an emotional Manifesto to take the message to the Toilers of the Far East in China, Korea, Japan, Mongolia, the Pacific Isles, Indo-China and the Dutch Indies.[21]

In 1959, J. H. Brimmell commented, 'These two gatherings – the Washington Conference and the Congress of the Toilers of the Far East – set the stage for the world struggle between Russia and the West.'[22] Undoubtedly, we could trace a line of development from the Conference and the Congress through to the Cold War including the rivalry in the third world, a line much reinforced if we take into additional consideration the pronouncements of the Third International. In a shorter perspective, however, we can now more clearly see the huge gulf between the mode of discourse employed in Washington on the one hand and in Moscow, Irkutsk and Petrograd on the other. Anxious to reduce the breadth of this gulf, the Soviet Commissar for Foreign Affairs, G. V. Chicherin, strove to make a clear distinction between the government on the one hand and the Congress and the Third International, the Comintern, on the other.

Soviet foreign policy and the struggle for recognition

On 21 December 1921, Chicherin wrote to Lenin

> The idea of the congress of the peoples of the Far East arose at a moment of extreme aggravation in relations before the Washington Conference... Now the situation is to the contrary. It is therefore, necessary, firstly, to avoid everything that might suggest the idea of a link between our government and the congress of the peoples of the East. Secondly, it is necessary to stop any noise rising up from this congress. This is extremely untimely right now. It is necessary therefore... to arrange its sessions behind closed doors and to give them the character of the undertaking of the communist party.[23]

No doubt, Chicherin did not want to spoil the chances of the Soviet government being invited to participate in the Genoa Conference.

While the Third International continued to advertise the new line of world revolution, the Commissariat of Foreign Affairs was looking for something more like business as usual. Already, with the departure of Trotsky after Brest–Litovsk and the appointment of Chicherin towards the end of March 1918, the shop was not so much shut as refurbished. As E. H. Carr rightly observed of the new Commissar's attachment to Marxism, it was 'rooted in his subtle and highly trained intellect rather than in his emotions'. As another historian Richard K. Debo appropriately put it, Chicherin combined 'a diplomatic background with proletarian internationalism, an unparalleled knowledge of languages with love of polemics, and an interest in world affairs with near legendary capacity for hard work'. He was therefore eminently suited to play the part of Lenin's 'Man Friday', as an American diplomat dubbed him.[24]

On 23 August 1921, *The New York Times* contained an interview with Chicherin, along with his message to the American people thanking them for their famine relief aid. Chicherin said

> The Russian people are hoping that the American people will very soon surmount the separating wall of calumnies and misrepresentations now preventing relations between the two countries. Since May 1918, Russia has desired peace and trade arrangements with the United States. Much has happened since then, but nothing that changes our desires.

Chicherin hoped that the American people would learn, through their own generous contributions to famine relief, more about the Russian people and their government. On the other hand, America's policy so far seemed to indicate that no relations would be resumed with Russia until private property was restored to those who held it before the revolution. Chicherin added

> We want to open our doors to foreign capital because we know that by this means we can carry out our reconstruction plans. But we never intend to resuscitate Russian capitalism. We have just recently denationalized small businesses, but the vast land estates, the large industries and the big factories are now national property and we intend for them to remain in the hands of the workers.

Asked by the interviewer, 'has the Russian Government abandoned its policy of world-wide revolution?', Chicherin replied

> That policy only was used by the Government in the first few months of its existence and then only as a war method, the same as both sides in the last war used propaganda to weaken their enemies. In peace the Soviet Government has not had such a policy. This is the first summer in seven years in which the country has not been engaged in fighting.

Chicherin suggested that the American people should distinguish between the Soviet Government and the Third International, which had a policy of world-wide revolution. The policy of the Third International was not the policy of the Soviet Government. The two organisations were quite separate. Soviet diplomatic missions gave no aid to the Third International. Mr Zinoviev, who presided over the Third International, was also at the head of the Petrograd Soviet, but he was not in the national Government. Propaganda for world revolution was not a part of the policy of the Soviet government, which had nothing to say about the government of other peoples. Chicherin was aware of the existence of this fear in America, and of much anti-Soviet feeling based on it.[25]

Chicherin declared: 'Our plans for trade cooperation with foreign capital were taken to America in 1918 by Colonel Robins... Our principal needs are agricultural machinery, general machinery, manufactured goods and the construction of new railroads...' All foreign trade would remain distinctly a government monopoly, however. Moreover, the USA would have to recognise this Soviet government before there could be a settlement of the debt problem and an international peace conference.

On 6 December 1921, the Soviet newspaper *Izvestiia* observed

> The principal force in the world is at present not Britain, not the Entente, and not the semimythical League of Nations, but the United States of America...a rare example of harmonious development of all economic resources...rendering the country independent and self-sufficient.

There was hardly a country which was not indebted to the USA, while the League of Nations, 'still-born from the very first', had become 'a regular hoax' after the refusal of the United States to take part in it'. Soviet diplomacy would have to take into account this change in the balance of the world's forces, but also realise that in many cases its interests coincided with those of its American counterpart. While a great barrier to the renewal of relations between 'the two great republics' was a complete ignorance of the actual state of affairs in Russia providing 'fertile soil for the growth of a false perception', a rapprochement of great mutual benefit would ensue sooner or later. The USA needed a market for her products and investment of her capital, while Soviet Russia needed such assistance for the development and exploitation of vast natural wealth.[26]

This was a theme taken up by Lenin in a speech 'On the Internal and External Policy of the Republic' to the Ninth Congress of Soviets on 23 December 1921, in which he argued that the powers blockading Russia were themselves vulnerable, and needed economic relations. Thus, he believed, there was already talk of another conference to follow that being held in Washington to which both Russia and Germany would be invited.[27] Trotsky also referred to the Washington Conference in 'There are no Fronts, but there is Danger', his report to the same congress on 26 December 1921. He attacked the so-called 'great democracies' for deciding the fate of the Far East without an invitation being extended to Soviet Russia. However, the FER had been constituted as 'a defensive formation prompted by the "reason of state" of the Russian working man in the Far East, who has endeavoured in this way to hold back the onslaught of Oriental imperialism'. Both the peasants and workers of the Far East had said to the imperialists of Japan, the USA and France

> You want democracy – well, here's a democracy for you, elected by us, on the basis of universal suffrage. You have promised that if Russia becomes a democratic republic you won't touch her – well, here's the Far Eastern Republic, as the flank of the Soviet Federation.

And behind the FER stood solidly the Soviet Republic and its Red Army.[28]

The search for 'normalcy' in Soviet foreign relations was brought about by internal as well as international considerations. The New Economic Policy introduced in March 1921 could not be for home consumption only. Large-scale industry and foreign trade remained under the control of the government, but individual entrepreneurs were allowed to operate without crippling restrictions. Abroad, commercial and other forms of agreement were pursued with foreign 'bourgeois', most notably Great Britain.[29]

However, neither the Civil War nor Intervention had yet come to an end.

US attitudes towards Soviet Russia

Soviet Russia appeared to be sneering at traditional democracy and flouting the norms of governmental behaviour. Commercial as well as financial commitments had been broken, and the prospects for raw material concessions or other international deals were not encouraging, especially since there was no stable market due to economic collapse. Along with social and political instability (party feuds as well as uprisings), Soviet Russia seemed unviable to many observers. One of these, John Spargo, who had gained something of a reputation as an expert on Russia,[30] produced early in 1921 a 'Memorandum of Suggestions for a Constructive Russian Policy' embodying the following principles:

1. Refusal to recognise the present rulers of Russia as possessing the qualities of a government entitled to the fellowship and co-operation of civilised governments.
2. Non-interference in the internal affairs of Russia, and the recognition of Russia's sovereign right to choose whatever form of government or economic organisation might seem to her best and most desirable, subject only to a just regard to the comity of nations and the established principles of international law.
3. Friendly action looking to the preservation of the patrimony of Russia during the period of her distress and disability. Just as the rights and

interests of an individual were protected during incapacity in civil law by friendly trusteeships, so the rights of Russia should be protected, and the principle asserted that no final decision adverse to her should be made in any matter in which she had a vital interest, until such time as she could be properly and adequately represented by her statesmen.

4   Refusal to sanction the dismemberment of Russia as a consequence of her temporary weakness. This did not mean, nor imply, any judgement of the claims set up by national and territorial groups which had declared their independence and separation from Russia. All that it meant was that these claims could not now be finally disposed of to Russia's permanent disadvantage and injury.

5   Refusal to give recognition to the Soviet Government, but no imposition of a blockade against trade with Soviet Russia.

Of the wisdom of this policy there could hardly be any serious doubt, Spargo asserted. Political developments had vindicated its principal features as emphatically as the conscience of civilised mankind had approved them. Every week made more clearly manifest the impossibility of Bolshevism, both politically and economically, and the certainty of its speedy disappearance. It was now evident to all thoughtful men that there could be no trade between Russia and any other nation, in volume sufficient to either nation, until the Bolshevik regime was swept away. Moreover, in every instance where other Governments, shaping their policies to suit temporary conditions, had departed from the broad basic principles laid down by the USA and made, or attempted to make, deals or compromises of any kind, the result had been failure.

Nevertheless, in Spargo's view, US policy was no longer adequate, but too exclusively anti-Bolshevik, too negative. In particular, it made no definite provision for assistance to the people in those areas where Bolshevism had been eliminated, nor for prompt and effective aid to the Russian people as a whole when they would turn to the great task of reconstruction after Bolshevism had collapsed completely.

A 'sane and constructive program' should be adopted towards the Baltic States and the FER, all carved out of Russia since the Bolshevik *coup d'état*. The USA should continue to refuse to countenance the dismemberment and 'Balkanization' of Russia, not losing sight of the fact that, exclusive of Finland and Poland which belonged to a wholly different category, '*the numerous states which have declared their independence are in reality Russian areas which have emancipated themselves from Bolshevism*'. (Spargo's own emphasis). It was highly probable that, after the elimination of Bolshevism, they would want 'to become autonomous units in a great united federative Russian Republic'. In a sense, therefore, nationalist separatism was 'a phase of Russia's healing from the fever of Bolshevism'.

While 'the principal modern imperialist nations' – Germany, Great Britain, France and Japan – had sought extensive dismemberment of Russia, the interests of the USA would best be served by the restoration of the unity of Russia within the boundaries of 1914, with the exception of Finland and Poland. The reasons for this difference in policy could be indicated historically. Imperial Germany had wanted

> to weaken Russia economically, politically and militarily; to establish a buffer zone of nominally independent but German controlled states between Germany and Russia; to secure and maintain economic control over these border states, so that they would in fact constitute a chain of economic colonies.

Similarly, British imperialists had wanted to weaken Russia and erect a chain of independent states in the Middle East. Ever since the days of Lord Palmerston the statesmen of imperial Britain had feared Russia as a potential serious challenger of British imperial interests in Asia. *The Times* of London on 3 March 1919 had declared that

> the doubt as to the future developments of Russian policy throws us back into the Asiatic politics of the mid-nineteenth century, and makes it doubly necessary that we should take special precautions against danger which, here, would fall first upon us...*As in Eastern Europe we hope to see a barrier of free states erected, so England, which has India to think of, wants to see a similar barrier erected in the Middle East* (Spargo's emphasis).

Meanwhile, French policy in recent years had been largely determined by the fear of a union of Russia and Germany. Spargo noted that

> when, on 23 December 1919, M. Clemenceau urged the erection of a barrier of barbed wire around Russia, he was ostensibly dealing with the temporary condition due to Bolshevism. In reality he was upholding the well established French theory that a chain of independent states between Germany and Russia, stretching from the Baltic Sea to the Caspian, would prevent the possible union of Germany and Russia.

Finally, Japan's motives for desiring the dismemberment of Russia were also easy to understand. Her statesmen well understood that the victory over Russia in 1905 could be reversed by fully efficient Russian forces.

Another important reason for Japan wanting to weaken Russia, especially as an Asiatic power, was to make it impossible for Russia to reach the Pacific by the overland route, either by her own occupation of the Trans-Baikal territory, or by the erection there of an independent state. Thus, in the event of war with the USA, or with any European Power or Powers, Japan would make it impossible for troops and materials to be transported across Siberia to Vladivostok and used against her.

While no interest of the USA coincided with any of these imperialistic motives, the most diametrical opposition was to those of Japan. It was of vital importance, therefore, to maintain the friendship of Russia, and to maintaining her integrity from Archangel to Vladivostok. Spargo observed

> In view of the world outlook, and especially Japan's recent policy in Asia, it is impossible to overestimate the potential importance to us of a friend and ally in command of an unbroken highway from the doors of industrial Europe to the shores of the Pacific.

But this did not mean there should be a reversion to the old centralisation policy of tsarism. On the contrary, Spargo concluded

> Every American ideal, tradition and interest led irresistibly to a view of the problem identical with that taken by the Provisional Government, immediately after the Revolution of March 1917, and by all Russian Liberals during the preceding half century, namely, the unity of all the territory of the former Empire of the Czar in a democratic, federative republic, not highly centralized as under the Empire, but de-centralized and giving to all national and territorial units the largest possible political and administrative autonomy consistent with the unity of the whole. The ideal, in other words, of 'The United States of Russia'.

While, according to Spargo, partly in misunderstanding of President Wilson's doctrine of 'the right of self determination', post-revolutionary Russia had gone through a period of territorial disintegration appropriately described as Balkanisation, by 1921 the only remaining independent republics were the Baltic States – Estonia, Latvia and Lithuania – and the FER in Siberia. In these circumstances, the following measures should be adopted. Immediate political and economic relations should be established with these states, although provisional rather than formal recognition should be accorded them. Whenever there arrived in Russia proper a competent government to which the USA gave formal recognition, the whole question of Russia's sovereign territorial rights, including her interest in these states, might be re-opened and reviewed without prejudice.

68 *Soviet Russia and the USA: the new diplomacy*

A declaration along lines such as these, Spargo believed, might persuade France and other states to follow suit. In addition, preparations should be begun for emergency relief and economic co-operation in the situation in Russia which would exist when the Bolshevik regime was either overthrown or fell through internal weakness.[31]

Spargo spelt out at greater length and in a more informed manner what many US officials were thinking about Soviet Russia in 1921. There was widespread agreement in the State Department and beyond that the Bolshevik régime could not last for much longer.[32] One view had been put succinctly by Indiana governor James P. Goodrich, who was to work for Herbert Hoover in Russia: 'Communist Russia would evolve into Capitalist Russia.'[33] Secretary of State Hughes himself was among those who would agree with Spargo's suggestion that, while the other world powers, France, Great Britain and Japan as well as Germany favoured the 'Balkanization' of Russia, the USA should oppose such fragmentation. On the other hand, at least a few voices were being given to the argument that the apparent Soviet melt down was no more than an illusion, and that greater efforts should be made for rapprochement with Russia as it was, not as it might be. For example, they were to be heard in the Senate as it debated the ratification of the Washington treaties, as we shall see in Chapter 5.

Herbert Hoover and US aid to Russia

The 'central figure in the American attempt to create a better world order' was Herbert Hoover, according to Walter LaFeber, who cites a speech made by Harding's future Secretary of Commerce in December 1920 as the US economy was sinking into postwar recession. Hoover told the American Bankers Association meeting in Chicago that 'our welfare is no longer isolated from the welfare of the world'. The 'vicious economic circles' of boom and bust could 'be broken in one way only. That is by the establishment of credits abroad... We have reached the position of many European states before the war'. However, such 'foreign enterprise' had to be underwritten privately, since government involvement would lead to 'evil ends' such as 'political pressures by foreign countries and by nationals within the U.S.' A test case for his philosophy of 'American Individualism' including his insistence that 'spiritual and intellectual freedom could not continue to exist without economic freedom' was provided by the Russian famine and American aid to relieve it.[34]

An abortive pilot scheme had been mooted in October 1918 by Woodrow Wilson's Secretary of State Robert Lansing, who put forward the suggestion that Herbert Hoover, who had already headed a relief mission to Belgium, could lead a similar venture in Siberia. This would serve the dual purpose of demonstrating American resolve to bring about 'an orderly government independent of Germany' at the same time as circumventing Allied demands for large-scale intervention. Hoover believed that such military ventures would result in the restoration of 'the reactionary classes in their economic domination over the lower classes', and favoured the economic approach. While asserting that 'communism and long term credits are incompatible' and that American ideas of industrial organisation could scarcely be reconciled with 'the philosophy of Messrs. Lenin and Trotsky', he also believed that to ban trade with Russia would be regarded as governmental intervention in economic life, and also strove to ease governmental regulations so that private firms could offer long-term finance to Soviet Russian organisations. However, although he had said at the outset that for world prosperity, nothing was more necessary than 'the recovery of productivity in Russia', he also predicted that that there would be 'no consequential trade' with it in the foreseeable future.[35] Hence, beyond charity, the importance of famine relief. Moreover, diagnosing the Russian Revolution as a 'food riot', Hoover believed that humanitarian aid would in itself help to undermine Bolshevism.[36]

A call for humanitarian aid to Russia in general came from Dr Fridtjof Nansen, the Norwegian Foreign Minister, on 3 April 1919. Addressed to the Allied leaders at the Paris Conference, Nansen's appeal met with a positive response from them on 17 April, although they pointed out the difficulty of sending supplies to Russia without a cessation of hostilities there. On 5 July, Chicherin too welcomed Nansen's initiative, but warned of the political problems resulting from the Allied Intervention and support for the Whites. These were intensified when the American Relief Administration (ARA) a private organisation directed by Herbert Hoover to alleviate difficulties throughout Europe, extended some of its first help in the summer of 1919 to the Russian 'Provisional Government' of Admiral Kolchak, Hoover himself looking upon the White leaders as the last hope of establishing, 'constitutional government and fundamental liberties' in Russia.[37] A considerable boost was given to the Soviet humanitarian cause on 13 July by an appeal of Maxim Gorky to the American people, with a positive response coming from Herbert Hoover ten days later.[38] However, negotiations dragged on with the Soviet government through 1920 without agreement before the arrival of the Harding administration.

Two years later, on 25 July 1921, Secretary of State Hughes was told that 'the crisis presents an opportunity which, if rightly used, may lead to the liquidation of the Bolshevist regime and the beginning of restoration'. The informant was none other than John Spargo, who went on to say that the ARA could be

> ... not only an agency through which we can hope to extend assistance and relief to the people of Russia without strengthening the Bolshevist

regime, but, what is more important perhaps, a group actively functioning in Russia, which, if it is properly and adequately supported by the generous cooperation of this and other nations, can develop into the representative government of Russia...[39]

One way of doing this was to negotiate as much as possible with an All-Russian Committee for Aid to the Hungry set up by a decree of 21 July 1921 and containing non-Bolsheviks, even non-socialists, as well as members of the Soviet Government.

A discordant note was struck on 2 August by Lenin in an 'Appeal to the International Proletariat': A serious famine was the consequence of backwardness and of seven years of war, first imperialist, then civil, thrust upon the peasants and workers by the landlords and capitalists of all countries. Those who were suffering needed help from their counterparts elsewhere who would surely answer the appeal even though oppressed by unemployment and high prices, since all who those who had lifelong experience of capitalist oppression would understand the plight of the Russian workers and peasants. They would also know or feel the need to help the Soviet Republic which was the first to take upon itself the noble but difficult task of the overthrow of capitalism. That is why the capitalists of all countries were taking vengeance on the Soviet Republic and preparing new plans of campaign, intervention and counter-revolutionary plots. But Lenin was convinced that the workers and peasants of all countries would be all the more energetic and self-sacrificing in the help that they extended.[40]

In fact, major relief was to come from the capitalist Herbert Hoover's ARA which, after negotiations with a Soviet delegation in the Latvian capital, Riga, signed a bilateral agreement on 20 August. The terms included arrangements for the conditions for the work of the ARA officials in Russia and for the departure from Soviet Russia of all Americans detained there. However, one of the US negotiators at Riga soon complained that they had been asked 'to formally state that our object was to bring relief to the famine-stricken regions of the Volga' and to accept several restrictions on the freedom of movement of the ARA officials. Apprehensive of further American dealings with the Whites, the Soviet representatives insisted on maintaining 'the right of search of our premises and their right to request the withdrawal of members of the mission engaged in political activity'.[41]

Lenin was not finished with his hopes of aid from proletarian sources. On 22 August he wired the President of the Comintern Zinoviev expressing his fears that the Riga agreement of two days before meant that aid from the USA would come via Hoover, not directly. Lenin therefore asked Zinoviev to make sure that the Comintern, while refraining from criticism of the American government for the time being, should notify workers to make their donations via Soviet Russian representatives abroad. Such direct aid would have the great advantage of being unconditional.[42] Moreover, within Soviet Russia itself, Lenin wanted to keep reliable hands on the purse strings. On 27 August, the All-Russian Committee for Aid to the Hungry set up earlier in the summer was formally dissolved,[43] Lenin fearing that its 'bourgeois' members were not sufficiently under party control. On 26 August, he had written to Stalin and all members of the Politburo that one of these suspect people should be arrested on a charge of 'anti-government speech' while the others should immediately 'be exiled from Moscow and scattered singly in provincial towns if possible away from the railway *under surveillance* [Lenin's italics]'.[44]

During the months of the Washington Conference, from November 1921 to February 1922, differences in attitude and reaction to the question of famine relief appear to have narrowed. On 5 November, Colonel William N. Haskell, the ARA chief in Russia, sent a confidential report to Hoover observing that scarcely a day was passing without 'some new concession to private ownership and right to trade' while seed distribution was under way for the following farming year. On 22 November, Lenin confidentially sent members of the Politburo a draft of a letter to Hoover saying that, according to Haskell, he himself would be prepared to come to Russia to help with the task of economic revival. Repeating what he said he had told Haskell, Lenin continued: 'Help to us from an outstanding organiser and a "captain of industry" in a country with principles of economic order opposite to ours would have extraordinarily great significance and would be particularly desirable and agreeable for us.' Lenin asked the members of the Politburo and Chicherin if they thought it advisable for him to give such a letter to Haskell or, in view of the unclear political circumstances, should he feign illness in order to avoid giving Haskell a letter of any kind.[45] On 30 November, an article in *Izvestiia* by A. Eiduk, a hero of the revolution now the Russian Representative on the staff of the ARA in Russia, praised ARA workers for their energy and commitment, although regretting that 'the food that has been delivered to the provinces has not yet reached the empty stomachs of the population'. However, another somewhat discordant note was struck by the Executive Committee of the Comintern on 13 December with the publication of its observation that, while the ARA was hogging the limelight and monopolising all publicity, 'the American workers have organised and are putting into operation their own class relief organization, which is aiding the starving Russian workers and peasants without exacting humiliating and tyrannic conditions'.[46]

On 16 December, Hoover confidentially proposed that more pressure should be applied to the Russians: 'It cannot be expected that American people will give charity in this volume while Soviet Russia does not strain

72 *Soviet Russia and the USA: the new diplomacy*

its every source.' Nevertheless, on 22 December, the US Congress voted $20 million for purchase, transport and distribution of corn, seed grain and preserved milk for famine relief and spring planting. On 30 December, the Soviet authorities placed at the disposal of the ARA $10 million worth of gold for further purchases. But an article in *Izvestiia* of 4 January 1922 suggested that 'bread alone' was not enough, going on to lament that Russian transport was in a miserable state, and that the USA should send locomotives, automobiles and spare parts to make up the deficiency. While such action would put Russia on her feet, it would also help to relieve unemployment and over-production in the USA, whose 'economic and political interests are at the present time identical with those of Russia'.[47]

Supplemented by medical supplies, US aid continued into 1922, if not without difficulties. And in the summer of 1923, the ARA's activities in Russia were wound up, the situation having improved enough for a farewell banquet on 18 July not to appear in bad taste. Chicherin was among those to make speeches, observing

> Just as in America in the beginning consisted of separate governments, connected with each other by a union, which gradually became one powerful united government, so our republics have now created one centre for the functions of all republics, including foreign affairs and foreign trade.

This one centre would organise economic policy in such a manner that future relations with the USA would be facilitated. The American and Soviet peoples had just began to know each other: with the activities of the ARA leaving an indelible impression, the two peoples would soon extend their hands to each other for the good of humanity.[48]

Cordial farewells could not dispel entirely the feelings of mutual suspicion engendered by the activities of the ARA in Soviet Russia. Later appraisals have by no means all been positive: E. H. Carr suggested that ARA 'clearly hoped' to use the relief programme to weaken the position of the Soviet Government; Peter J. Filene characterised ARA activities in Russia as 'more devious than frank counter-revolution'; and William A. Williams found Hoover guilty of using them exclusively for counter-revolutionary purposes.[49]

Certainly, the ARA's head undoubtedly favoured Kolchak and other White leaders and spoke in support of the quarantine of their Red opponents in 1919.[50] Moreover, although his later outrage at the charge of ARA espionage appears justified in the full account of Bertrand M. Patenaude,[51] Hoover hoped to undermine Bolshevism by negotiating to bring aid to the starving and the sick, as we have seen.

In a sense, then, the new diplomacy was already turning out to be devious like the old. Meanwhile, in his assertion that the Third International was separate from the Soviet Russian regime, Chicherin was demonstrating that a People's Foreign Commissar could lie on behalf of his country as much as his Tsarist predecessors.

As we shall see in Chapter 4, more examples of Soviet deviousness could be found in some of the policies of the FER.

4 The Far Eastern Republic
A Trojan Horse?

On 4 March 1921, a letter was sent to the White House in Washington DC from the Executive House in Chita, to President Harding of the USA from the President of the Republic of the Far East and Minister for Foreign Affairs A. M. Krasnoshchekov. In the name of his young republic, Krasnoshchekov asked 'Honorable Mister Harding' to allow him to offer congratulations 'upon the acceptance of the high office, the greatest gift of the free people of the greatest Republic of the USA'. The letter included the observation: 'the shining example of the great American democracy and the ideals it stands for serve as a source of inspiration and encourangment [sic] to our people fighting against terrible odds...'[1] A letter of the same date was sent to the Chairman of the Senate and the Speaker of the House of Representatives from the Constituent Assembly of the Far East observing that

> Upon the vast territory east of the Baikal [sic] to the Pacific, a new independent democratic state is being organized, separate and distinct in its form of government and social structure from the system prevailing in Soviet Russia... It is the earnest hope of our people that the new Administration and Congress true to the great American ideal of freedom and self-determination will lend a helping hand to our young Republic in its struggle against intervention and for separate independent existence.[2]

Obviously, there were high hopes that the new US administration would give a full measure of attention to the FER and its problems, the greatest of which was the Japanese intervention. Let us turn our attention to this problem before considering in detail the formation of the FER, its Constituent Assembly and its participation in the Dairen Conference with Japan. But let us not forget that our major purpose is to illumine problems of international relations in the context of the Washington Conference. The attempt of a delegation from the FER to influence the outcome of that conference will be the concluding theme of the chapter.

The Japanese intervention

According to Raymond Leslie Buell writing in 1922, Japan followed its own historic impulses as well as the example of all the Western empires. Spurred on by her lack of resources and possessed by the 'Evil Spirit of militarism', Japan sought to exploit the 'fathomless, but unused wealth' of the nearby continent: 'The resources of China will supply Japan indefinitely, but now they are scarcely exploited. The vast stretches of Manchuria, Mongolia, and Siberia will raise the grain necessary to feed the multiplying millions in Japan, but their fields are still unplowed.'[3] Later assessment would find less of the 'Evil Spirit' and more of the *realpolitik* that the Japanese had learned – if they needed to – from Germany and the other Western powers. For Japan, comments Frederick R. Dickinson, the First World War was 'more of a domestic political struggle over national identity than it was a strategic battle against a foreign enemy'. He goes on to observe that, at the very least, 'both Japanese admirers of Great Britain and their chief rivals, men inspired by Imperial Germany, agreed on one thing in 1914: the importance of Japanese imperialist expansion on the continent.'[4] We can make no exact assessment of the relationship between indigenous tradition and foreign example. However, we can emphasise the suggestion that the later the application to join the society of imperial powers, the more the energy that had to be exerted to gain and consolidate membership. Hence to a considerable extent the militarism of Japan, and the aggressive policies associated with Japanese intervention in the Far East. Having already considered this subject to some extent under the headings 'Intervention in Russia' and 'Open Doors and Monroe Doctrines' in Chapter 1, let us turn our closer attention now to the most significant aspects of it for our overall purpose.

Towards the end of the nineteenth century, the conflict between Tsarist Russia and Japan, which culminated in actual warfare, was brought about by the similarity of the policies of the two countries in Korea and Manchuria especially, and to some extent in Mongolia.[5] Although both sides professed the principles of independence, they were actually aiming not only to gain a foothold in those regions, but also to establish themselves there both economically and politically. In 1894, Japan acquired rights to the Liaotung peninsula as a result of war with China. However, she was obliged to return this district to China after protests from France, Germany and especially Russia. Japanese resentment grew in 1896 when Russia acquired a valuable concession in Manchuria, namely, the zone for the construction of the CER. In 1898, this resentment reached fever pitch when Russia obtained the lease of the Liaotung peninsula including Port Arthur, and then, after a further two years, under cover of the Boxer uprising, occupied Manchuria. The effort of Russia in 1901 to legalise this seizure immediately aroused the opposition of Japan; the underlying threat of aggression on the part of Tsarist Russia in Korea forced Japan to think of open conflict or reconciliation to defeat. The conclusion of the Anglo-Japanese alliance in 1902 brought forward the first alternative.

The defeat of Tsarist Russia in the war of 1904–5 encouraged Japan to think of expansion not only into Korea, annexed in 1910, but also into Southern Manchuria and beyond, Southern Sakhalin and beyond. In the view of the FER's own history of the intervention, Japan began to display open tendencies towards establishing a foothold on the Far Eastern shores of Russia itself. These tendencies were at first revealed in determined if unsuccessful efforts to dominate Far Eastern fisheries and to obtain navigation rights in the River Amur. In spite of these efforts, Japan nevertheless concluded a number of secret agreements with Tsarist Russia aimed at curbing the ambitions of the other great powers to establish themselves in China. G. A. Lensen went so far as to observe: 'There is a thin line between love and hate. In the decade following the Russo-Japanese War Tsarist Russia and Japan abruptly shed their hostility and became friends.'[6]

When the First World War kept Tsarist Russia busy on the German front and left the Far East exposed, in 1915 the Japanese imposed their notorious 21 Demands upon China concerning Shantung and Manchuria. They also raised again the coastal fisheries and navigation questions, almost obtaining a favourable solution of them. As the USA entered the war, Wilson's administration strove for collaboration with its allies for stability in China, but also entered into direct negotiations with Japan leading to the Lansing–Ishii agreement of 2 November 1917, which recognised that 'territorial propinquity creates special relations' between countries and that Japan had 'special interests' in China. The two sides agreed that China's sovereignty must not be impaired and that they would both maintain the 'open door' principle. Secretly, they committed themselves further not to take advantage of the European war to seek 'special rights or privileges which would abridge the rights of subjects of other nations'.[7]

Nevertheless, with the Revolution of 1917, and particularly with the outbreak of the civil war, Japan devised a programme to dominate the Russian Far East both economically and politically, using the same methods that had been applied by both Japan and Tsarist Russia in China and Korea. The characteristic main feature of this policy was cautiousness. First, from December 1917 to August 1918, playing upon the feelings produced in Great Britain and France by Russia's abandonment of the war, Japan aroused the Allies against the Russian Far East, and particularly against Vladivostok, by suggesting that the region was one in which the lives and property of foreigners were in danger, and that it would therefore require a prolonged presence of warships and landing parties. When France and

Great Britain had decided upon an active policy in Russia, hoping to overthrow the Soviet government with the aid of all the anti-Bolshevik elements and thus to force Russia back into the group of belligerent nations, the Japanese assumed a modest position of watchfulness until Great Britain and France succeeded in drawing the USA into the intervention. Then, after the question of sending troops into Russian territory had been decided upon, Japan still waited for the 'invitation' of her new Far Eastern competitor, the USA.[8] As Walter LaFeber puts it, 'Japan was becoming the great Asian power, but it still needed the Americans'.[9]

To resume the FER's own account, the Japanese intervention began on 30 December 1917 when a warship sailed unexpectedly into the port of Vladivostok, and the Consul-General issued a declaration to the Mayor of Vladivostok and the Chairman of the Maritime Province Zemstvo Board stating that

> This decision was made with no other purpose than that of defending Japanese subjects, which is a duty incumbent upon the government... The Imperial Government has, moreover, no intention whatsoever of meddling in the question of the political structure of Russia, which will be determined by the Russian people, and the object of the present expedition has no connection whatever with this question.[10]

As could only be expected, the Mayor and Zemstvo Board protested against the violation of the sovereign rights of the Russian Republic. The Japanese did not respond, but the consuls of Great Britain and the USA sent the regional government on 16 January 1918 an expression of 'feelings of uneasiness on the part of those countries having considerable material interests here' which they considered sufficient justification for intervention. A second Japanese ship was followed by others, from Great Britain and the USA in particular.[11]

On 28 June 1918 Vladivostok and its environs were seized by the Czechs (strictly speaking Czecho-Slovaks) who had overthrown Soviet power in Siberia. Their commander joined with local Allied counterparts to issue a proclamation to the local population on 6 July including the observation

> The authority of the Zemstvo and of the City Government is recognized in local affairs, but the military force and the police shall be strengthened by such numbers of Allied troops as may be found necessary for eliminating the danger threatening from Austro-German agents and their influence, who, according to information in our possession, are active in the city.

Thus the intervention was taken a significant stage further.[12]

78 The Far Eastern Republic: a Trojan Horse?

Under the cover of the above excuses, the FER account alleged, the Japanese in particular sought to create an army opposed to Soviet power led by Cossack atamans and former Tsarist officers and including 'ignorant natives of the Buriat and Mongolian tribes, as well as Chinese Khun-Khuses [bandits]'. While the French and British were framing great plans for the renewal of the Russian participation in the war with Germany, the US authorities formulated the task of their troops as the 'guarding of supplies that might later be of assistance to the Russian troops and also the giving of aid such as the Russians would be ready to accept in the organization of their own self-defense'. Nevertheless, the USA, like Great Britain and France and others and especially Japan, became more involved in the business of intervention, in spite of assurances about the non-violation of Russian territory and political sovereignty and non-intervention in internal affairs. In a declaration of 5 August 1918, the USA assumed officially the political responsibility for the entrance of Japanese troops: 'The United States and Japan are the only powers now able to act in Siberia with sufficient forces to carry out even those modest aims that have been indicated above.'[13]

Although the World War came to an end in November 1918, the intervention did not cease: indeed, further justification was found for it. For example, an allied agreement of 14 March 1919 set up a Railroad Commission to guard the Chinese, Ussuri and Siberian railways.[14] Later, this Commission was to complain of Japanese attempts to take it over.

In September 1919, the British interventionists left the Far East, and hopes rose that they would be followed by the others. On 24 November, Chicherin offered to negotiate with the Japanese, but received no reply. Concern about the Japanese was no doubt on Lenin's mind when, as the Fifth Red Army advanced in Western Siberia, Lenin sent his congratulations on the seizure of Novonikolaevsk (later Novosibirsk) on 15 December 1919, but added the warning 'Remember, that it will be a crime to go too far to the East.'[15] In January 1920, the USA notified Japan about its intention to withdraw its expeditionary force, the last units of which departed from Vladivostok on 1 April. But the Japanese stayed on, issuing a declaration on 31 March to the effect that

> as no other country is geographically so closely connected with Siberia as our empire, and whereas the political condition of the Far East is such as to threaten not only the life and property of our citizens living in Siberia, but also to make a breach of the peace of Korea and Manchuria, we regret to state that it will be impossible to evacuate our troops from the Far Eastern territory.[16]

The formation of the FER

The formation of the FER was intimately connected with the ongoing problem of the Japanese intervention and the Soviet hope to stimulate opposition to it among the international community, especially by the USA. On 20 January 1920, N. N. Smirnov, the chairman of the Siberian Revolutionary Committee, reported to Lenin and Trotsky that a new move was being suggested by the Political Centre created at the end of 1919 in Irkutsk by the Menshevik and Socialist–Revolutionary Parties. Their aim was the creation in the Far East of a democratic republic independent of Soviet Russia which, in Smirnov's words, would 'break the blockade with the help of America and clear the Far East of the Japanese exclusively through American pressure'. In the event of war, he believed, the dissident Political Centre would come under Bolshevik control. The Revolutionary Military Committee of the Fifth Army, of which Smirnov was also a member, therefore proposed to recognise the buffer state stretching from the River Oka to Vladivostok. The Czechs and the Japanese should be fully informed about this measure, which the Political Centre could use as a basis for insisting on the retreat of the Czechs beyond Lake Baikal. Meanwhile, the Fifth Army would in effect take over the army of the Political Centre, which would be persuaded to move from Irkutsk to Chita, with the frontier between Soviet Russia and the new republic becoming Lake Baikal. The Revolutionary Military Committee considered 'the temporary existence of a fictitious state useful for purely strategic considerations'. But it could hardly be made secure for more than four weeks. Smirnov concluded by asking Lenin and Trotsky for their views about how to play the card of the buffer state.[17]

On 21 January 1920, Lenin and Trotsky sent a telegram to the Revolutionary Military Committee of the Fifth Army accepting Smirnov's suggestion about the buffer state and the expulsion of the Czechs.[18] On 18 February, the Bolshevik Central Committee directed the Siberian Revolutionary Committee to support the buffer state and to quell all opposition to it.[19] On 19 February, Lenin wired Trotsky agreeing with him that opponents of the buffer state should be roundly censured and suppressed by the party so that everybody in Siberia could make a reality of the slogan 'Not a step further to the East, strain every nerve for the speedy movement of troops and trains to Western Russia'. They would be idiots and criminals to allow a stupid move into the depths of Siberia, when the Whites were reviving and the Poles attacking.[20] No doubt, the execution of Kolchak on 7 February had also relieved pressure to the East. However, the Japanese intervention was continuing, less urgent than the threats confronting Soviet Russia in Europe, but remaining a painful thorn in its Far Eastern side nevertheless.

80 The Far Eastern Republic: a Trojan Horse?

According to the FER's own short outline history which we will follow closely, at the time of the fall of the reactionary government of Admiral Kolchak in February 1920, White leaders such as General Rozanov in Vladivostok, Ataman Semenov in Transbaikalia and Ataman Kalmykov in Khabarovsk and others were still employing throughout the Far East and the whole of Siberia 'a system of incredible despotism and cruel repressions, violating all civil liberties and popular rights'.[21] This system aroused the opposition of even moderately minded democratic zemstvos and autonomous municipal administrations, and they began to collaborate with the partisan movement which was to include within its ranks not only the 'middle' peasants but also the wealthiest peasants who owned large tracts of land. Workers in their organisations and other democratic bodies from the cities joined in, too, and the reinforced partisan movement managed to confine the reactionary governments to the large cities which were cut off from each other.

At the beginning of 1920, the popular revolutionary movement was asserting itself in the Amur region and Maritime Province. While in the Amur region the interventionists were exclusively Japanese, in the Maritime Province there were also Americans and some Czechs, who were at least partly guided by the principle of non-interference in the internal affairs of the Russian people. In the Amur region, therefore, the opposition movement became accustomed to the thought that 'only union with kindred Soviet Russia will assure the success of their efforts to free themselves from their native and foreign oppressors'. In the Maritime Province, on the other hand, the revolutionary and democratic forces came to the conclusion that they must secure the support of at least some of the Allies, and that they could achieve this only if they accepted the principles of democratic government – 'Thus was originated and strengthened in the Far East the idea of its organization into an independent democratic state, founded on the recognition of civil liberties.'[22]

In the month or so following the fall of Kolchak, Semenov managed to hold out in Transbaikalia, but Rozanov was overthrown in Vladivostok and Kalmykov fled from Khabarovsk. Already in March 1920, negotiations began between the Maritime Province and the Amur region concerning the creation of a united government for the liberated Far East. But a formidable stumbling block was created by the Japanese interventionists, who continued to support Semenov and to inhibit the democratic movement in every way possible.

However, at the end of March 1920, a popular movement swept the Semenov forces from Pribaikalia to the west of the great lake, and set up a democratic administration formed by autonomous zemstvo organizations and representatives of socialist and democratic organizations in Verkhne–Udinsk

[Ulan–Ude] to the east of it. There on 6 April, the creation was proclaimed by a regional conference of an independent republic including Transbaikalia, the Amur region, the Maritime Province and Sakhalin, with a democratic government and all civil liberties. Then the conference formed a provisional government and entrusted it with the task of uniting all regions into one republic and of appealing to all nations, through their governments, inviting them to establish friendly relations with the guarantee of full inviolability of person and property for all foreigners.

The Verkhne–Udinsk declaration of 6 April 1920 set the standard for the subsequent struggle for independence. But at no time was it suggested that the national bonds binding the region to the rest of Russia should be broken. On the contrary, the separation was seen from the beginning as no more than the consequence of the prevailing international circumstances and isolation from the mother country. For its part, the Soviet Russian government sent on 14 May a note signed by the People's Commissar for Foreign Affairs recognising the FER and its provisional government.[23]

As for the Japanese, their response to the request for their withdrawal of the government of the Maritime Province of 2 March 1920 was to send more divisions there. During the course of a Russian counter-attack, there occurred what became known as the Nikolaevsk 'incident' or 'massacre' when several hundred Japanese were killed by partisans in a town near the mouth of the Amur River in March.[24] As part of their retaliation, the Japanese consolidated their occupation of the northern part of the island of Sakhalin 'until a satisfactory settlement of the Nikolaevsk affair could be obtained from a government Japan recognized'.[25]

On 25 May 1920 the revolutionary administration of the Amur region passed a resolution of adherence to the Verkhne–Udinsk declaration of 6 April, recognising the Verkhne–Udinsk government as the Central Government of the FER in view of the circumstances obtaining in Vladivostok. A preliminary conference of the representatives of all regional governments was held in Verkhne–Udinsk in September 1920. At this conference, full agreement as to the bases of unity and the formation of a single democratic authority was all the more easily reached since the recognition of democratic principles had already been previously proclaimed in all parts of the country in almost identical expressions in the representative organs of the regions.

Obstacles still had to be overcome. The Japanese military command persisted in demanding the recognition of Ataman Semenov in Chita, while on 11 September, the Japanese semi-official information bureau issued a report under the heading 'The treacherous attitude of the Verkhne–Udinsk government in connection with the project of the creation of a buffer state'.[26] This report contained accusations as to the equivocal attitude and bad faith of the Verkhne–Udinsk government, reproaching it for the disagreement between the various Russian local governments, which distrusting each other, were waging a struggle for hegemony. In fact, this was a complaint about the non-recognition of Semenov.

In November 1920, Chita fell to the revolutionary troops and Semenov was put to flight towards Manchuria. A Unity Conference of all the various governments of the Far East met immediately in Chita, and on 9 November endorsed the declaration of 6 April concerning the independence of the republic, the establishment of a democratic administration the basis of which was to be the introduction of all civil liberties and the preservation of the principle of private property. A new declaration announced that: in the course of the next two or three months a Constituent Assembly of the Far East would be called on the basis of a universal, equal, direct and secret suffrage; out of the membership of this conference there was to be elected a single provisional government of the Republic; at the moment in which it was elected, all existing governments would have to give up their state prerogatives and would become organs of the local autonomous administration until new elections took place on the basis of the law concerning this administration. The declaration granted an amnesty to remnants of the White Armies surrendering their arms and permitted them to return to peaceful work.

Immediately afterwards, the conference elected the Provisional Government of the FER, the main task of which was the calling of the Constituent Assembly. In such a manner, the task of uniting the Far East in one single state was formally accomplished, and the entire territory with the exception of Sakhalin and the district of Nikolaevsk on the Amur, which were still occupied by the interventionists, was united under the rule of the Provisional Government. While enemies still had to be overcome, an important kindred spirit was Soviet Russia, which on 28 October, even before the conference had begun, had sent greetings to it expressing the hope that unity would be successfully attained and that friendly relations between the young republic and the mother country would be strengthened.

While continuing their intervention and their support for Semenov's army, the Japanese military command also tried by means of memoranda and unofficial communications to restrain the Vladivostok administration and the Assembly of the Maritime Province from the recognition of the decisions of the Unity Conference and from submitting to the single government that was elected there. At the same time, agents of the Japanese General Staff in Vladivostok were conducting an underground activity with a view to creating general confusion and were spreading rumours about the possibility of a reactionary coup with the help of the Japanese. In spite of all this, however, the Assembly recognised all the decisions of the Unity Conference and of the Provisional Government of the entire Republic.[27]

In November, detachments of Semenov's army seized the station of Grodekovo and other points of the Ussuri railway, further disrupting communications and transport. They also created there a new Chita with its own laws and authorities without any regard to the democratic organs and law of the FER. Moreover, the Japanese military command took a number of further harmful steps, including the assumption of jurisdiction over almost all fisheries of the Maritime Province. Notwithstanding all difficulties and obstacles, however, the Provisional Government of the FER published on 12 December 1920 its decision for elections to a Constituent Assembly to be held throughout its entire territory on 9 January 1921. The elections were duly held on the appointed day, although the Constituent Assembly, due to convene on 25 January, did not actually begin its work until 12 February.

The FER's constituent assembly

According to *A Short Outline of the History of the Far Eastern Republic*, which we continue to follow while recognising its propagandistic nature, the rights and interests of the people and the introduction of a strict democratic order and constitution were fully guaranteed in both the voting procedure and the composition of the elected body. The elections were held on the basis of the most democratic suffrage, according to the system of proportional representation, while the election campaign took place with complete freedom of written and oral propaganda for all parties and groups of the population. Even remnants of Kolchak's army led by General Kappel were allowed to vote, and elected two generals, who did not, however, take part in the activities of the Constituent Assembly, preferring to organise conspiracies and to prepare reactionary upheavals under the protection of Japanese bayonets. Overall, the number of voters who participated in the elections was very large, as high as 80 per cent in many districts, never lower than 60 per cent.

The largest number of representatives was sent by the peasantry, the largest part of the population: approximately 220 deputies known as the group of the revolutionary toiling peasantry, or the group of the majority, formed about 60 per cent of the total membership. The next largest number of delegates was the 80–90 representatives of the working class and most revolutionary elements of the cities forming the communist group. 30 delegates representing the wealthiest peasants were known as the group of the peasant minority, while a total of 58 delegates were formed into small groups representing Social Democrats, Right Socialist Revolutionaries and the wealthy bourgeoisie. While the group of the majority predetermined the result of the voting, many of the most important questions of principle were settled by unanimous vote.

The first of these was the adoption of a general edict recognising the decisions of all regional representative organs and of the conferences of the regional governments on the formation of an independent state – the democratic FER. All foreign interference of whatever kind was considered to be a brutal outrage, and a violation of basic international law and civilisation. The general declaration stated that the foundations of the state organisation of the republic should be the principles of real democracy and self-government, put into effect by popular representation on the basis of universal, equal, direct and secret suffrage, guaranteeing to all citizens political liberty and the preservation of the principle of private property. In a separate article the declaration also stated that the republic intended to take measures for the invitation of foreign capital and initiative for the development of the natural resources of the country.[28]

The ensuing act of the Constituent Assembly was the adoption of solemn appeals to the governments and the nations of the whole world, and particularly to the governments of the larger powers, the USA, Great Britain, France and Japan, which had participated in the landing of their troops in 1918 on the territory which became part of the FER. In the first of these appeals, the Constituent Assembly informed the governments and the nations of the creation of an independent FER and declared that it was necessary for the successful development of the new democratic country that the FER should be accepted with equal rights into the family of the other independent nations and that its territory should be liberated from foreign troops and intervention.

In particular, in its note to the Japanese government, the Constituent Assembly characterised the situation which was created as a result of the activities of the Japanese military command on the territory of the republic. In the memorandum to the government of the USA the Constituent Assembly referred to the declaration of the American government of 5 August 1918 which 'most sincerely and solemnly' declared to the Russian people that the intervention did not mean any interference in its internal or even local matters, that the exclusive and the only aim of the intervention was to offer such help as would be acceptable to the Russian people themselves in their aspiration again to become masters of their own affairs, of their own territory and of their own destiny. In recalling these promises, the Constituent Assembly raised the question of the responsibility for the still existing military intervention which expressed itself in continuous brutalities by the Japanese military command, in open assistance to reactionary groups, and in endless violations of the rights and the interests of the population of the FER. Finally the Constituent Assembly expressed the hope that the government of the great democratic republic would recognise the independence of the FER.

With a feeling of bitterness, *A Short Account* remarked that not one of the governments of the large countries, except China, answered the address and the appeals of the young democratic republic of the Far East to aid it in its efforts to defend its rights to an independent existence and to develop and strengthen its democratic state organisation.

After the formulation of the above addresses, the Constituent Assembly entered upon the elaboration of the fundamental laws which were the bases of the democratic constitution of the country. The discussion and adoption of these laws took up the greater part of the working time of the Constituent Assembly. In their main, essential features they represented a development of the theses expressed in the declaration which was adopted by the Constituent Assembly at the very beginning of its deliberations.

The full text of the constitution, issued separately among other official documents, contained the following sections: general principles of the state organisation of the republic; the domains of the republic; the rights of the citizens; the local organs of the central government and of the autonomous administration; fundamental principles of the economical structure of the republic; the defence of the republic; revision of the fundamental laws; the emblem and flag of the republic; statement about the first National Assembly and the election of the government of the Republic.

After completing the Constitution and after adopting the motion concerning the first National Assembly of the republic, the Constituent Assembly, in accordance with the Constitution, instituted a permanent government consisting of seven members which took over the full civil and military authority in the territory of the FER subject to the fundamental laws of the country. Immediately after an appeal to the population of the country, the Constituent Assembly declared itself dissolved on 26 April 1921.[29]

The continuation of the Japanese intervention

During and after the deliberations of the Constituent Assembly, the Japanese interventionists and their henchmen, the Russian Whites, continued their activities. Allegedly, from the end of 1920 to the beginning of 1921, Japanese and French representatives corresponded about the transfer of the troops of General Wrangel from the Crimea to Vladivostok to continue the fight against the FER. In March 1921, a secret treaty was said to be signed by Japanese, French and White Russian delegates confirming complete Japanese domination of Siberia, including all concessions, and control of the CER. Chicherin complained about this to Curzon, among others, receiving short shrift from the British Foreign Secretary. In May 1921,

Japanese and Russian White forces combined to take over Vladivostok again

> Coupled with the Japanese occupation of Sakhalin and the district of Nikolaevsk, the passing of the Maritime Province into the hands of the interventionists and reactionaries... opened a wound in the body of a weak democratic country, still dripping with the blood of the Russian people.[30]

On 31 May 1921, the US State Department sent a note recalling Japanese assurances to the Allies about the evacuation of the Far East and refusing to 'recognize as valid any claims or titles arising out of the present occupation and control' or to 'acquiesce in any action taken by the Government of Japan which might impair existing treaty rights or the political or territorial integrity of Russia'. Moreover, in the State Department's assessment, 'continued occupation of the strategic centers in eastern Siberia... tends to increase rather than allay the unrest and disorder in that region'.[31]

On 2 June 1921, the FER government sent a note to the government of Japan complaining about the activities of Semenov and others in Vladivostok and the manner in which, together with those of the Japanese forces, they had impeded the work of the FER's Constituent Assembly. Nevertheless, an unnamed member of an American mission to the FER in Chita had said that he felt as good and as calm as he would in his democratic homeland, although he also recognised that order could not be fully restored in the FER until the departure of the Japanese.[32] (Although no reply ensued, on 29 June Chicherin was to wire the FER's Foreign Minister I. L. Iurin not to believe the 'honeyed words' of the Japanese, but to work for precise and businesslike talks with them while telling them unofficially that they could negotiate with Soviet Russia's representative Karakhan in Warsaw[33].)

Meanwhile, according to *A Short Account*, 'a new faithful tool of the Japanese militarists' appeared in the shape of Baron Ungern Sternberg who, immediately after Semenov had been driven from Transbaikalia, went to Mongolia to commence activities there against the republic. Stirring up the Mongolians against the Chinese, he took Urga [Ulan Bator], their capital, in February 1921, and used it as a base from which to prepare an attack on the republic from the west, while Semenov was launched from the east. But the people of the Amur, even the wealthy Cossacks, would not support Semenov, while Ungern was defeated near Verkhne–Udinsk at the end of June 1921. Driven back to Urga, which was temporarily taken by a combined force of the Soviet army and the 'popular revolutionary army' in July, Ungern escaped only to be taken prisoner by the Reds in August.[34]

The Far Eastern Republic: a Trojan Horse? 87

On 18 June 1921, the US Department of State complained to the Japanese Embassy in Washington DC about the activities of Semenov and Ungern Sternberg in collusion with the Japanese throughout the Far East, especially in Mongolia and Manchuria. On 8 July, the Japanese Embassy replied at length to the US memorandum of 31 May asserting that the Japanese forces could not leave the Russian Far East until the rights of Japanese residents were guaranteed and the frontier with Korea made secure, and insisting again that Northern Sakhalin had to be occupied in reprisal for the outrage at Nikolaevsk. An *aide-mémoire* followed on 14 July in response to the State Department's note of 18 June disclaiming collaboration between the Japanese forces on the one hand and those of Semenov and Ungern Sternberg on the other.[35]

While the armed struggle continued, civil activity by no means stopped after the closure of the Constituent Assembly. Immediately after the establishment of the government the formation ensued of a Council of Ministers, which according to the Constitution was responsible to the Government and to the National Assembly. The Council of Ministers was formed on a coalition basis with the participation of the opposition formed from right and moderate socialists. For the period beginning 1 May 1921 the Council of Ministers elaborated and submitted for sanction by the government a number of very important laws and measures referring to the most varied concerns of state policy.

Under this heading were laws establishing the functions of the administrative organs, governing the elections to the regional Assemblies of Representatives and providing for the people's control, regional emissaries and local autonomous administrative organs. There were also measures covering the levying and collection of taxes, among which the most important were a national, progressive income and property tax, a grain tax, a tax in kind on commercial and industrial enterprises, as part of a fundamental industrial tax. Regulations were introduced for the estimates and records of general and state revenues, and concerning the unity of the treasury.

In addition, there were statutes regulating economic life including: the private gold industry; land-property relations between the Buriat–Mongol and the Russian populations; the industrial establishments of the state; and the granting of concessions for the exploitation of mineral resources and forest areas.

In consideration of the extraordinary events in the Maritime Province, a special law was issued, prohibiting arrangements and agreements with the insurgents calling themselves 'the Pri-Amur [Merkulov] Government', and suspending payments to the treasury in the territory occupied by the insurgents.

In the regional and district centres there were organised administrative bodies, which introduced reforms in accordance with the fundamental statutes of the Constitution adopted by the Constituent Assembly. The most important manifestations of this reorganisation of public life in the various localities were the elections and deliberations of the regional National Assemblies that took place in July and August 1921. In those parts of the Maritime Province which were seized by the reactionaries almost the entire population of the occupied territory started an active struggle against the usurpers.[36]

When the opportunity arose for a possible peaceful resolution of this struggle, the government of the FER entered into negotiations with the Japanese government at Dairen, Manchuria. At that point, *A Short Outline of the History of the FER* comes to its conclusion

> And from this history the people of the Far Eastern Republic draw the conviction that their efforts will not be in vain, that after all the time will come when they will be liberated from the bloody blight of armed foreign intervention, when they will be in a position to undertake the peaceful economic reconstruction of their entire territory.[37]

These and the preceding observations and declarations were aimed at winning over to the cause of the FER as many Americans as possible at the time of the Washington Conference. Before then, we need to note, several Americans on the spot had formed a favourable impression of the government based in Chita. For example, D. O. Lively, former director of the American Red Cross in Siberia, was convinced after a private visit in March 1921 of 'the abiding faith the people have in the future of the Republic of the Far East'. He had never seen men more serious of purpose or harder working. Lively declared: 'It is my belief that if the democracy that is sought to be established in the buffer state is permitted to have life, that its influence will spread over Russia'.[38] In May, a Mr Greenberg of the Robert Dollar Company reported from Chita that the FER government was 'surprisingly liberal'. The best men available filled government posts 'regardless of their political views'. While making plenty of criticisms, the people 'feel that the present government is better than any other that they might elect'.[39]

There were contacts with US diplomats, too. Echoing some of the sentiments expressed early on 4 March 1921 and cited at the beginning of this chapter, on 22 March the FER's Constituent Assembly sent out a Declaration to the governments and nations of the world, attaching a memorandum to the US government in particular, asking it when it would require a definite end to the intervention which began in 1918 with its invitation to the Japanese Government for military co-operation in the Far East.[40] On 26 March, Ignatius L. Yourin [Iurin], President of the FER's Mission to China, wrote to the American Minister in China Crane informing him of the achievements of the Constituent Assembly and of the availability of concessions for the exploitation of its rich natural resources. Iurin also expressed the hope that the USA and FER might exchange representatives. On 6 April, Secretary of State Hughes wired Bell, the Chargé in Japan, apprising him of the decision to send the military attaché's assistant Major J. W. Davies to Chita, adding that 'the sole purpose of his mission is to obtain information as to existing military, economic and political conditions in what is known as the Far Eastern Republic.' Davies was 'to carefully avoid any statement regarding the possible future policy of the United States regarding Siberia.' On 9 July, Bell relayed from Tokyo a report on conditions in Chita from Major Davies and his companion James F. Abbott, commercial attaché in Japan, who had reached Harbin after visiting Chita from May to June. The report stated: 'Conditions in Chita continue normal and are improving commercially. No internal disturbances...Japan and Semenoff influence in Chita insignificant. ...Prospect for harvest good. No reason why Americans should not travel freely...Good opportunities for investment development...' Then, on 9 September, Hughes instructed Bell to send Consul John K. Caldwell from Kobe and Vice Consul Edward B. Thomas from Harbin to Chita as observers.[41]

The first book in English on the FER, published in 1922, typified its leaders as

> men who without exception have struggled to throw off the yoke of an oppressive autocracy, long since become a disgraceful anachronism in the political world. Their theorizing led them further in argument than they can hope to go in practice. Faced with the actualities of constructive work, they have resigned many of their dreams to follow the example of successful State builders elsewhere.[42]

From the Soviet Russian side, however, there were many complaints about the 'White Guard' colour of the FER while A. M. Krasnoshchekov, the first Prime Minister was deemed by the local representative of the Cheka to be an adventurer 'dreaming of the creation from the FER of some kind of Mexican republic conducting a separate policy'. On 7 April 1921, Krasnoshchekov wrote to Chicherin: 'I ask for the protection of the FER from the descent of the Varangians in the shape of upstart generals...and Alexanders of Macedon with broad imperialist plans.' However, some of his colleagues found him insupportable, and they successfully requested his dismissal in July.[43] The Bolshevik Central Committee sent Ia. D. Ianson from the Commissariat of Foreign Affairs to be Minister of Foreign Affairs and V. K. Bliukher from the Revolutionary-Military Council (Revvoensovet) to be commander of the army. The government of the FER was now effectively under the control of the RSFSR as it began to parley with Japan.[44]

The Dairen Conference: 26 August 1921 to 20 February 1922

In June and July 1921, the Deputy Foreign Minister of the FER I. L. Kozhevnikov held talks with the Japanese vice-consul in Harbin Shimada. By 3 August, the Japanese accepted the FER's proposal for full-scale negotiations. The Dairen Conference duly opened on 26 August, with the FER delegation including Kozhevnikov and Dr F. N. Petrov, deputy chairman of the Council of Ministers of the FER. The Japanese delegation was led by Matsushima, formerly second secretary of the Japanese Embassy in St Petersburg.

'Almost at once the negotiators were at loggerheads', Lensen noted. 'It was the position of the Far Eastern Republic that Japan withdraw her forces from Siberia. The Japanese, on the other hand, demanded the conclusion of a treaty prior to evacuation.'[45]

On 6 September 1921, the FER introduced a draft agreement with pious hopes for peace as well as a guarantee of Japanese economic interests in the FER. The problems of compensation for the Nikolaevsk incident and the occupation of Northern Sakhalin were to be decided after normalisation of relations. On 15 September, Bell in Tokyo reported that 'Japan is unwilling to deal with Chita on a basis which would imply recognition of Chita as an independent country.' He also relayed the views of the US consul at Dairen dated 14 September

> If Chita unwilling to permit concessions Japan will break off negotiations and if nothing comes out of Washington Conference it is clear will demand even greater concessions later. However, if Chita allowed to have representatives sent to Washington they can afford to break off present conference with Japan.

The consul's opinion was that 'the only way to prevent cession administrative or territorial rights to Japan is to permit the despatch of informal representatives to Washington'.[46] Support for this view could be drawn from the Japanese response to the FER's draft agreement of 6 September, a list of demands put forward on or around 26 September for settlement of its differences with the FER which became known as the '17 points'. These included making the port of Vladivostok exclusively commercial under foreign control; establishing the freedom of navigation on the Rivers Amur and Sungari and along the coast, mainly for fishing, along with the extension of

'Open Door' principle to agriculture, forestry and mining; and conceding a lease of Northern Sakhalin for 80 years as a solution of the Nikolaevsk incident. There were three secret articles: binding the FER to neutrality in the event of an armed conflict between Japan and a third power; allowing the Japanese to evacuate the Maritime Province how and when they chose; and delaying the evacuation of Sakhalin until the lease was agreed.[47]

On 29 September 1921, the FER's foreign minister Ianson sent from Chita a note to Matsushima the head of the Japanese delegation in Dairen a complaint about negotiations concerning the CER being carried on in Vladivostok by the Merkulov government, attributing the responsibility for such 'illegal and rapacious misappropriation' of the FER's property to the support given by the Japanese forces to the Russian counter-revolutionaries.[48]

The Mensheviks and Socialist-Revolutionaries in the FER government were opposed to any concession to the Japanese, and left the government before the end of September in protest at the Moscow government's support of compromise. Soon afterwards, Moscow appointed Iu. Markhlevsky as unofficial leader of the FER delegation, although he did not arrive in Dairen until December 1921, accompanied by Bliukher. Markhlevsky did not participate in the talks, but became the actual head of the FER delegation.[49]

Late in September, too, talks were held in Moscow with a delegation from China, and a proposal put forward for a Russo-Chinese agreement.[50] The Soviet side in the talks was led by the deputy Commissar for Foreign Affairs L. M. Karakhan, an expert on Asian affairs. Influenced no doubt by what he had learned in these talks as well as from those in Dairen, Karakhan wrote to Chicherin on 13 October 1921 that the FER, created as a barrier and a buffer between Soviet Russia and Japan, had already played out its role; having been useful in its day, it was now positively harmful. The RSFSR needed to talk to Japan directly. Unfortunately, the FER had created the illusion that Japanese appetites could be satisfied without taking into consideration the needs of Soviet Russia, while the FER's representatives had shown themselves to be ill-disciplined in general. The talks in Dairen had shown everybody that a buffer was harmful in the current phase of the international situation, on the eve of the Washington Conference. Japan, China and the USA were all making haste to bring their influence to bear on the Far East and then to come to Washington with decisions already prepared. This tendency had to be used to force the FER to talk to Moscow about the fate of the Far East. It would not be difficult to 'sovietise' the FER, because the present internal Soviet régime (i.e. the New Economic Policy) came close to theirs. Soviet Russia would have to carry out this policy gradually, beginning with the inclusion of the FER into the RSFSR and the unification of foreign and military policy. But the decision would have to be taken quickly, so that an understanding could be reached with Japan before Washington in such a manner that all Japanese illusions about making gains without Soviet involvement would be shattered.[51]

At this time, there was no support for Karakhan's position in Moscow. As the Dairen Conference faltered and the Washington Conference approached, the importance of the FER for Soviet Russian bargaining purposes appeared not smaller but greater.

On 17 November 1921, the FER's Foreign Minister Ianson wrote to Chicherin that the Japanese had agreed to evacuate Northern Sakhalin if the FER initiated compensation for the 'Nikolavesk massacre' and guaranteed a sympathetic settlement of the fisheries question with the representatives of the RSFSR as well as of the FER. The Japanese insisted on political and economic guarantees, without which they might well start dealing with others (i.e. the Merkulov régime). Petrov, one of the leaders of the Far Eastern delegation at Dairen, was pessimistic about the conference that had opened in the USA on 12 November, stating that 'Washington will give us nothing and therefore we must agree with the Japanese.' On 21 November, Ianson wrote to Chicherin that the Japanese would leave the Maritime province if the FER signed a treaty in the spirit of their 17 points, including leases on Northern Sakhalin and the mouth of the Amur for sixty years. The Japanese were refusing now to admit Soviet Russian representatives to the talks while threatening to organise a new counter-revolutionary group in the Maritime province. Nevertheless, Ianson believed that the talks should be continued until news came through from Washington about how the Far Eastern question had been posed there.[52]

On 11 December 1921, the US Ambassador in Japan Warren wrote to Hughes that a partial relief for the Japanese troops in Vladivostok that had been postponed 'in view of the negotiations on commercial relations and other problems now in progress at Dairen with the Chita government' would in fact go ahead because of the continuing unstable situation.[53] On 24 December, Warren relayed to Hughes a communication from Caldwell in Chita intimating that he had been informed by the FER Minister for Foreign Affairs that 'the Japanese at the conference at Dairen have become more insistent in their demands since the Washington Conference opened and that they now positively demand certain previously discussed concessions which heretofore they seemingly were willing to modify'. An attack in the Maritime Province including the seizure of Khabarovsk by 'so-called White Partisans' had happened at the same time, and Japan was believed to be responsible for this.[54]

On 24 December 1921, the correspondent of the *Chicago Tribune* wired that the Japanese at Dairen were reluctant to give up many rights which they had acquired during and after the First World War, referring to 'certain unspecified secret agreements with Kerensky, Kolchak and Merkuloff governments which believed give Japanese preferential rights maritime province also providing return money Japan advanced wherewith waged warfare against Chita government'. Japan appeared to be 'keeping province upset by playing financing one faction against other obtaining treaty promises in return'.

Markhlevsky seems to have reinforced the FER delegation's opposition to Japanese demands. On 3 January 1922, the FER delegation at Dairen sent a note to its Japanese counterpart objecting to several of the '17 points'. However, in another note of the same date, the delegation expressed a readiness to give Japanese entrepreneurs concessions in the northern part of the island of Sakhalin in response to the evacuation of the Japanese troops. Although not accepting responsibility for the incident at Nikolaevsk, the delegation stated its readiness to help solve the ensuing problems.[55]

Not for the first time, negotiations were deadlocked by 20 February 1922, nearly two weeks after the closure of the Washington Conference.[56]

The Washington Conference

On 3 October, 1921 Chicherin wrote to the FER's Foreign Minister Ianson that the Dairen Conference was for Japan no more than a new way of seizing the Far East. At the same time, with preparations under way for the Washington Conference, the USA was also contemplating economic infiltration. On 7 October, he reported to the Politburo that the FER served 'as a temporary fig-leaf' of a buffer state, with centrifugal tendencies that must be restrained but still of use to the central government in Moscow.[57] The FER could still help to resist infiltration. Its Trade Delegation could be useful as an agent for the Soviet government.

On 4 October, the US Minister in China Schurman wrote to Secretary of State Hughes that

> Much more importance is attached by intelligent public opinion here, American included, to the Far Eastern Republic as a factor in the problems of the Far East than by public opinion in the United States. Such opinion here holds that not receiving a mission for strictly commercial purposes nor giving an invitation to the Washington Conference has a tendency to throw the Far Eastern Republic into the arms of the Japanese. It was stated to me last Friday by Yourin himself that American action to help his people might be taken too late. I learn from other sources that there is a danger of the Far Eastern Republic reaching an agreement before the Washington Conference convenes. This would be done by the cession of Northern Sakhalin to the Japanese. Probably no such cession would be made if the United States could admit a commercial mission.

This kind of advice no doubt helped persuade Hughes to authorise visas for the members of the FER's Trade Delegation, extending to them 'informal assistance but no official recognition'.[58]

By September 1922, after the Conference was all over, the Delegation gave its own account of its activities in the USA, which we will use fully, with interjections from other sources. En route, its members had talks with Schurman and others in Peking, giving a press conference attended by about fifty journalists. On 4 December 1921, the Delegation arrived in Washington DC, where it understood that the FER was to be given the same rights as other former constituent parts of the Russian Empire such as Latvia and Lithuania. The delegates shared their tasks among themselves in the following way. P. N. Karavaev was to be in charge of information and confidential correspondence while B. E. Skvirsky was to manage all discussions and relations with Americans. A. A. Iazykov, whose name was printed in the report in capital letters to emphasise his importance, was to exert overall control as chairman.

The delegates soon met old friends, in particular Alexander Gumberg, formerly secretary and interpreter for the Robins Red Cross Mission to Russia. Maintaining his links not only with the Soviet and FER governments but also with American political and journalistic circles, as they saw him, Gumberg was useful to them as translator, interpreter and intermediary with American government and society. They appointed him to the position of delegation secretary. In the assessment of James K. Libbey, although he could have applied himself more energetically to his duties, nevertheless 'Gumberg played a major role in whatever success the delegation achieved between December 1921 and February 1922.' His contacts included William Boyce Thompson, chair of the Advisory Commission attached to the Washington Conference. Gumberg also introduced the delegation to officials of the State Department, members of Congress and to a number of journalists and intellectuals.[59]

The FER delegates found contact with the State Department difficult, owing to its ties to reactionary representatives of the old Russia such as the ambassador of the Provisional Government, Boris A. Bakhmetev.[60] Having been told to expect as much by some of the sympathisers they had met in China, they soon became convinced on the spot that the problem was much more profound, closely connected as it was with the overall attitude of the dominant political forces in the USA to the Russian Revolution. They referred to the influence of J. P. Morgan on both Wilson and Harding, and cited Nathaniel Peffer who in the periodical *Century* had called the Russian division of the State Department the 'Tsarist Division' and their policy towards Russia an integral part of the 'Red Scare'. Miles, who had been head of the Russian Division, was now the Conference Secretary. The present head, Poole, had been Consul General in both Moscow and Vladivostok and was closely associated with Bakhmetev. He had resigned from the diplomatic service after Woodrow Wilson's note to the Russian people of March 1918, fearing that American policy was becoming too friendly towards the new régime. The heads of the Far East division of the State Department Macmurray and Clifford were hand in glove with Russian monarchists, while Hughes, Fletcher and Dearing, assistants to Hughes had all been appointed by Wilson and retained old prejudices. More moderate in their attitude to Russia were Leonardi and Jameson, especially the latter. Such was the estimate by the Far Eastern delegates of some of the officials with whom they had to deal.

If the attitude of these officials was so negative, why had the Delegation been allowed entry into the USA? Its members believed that the necessary leniency had been shown to them because of the fluid situation in the Far East brought about by the Japanese intervention in particular. Therefore, the Russian division of the State Department could not be entirely hostile to the delegates, who were received in the first few days, either altogether or individually, by Poole, Macmurray and Dearing. The emissaries from the FER were given to understand that recognition of the Delegation was improbable, since the question would have to be decided by all the countries represented at the Conference. A meeting with Hughes was to be considered.

Meanwhile, the delegates could still work for the political and economic rapprochement of their fledgling republic with its older sister, the USA. In particular, they could set about engaging public attention and sympathy, to which end Skvirsky made use of press contacts, including Junius Wood, Malcolm Davis who had been in Siberia from 1918 to 1921, Charles Morits, Elmer Davis from *The New York Times*, Evans and William Hard, a talented journalist from the radical press. Another significant figure was to be H. W. Nevinson of *The Manchester Guardian*, who was to play a big part in the publication of 'secret documents', of which more later. According to the Delegation's report, Nevinson said over and over again on learning about the ramifications of the intervention, 'We knew nothing about this'. Sympathisers with the FER included an engineer Charles H. Smith who had been in Siberia, General Graves, formerly commander of the US expeditionary force and representative of the USA on the International Council of the CER, and his son Major Graves, all considered to be converts to anti-interventionism and friends of the Russian people. The delegates believed that General Graves had been instrumental in stopping official recognition of the régime of Admiral Kolchak while acknowledging that the people of Siberia as a whole were adherents of the Bolsheviks. They also understood that Smith had been sympathetic to their cause in a report to Herbert Hoover.

The FER delegates described how, through the good offices of their sympathisers, the delegates of the FER met Rabinov, Reinsch and Branham.[61] Rabinov was an émigré businessman offering introductions and other assistance in the furtherance of economic aims. Dr Reinsch, formerly US Ambassador in Peking, arranged a meeting with Yen, one of the advisers of the Chinese Delegation. But the Chinese representatives appeared to be too passive, hoping for the support of the USA: the representatives from Canton were more friendly than those from Peking, but they were also unrecognised. Lucy Branham, a suffragette reminding the delegates of a member of the old Russian intelligentsia, had been in the Urals in 1921 and suffered much deprivation. She introduced the delegates to 'the most progressive and worker elements in society', and took them to her talk on the Russian famine at the Penguin Club. According to Katherine A. S. Siegel, Branham was known as 'the suffragette history professor' of Columbia University, and led the Women's Committee for the Recognition of Russia formed by the Women's International League for Peace and Freedom (WILPF). She had accompanied Armand Hammer on his visit to Soviet Russia in 1921.[62]

In order to put their case more widely, the delegation decided to arrange two of the publications which we have already made use of above, one on the history of the FER, the other on the Japanese intervention. These were to be given wide distribution, and the second of them to be entered into the Senate record.

In the first half of December, the delegates were received by Secretary of Commerce Herbert Hoover, who encouraged them to talk about trade and investment possibilities, as well as about the Japanese intervention. For the first part of the interview, Hoover was mostly silent, although nodding frequently. But then he asked about the economic situation within the FER, and whether or not the FER would enter the Russian Soviet Republic.[63] Rabinov arranged a meeting with Senator Lodge, which led to further meetings with Senator France, Senator Goodrich and others.

On 20 December, 'An Appeal to All Nations by the National Assembly of the Far Eastern Republic to the Peoples and the Governments of the World' was sent to US Secretary of State Hughes as Chairman of the Conference. The message pointed out that the Japanese invasion had already lasted for up to four years. Japanese troops were still pouring into Vladivostok, and occupied practically all the Russian Pacific shore. They had made a provocative attack on Nikolaevsk in 1920. The mouth of the River Amur had been closed to the FER's commercial ships and used as a base for attacks on the Republic, while no Russian could enter the lower part of the Amur or Sakhalin without Japanese permission. The Japanese were selling the FER's timber, fish and minerals.

Contrary to the agreement of 29 April 1920, the 'Appeal' claimed, no Russian armed forces (except a certain number of militia, reserves and staff guards) were allowed in the Japanese zone. However, the Japanese had openly allowed and aided the organisation of armed anti-government forces, thus paralysing the efforts of the Russian forces to restore normal life. The Maritime Province had been separated from the rest of the territory of the FER. Moreover, when the FER had resisted the Japanese demands at Dairen, the Japanese gave aid to Merkulov as he organised an attack on the FER.

The 'Appeal' concluded with a complaint about the policies of the great powers which, it said, amounted to worse than nothing, silently sanctioning Japanese violence and giving Japan freedom of action in the Russian Far East. At the present time when the governments of the great powers were meeting in Washington where the problems of the spheres of influence were to be discussed, they would decide the fate of the FER without any consultation with the National Assembly which was also in session.[64]

On 28 December 1921, Iazikov as Chairman of the Delegation sent a note to Hughes including the statement

> The fact of non-recognition of our Government by the Powers participating in the Conference does not obviate the fact that we represent a Government which was elected by the population of the entire Republic whose fate is being decided at the Conference.
>
> At the same time when the Conference is trying to establish peace on the shores of the Pacific Ocean, troops are being brought into the territory of the Far Eastern Republic in order to create a new 'civil war', and the armed invasion of our territory continues.[65]

Meanwhile, the FER delegates were considering another approach to the predicament of their non-recognition – the question of the publication of two sets of documents on Japanese relations: with Semenov; and with Wrangel and France.[66] To begin with, they had thought of publishing the first set only, but then the possibility had arisen of the Conference closing by Christmas 1921 without discussion of the Siberian question. Moreover, the French appeared to be unpopular at the Conference owing to their stand on the submarine question, which had been compared to German policy during the World War. So, after taking advice from Alexander Gumberg and some of their journalist friends, the delegates decided to send both sets of documents to the newspapers on 31 December 1921. Some newspapers asked for exclusives, but they were refused. However, the delegates decided to make an exception for Nevinson of *The Manchester Guardian*, so that he could arrange publication in the United Kingdom for the same day as in the

USA.[67] Nevinson had a long conversation with Skvirsky, who said that the FER delegation believed that every word of the documents was true, and that 'the best way for the Japanese to disprove them would be to evacuate Siberia', adding that it was the moral duty of the powers who had participated in the intervention to see that the Japanese army was withdrawn.[68]

When the news broke, the French delegation issued enraged denials, while the FER delegation's apartments were stormed by journalists seeking further information. Charles H. Smith the engineer confirmed the existence of ties between the Japanese on the one hand and the French in conjunction with Wrangel on the other. Hughes was reported as saying that the publication of the documents was favourable to US interests, while Senator Borah was said to have observed that the documents reflected the actual situation in the Far East. The Hearst press took up the Siberian question, and commented on State Department policy towards it. Even the anti-Bolshevik Miliukov was said to have observed in the journal *Poslednie Novosti* [*Latest News*] that it would be good if the publication of the documents helped to solve the Siberian question. But the FER account said that Miliukov was wrong to suggest also that the publication would kill off the delegation, arguing that 'the leader of bourgeois liberalism' was turning out to be as 'short-sighted' on this question as on many others. Even if the chances of the delegates joining in the conference were now non-existent, they believed that the few words they could have spoken there would have made far less impact than the publication of the documents. Some support for this assessment came from the Washington correspondent of *The New York Times* who stated: 'Whatever the effect the incident has on the standing of the delegation from the Far Eastern Republic, which gave out the documents, it has at least brought the Siberian question squarely before the eyes of the world.'[69]

On 5 January 1922, to reinforce its case, the delegation produced a further long memorandum on the intervention from 1918 onwards while trying still to achieve recognition of the FER.[70] Meanwhile, the Japanese were being forced in the direction of compromise on the questions of Shantung and Manchuria, they believed.

Talks ensued between the FER delegates and Senators Borah, France, Hitchcock, Johnson, McKinley, Shortridge and Willis, as well as former Senator Sutherland, recently made director of the Advisory Committee appointed from various walks of life and different regions to help gain public support for the Conference.[71] The delegates divided the senators into three groups. The first of these, including Borah, France and Johnson as well as the Democrat leader Hitchcock, constituted a minority in favour of recognition of the FER. Johnson was from California, the delegates noted, and therefore looked upon the Japanese 'with no greater sympathy than any of our partisans'. The second group, which included McKinley, Willis and others, were well disposed towards recognition, but pointed out that such a step depended on the President and his administration. The third group, among them Moses and, up to a point, Sutherland thought that intervention should end but that recognition of the FER might lead to war. They had no great interest in the new republic and did not want to spoil relations with Japan. The FER delegates commented that this third attitude followed the line of the Harding administration's foreign policy, which was determined by 'the aspiration of the ruling classes to put off all possible foreign conflicts, to lessen any contradiction threatening a clash with rivals even in foreign markets'.

At the Conference itself, in the estimate of the FER account, Baron Shidehara's statement consisted of parts of the truth and one big lie – that Japan was carrying a heavy burden in the name of civilisation now that the other interventionists had left. Hughes made some effort to hold Japan to its word on evacuation, but the decision of the Siberian question was left more to events. The FER delegation sent a note to Hughes on 28 January 1922 maintaining that the People of the Far East

> still have confidence that the American people will not tolerate the oppression of a kindred-spirited, democratic people by a military absolutism, and believe that in their struggle for national independence the people of the Far Eastern Republic will have the active sympathy of the American people.[72]

However, to their complaints about the delay, the US administration replied, in the words of the FER delegation's account, that it would ensure that Japan would keep to its gentleman's agreement.

On 10 February 1922, just after the Conference was concluded, the FER's Foreign Minister Ianson sent a note to the Japanese Ministry of Foreign Affairs pointing out that Shidehara's statement at Washington was in contrast to the demands made at Dairen and giving further examples of Japanese treachery, for example, the supply of more arms to the FER's White opponents.[73] 'Trojan horse' or not, the FER provided reminders of the necessity for an end to intervention and the restoration of 'normalcy' in international relations. Moreover, while some of its delegation's contacts in Washington DC and New York, for example, with members of the radical fringes, might not have been of much of a help to the Soviet cause, meetings with Senators and other leading figures almost certainly were.

5 After the Washington Conference
Conclusion

On 26 January 1922, *The New York Times* published a leading article entitled 'Japan and Siberia', comparing the Japanese answer to the question when it would withdraw its troops from the Russian Far East to the British commitment forty years previously to leave Egypt as soon as a stable government was set up. British forces were still in Egypt, however, and in greater numbers than before. Similarly, the USA still had soldiers in Haiti and San Domingo, as well as marines in Nicaragua: 'Our Government is always consumed with anxiety to remove military pressure from those countries and to leave them freely to develop their own institutions. But somehow the exact hour does not arrive.' It was obvious, therefore, that 'the Siberian question is not one to start a shower of stones thrown from international glass houses'. Nevertheless, it was a matter of vital interest, and, while Japan had first sent an army to the Russian Far East in 1918 on the initiative and appeal of the USA, as much as possible of the objects of the intervention – to support the Czecho-Slovak evacuation, to help Russians to set up self-government and to protect military stores at Vladivostok – had been achieved. American troops had been brought home but the Japanese were still there.

Plausible reasons could be given: while Japan could well be the first to suffer from any 'Bolshevist eruption' in the Far East, she also possessed valid claims to be adjusted before she withdrew with honour. On the other hand, her control of Vladivostok and its hinterland as well as of the island of Sakhalin meant domination of a long stretch of the coast. Furthermore, from the Pacific terminals the railway linked up with Russia and Europe, while the long southern frontier of Siberia flanked Manchuria and Mongolia. The forthcoming Nine-Power Treaty concerning China and Siberia would have to make firm stipulations concerning 'the destiny and the trade' of these countries, or 'serious disquietude' would be found 'in the minds of thoughtful and far-sighted American statesmen'.

On 6 February 1922, the day that the Nine-Power Treaty was signed, among the headlines on the front page of *The New York Times* were 'JAPAN

GAINS MOST, RUSSIA THE LOSER, IN THE CONFERENCE' and 'JAPAN SUPREME IN ASIA'. A special correspondent sympathetic to the FER, Elmer Davis, observed that the Conference had done nothing to free Siberia. Japan had promised to leave, for the third or fourth time, but the fact that the promise had been made so often, while she had actually left Shantung, aroused scepticism. Sooner or later, if Japan did not quit Siberia, the Russians would certainly fight to free it.

Ratification of the treaties and the FER delegation

On 10 February 1922, President Harding addressed the US Senate, which was about to begin a long debate through to the end of March on the ratification of the Washington Treaties. 'We have seen the eyes of the world turned to the Pacific,' the President said. 'With Europe prostrate and penitent, some feared the likelihood of early conflict there. But the Pacific had its menaces, and they deeply concerned us. Our territorial interests are largely there...Our earlier triumphs of commerce were there.'[1] On 15 March 1922, in a leader with the title 'Russia and the Treaty', *The New York Times* somewhat facetiously observed that 'the best, near-best and semi-best minds in the Senate' were discussing the possibility of a Russian attempt to drive out the Japanese involving operations against Southern Sakhalin protected by the Four-Power Treaty and consequently obliging the USA, the UK and France to join in the conflict on the Japanese side. The tone of the leader became more mocking: 'Arguments based on possible occurrences in the fourth dimension and the year 31920 AD are hard to answer, but let us see what are the possibilities on this planet and during the life of this treaty.' In the ten years that the treaty had to run, the leader continued, Russia would not recover enough to fight Japan, and would certainly not acquire a navy capable of taking a war to the islands covered by the treaty. But the Senators also chose to discuss the hypothetical question of the treaty being renewed. Might this involve the USA in a war on the side of Japan against Russia and China, and then in another against a Japanese–Chinese alliance, a Senator had asked? The fact of the matter was that the American government had declared that Japan had no business in Siberia, so there could be no moral obligation to fight to keep her there. *The New York Times* leader moved on to another point which seemed 'so important to Senatorial scaremongers' – the exclusion of Russia from a conference of the signatory powers. But Japan would be the last to ask for such a conference about Siberia, since she knew well that possibly the UK, probably France and certainly the USA would tell her that 'she had got herself into trouble and could get herself out without help from outside'.

If *The New York Times* had any inkling of what was to ensue less than twenty years later, it would not have been so dismissive of the Senate discussion. Of course, some of the Senators could be as facetious as the newspaper. During discussion of the Yap Treaty, Mr Watson of Georgia asked, if Japanese nationals should violate the treaty and the Japanese Government refuse to interfere to enforce it, what would the US Government do? Mr Reed of Missouri answered: 'We would do exactly as we would with reference to any other violation; we would have a Washington Conference and yield to Japan.'[2] There was also a considerable amount of what *The New York Times* might not be alone in finding irrelevancy, Mr Watson regretting that 'we are now going back into the European system from which our ancestors had fled' across 'the dangers of the ocean in those days when the vessels were mere little tubs' and at the risk 'of conflict with the savage, with the wilderness, with the diseases incident to a new land'. But they also enjoyed the 'absolute democracy' to be found in 'the *Mayflower* compact, written while the little vessel was still tossing up and down on the waves'.[3] On the other hand, most of the focus of the Senate was on the more immediate situation. In an address entered into the Record at the suggestion of Mr Borah, former Under-Secretary of State Norman H. Davis observed that 'The settlements in the Far East may all be upset unless Europe is straightened out', both economically and politically. Mr France of Maryland argued that it was a mistake in Paris and Washington alike not to invite Germany and Russia to the conference. Mr Reed of Missouri protested that the Washington treaties were forcing into each other's arms these two prostrate giants of the eastern [*sic*] world.[4] Some wider cultural considerations were injected into the Senate debate, too. Mr Watson insisted that 'We are paganizing ourselves to assist the [Japanese] Buddhists to rob the Christians of Russia and Korea. Can that be defended in any form where reason prevails?' Mr Robinson of Arkansas warned that for the first time in history that he could recall 'the Caucasian race in parts of Russia is held in subjection by representatives of the yellow race. Japan will not recede; Russia must attempt to drive her back...'[5]

Is it possible to detect any influence on the Senate debate from the FER's delegation? As the Washington Conference came to an end, Senator Borah advised going to the people, so, early in 1922, Skvirsky embarked on a series of speaking engagements among them: 'The Future Peace in the Far East, the Washington Conference and the Far Eastern Republic' to the National Council on the Limitation of Armaments in Washington DC on 14 January; 'Some Facts about the Far Eastern Republic' to the Foreign Policy Association in New York City on 4 March; and 'The Far Eastern Republic of Siberia and Its Relation to the International Problems of the Pacific' to the Civic Club, Brooklyn, also in New York City, on 29 March. To the Foreign Policy Association, Skvirsky remarked: 'The United States herself went through a difficult struggle for her independence and can understand and sympathize with the Far Eastern Republic.' To the Civic Club, he observed

> The aggressive spirit of Japan and the methods used in her aggression have had such an effect upon the peoples of China and Korea that they nearly forgot the historic aggressions of the western nations. Japanese deeds eclipsed those of the rest of the world. Japan wants to dominate China, Korea, the Russian Far East, and to force out gradually all the other nations.

Skvirsky argued: 'it is in the interest of the United States to support the Siberian Democratic Republic', adding 'western civilization was the first in aggression. It must be first in justice'.

On another occasion, the organisation, The Sword of Peace and Freedom, sponsored a banquet in Washington DC for the recognition of Soviet Russia, at which Senator France and the former ambassador to China Dr Reinsch spoke. Links with journalists were strengthened, too, with William T. Newton of *The New Republic*, Miss Kirchwey of *Azia*, Mr Little, Mr Billard and Miss Harrison of worker newspapers, the editor of *The New York Globe* Bruce Bliven and the editor of *The Christian Science Monitor* Harding.[6] Among others, Admiral Caine, Professor Pitkin of Columbia University, who found a 'Jeffersonian' aspect to the FER, and Raymond Robins also showed sympathy. Altogether, the FER delegation believed that it had been so successful in its search for support that the Whites believed that tens of thousands of dollars had been spent on buying over the American press.[7] In the Senate debate on ratification of the Washington treaties, too, there was palpable evidence of the influence of the FER delegation, too. For example, Mr Robinson of Arkansas made several references to press reports concerning Skvirsky's allegation that France and Japan were conspiring together to exploit Siberia with Marshal Joffre as an intermediary.[8]

On 13 March 1922, Ianson, the FER's foreign minister in Chita, sent Hughes a note complaining that the puppet Merkulov government in the Maritime province was planning to take FER state property with it when it evacuated Vladivostok. Ianson asked Hughes for the USA's intercession on this matter and for the prevention of the arming of elements hostile to the FER. On 4 April, Iazikov, the head of the FER delegation in Washington, sent Hughes a note stating

> The present situation in the Russian Far East is once more very critical and may result in more bloodshed. I believe that only immediate action in accordance with the declaration of the Government of the United

States at the Washington Conference regarding the withdrawal of the Japanese troops from Eastern Siberia may prevent the Russian Far East from once more being plunged into chaos.[9]

The FER delegation's account described how it was involved in a campaign against Semenov and Bakhmetev which met with a large degree of success. Major Graves denounced the White general in a newspaper article, while a bankrupt fur firm, Iurvet,[10] hired a lawyer to recover $100,000 from Bakhmetev. Semenov was sent to jail, then allowed out on $25,000 bail. Both Smith and General Graves testified against Semenov. Colonel Morrow, a member of Graves' staff, called Semenov a butcher slaying Russians to left and right, and killing two American soldiers. As a consequence of this last allegation, the American Legion turned against Semenov. An insurance company withdrew a loan to Semenov, giving patriotic reasons, and the White general found himself back in jail, in a neighbourhood inhabited by poor Russian Jews, who whistled him each time he appeared. A Senate commission set up at the instigation of Senator Borah turned on Bakhmetev, who had received Semenov, and the ex-ambassador left town. The State Department declared that an ambassador could not be summoned to appear before the Senate, but Borah retaliated, asking what had become of $187 million given by the US Treasury to Bakhmetev.[11] Senator Norris also spoke. The State Department defended Semenov and a monarchist group led by Brazol and K-O,[12] denounced Bolshevik intrigue and insisted on Bakhmetev's immunity. This stretched, apparently, to 'the right to receive spirituous drinks, which are very valued in this dry country'. About the middle of April, allegedly 'in error', a telegram from Moscow about the transfer of $10,000 to the FER delegation was given to Bakhmetev, who passed it on to the State Department. As a consequence, Skvirsky predicted, an article would appear in *The New York Times* stating that the delegation had received $10,000,000 from Moscow and therefore definitely proving that the existence of an independent FER was a fiction. There was also 'a great and joyful emotion' among the translators in the State Department, Skvirsky believed, when they read in a January number of *Izvestiia* that Ianson had been chosen by the All-Russian Central Executive Committee (VTsIK) as the FER's delegate to the forthcoming Genoa Conference. When asked about this by newspaper reporters, Skvirsky had replied that the RSFSR and FER were in close collaboration concerning Genoa, but the Central Committee would no more choose a delegate from the FER than from Poland, adding that a Soviet correspondent could make mistakes about Genoa such as could often be found in the US press.[13] The case was to reach an impasse when Bakhmetev wrote to Hughes on 28 April 'I am prepared, if the United States Government so desires, to retire and terminate my official duties'.[14] The Secretary of State had no objections. Having settled the Provisional Government's financial affairs to the US government's satisfaction by early June,[15] Bakhmetev left for France at the end of July. Semenov suddenly disappeared from jail and returned to Japan.

As well as battling against its White opponents, the FER delegation continued its publications and gave renewed emphasis to economic activity. Its correspondence with its government back in Chita through to August contained requests for further information on such subjects ranging from the co-operative movement and railroads, furs, minerals and timber to schools and the armed forces.[16] In the USA, there were extended discussions with the Sinclair Co, represented by an engineer Beech, and negotiations with Fuistek and Co[17] for a big fur deal. Railroad companies involved in talks included Baldwin [Boldvii] Locomotive. The Pacific Steamship Company showed interest, too. General Graves was among those concerned in an approach for a gold concession.

But General Graves was forced to go to the Philippines, and the situation of Raymond Robins became difficult. The anti-Soviet State Department was among those agencies making things difficult for those who showed more sympathy. By the spring of 1922, however, the Soviet situation was taking a turn for the better. Senator France's visit to Soviet Russia in the fall of 1921 helped to bring about an agreement between Litvinov and Hoover's ARA. An amount of $20 million was assigned to Soviet Russia as well as a considerable quantity of medical supplies. Lucy Branham and women's organisations had a considerable influence in this regard. Talks in Riga and Berlin helped to pave the way for an invitation for Soviet Russia to attend the Genoa Conference. The FER delegation could not comment on Genoa, but continued to distribute information about Soviet Russia.

A reactionary campaign supported by *The New York Tribune*, *The Public Ledger* and the American Federation of Labor leader Samuel Gompers along with Russian émigrés was among the reasons why the USA did not go to Genoa, in the estimate of the FER delegation.There was a campaign to win over the AF of L, but Gompers proved too strong.

The campaign for recognition of Soviet Russia continued in the Senate, but both Hoover and Hughes were among those opposed. On the other hand, a campaign in the press and by women's organisations helped set up US representation in Chita. However, the delegation came to believe ever more strongly that the question of the recognition of the FER would be resolved in connection with that of the RSFSR.

Literally, the FER was getting on to the map. When the delegation first arrived in Washington, correspondents asked 'Is your republic to the East of the Caspian Sea?' Towards the end of its stay, the FER appeared both in US school maps of Asia and in a large map of Russia produced by the

Library of Congress.[18] However, figuratively, the writing was on the wall, and the days of the FER were numbered. Other members of the Special Delegation left Washington, although Skvirsky stayed on, assuming the title of commercial representative of Soviet Russia, then semi-official Soviet consul and head of the Soviet Information Bureau.[19]

The Dairen Conference: 20 March to 16 April 1922

As the Washington Conference came to an end and in the months following, there were pertinent developments not only in the US capital but also in the Russian Far East. Both military and political, these developments were undoubtedly significant in their own right but also helped to reinvigorate the Conference at Dairen.

Early in 1922, at Trotsky's initiative, the head of the secret police F. E. Dzerzhinsky was sent to Siberia on an inspection visit. (The timing might have been significant, incidentally, since on 8 February the Cheka was abolished and replaced by OGPU.) On 1 February, Dzerzhinsky wrote that the army was starving. It had about 142,000 rations and about 180,000 mouths to feed. As a result of famine, cold and difficult conditions in general, signs of disintegration were apparent. More and more Red Army soldiers and even recruits were caught up in banditry. Moreover, the army was politically engaged in requisitions, which in Siberia had taken the form of extorting grain from the peasants with the most repressive measures. Even the most reliable detachments were involved. The danger from this was very great indeed. It was necessary to give this matter urgent attention and to take appropriate measures, since the Red Army in Siberia was of great importance.[20]

As far as the FER's army was concerned, Ianson had sent a telegram to Chicherin stating that on 15 December 1921 'Our position on the Khabarovsk front is completely unstable. The army can in no way free itself from the partisan spirit with all its consequences. We are applying our strength as far as executions.'[21] Still in February 1922, perhaps sensing a military weakness, the Army of the Maritime province supported by the Japanese, attacked on that very front, taking Khabarovsk itself on 5 February. But the FER's forces, partisans and all, struck back, defeating its opponents in the biggest clash of the Far Eastern conflict, 1920–2.

These events did not prevent, but perhaps even stimulated, the economic union of the FER and RSFSR on 18 March 1922. A few days previously, L. M. Karakhan, the Soviet deputy Commissar of Foreign Affairs, had just observed to the Politburo on the draft of the agreement that 'the task of the agreement is to show to the whole world that in fact and actuality the master of the FER is Russia. Our wording is open and without any diplomatic flummery secures all the natural resources of the FER for Russia'. The FER had its own draft, stating that on the basis of reciprocity, 'the preference in the exploitation of the resources should be for Russia'. Karakhan commented: 'In real relations with the FER, the difference in these formulations has no practical business significance. Politically our formulation has all the advantages.'[22]

In part, perhaps, because of this economic union, and in part, more likely, because of the military reverse of the forces of the Maritime province, the Japanese reinvigorated negotiations with the FER at Dairen following a directive from Foreign Minister Uchida on 20 March 1922.[23] Just possibly, the US Consul in Chita played his part here. Certainly, he was asked several times to intercede with his government on behalf of the FER.[24] Just possibly, too, the Japanese were also responding to a note delivered to their delegation by the FER delegation from Ianson, the FER Foreign Minister, on 14 March. The note observed that, in response to FER protests, the Japanese had either said nothing or declared that their troops were observing strict neutrality. Allegedly, Japan was observing the agreement of 29 April 1920 concluded between the Japanese Command and the Zemstvo Government of the Maritime Province, that the Japanese troops never had allowed and never would allow armed rebels to enter the zone defined by that agreement. However, Ianson's note continued with support from several witnesses that the Japanese command had in fact rendered assistance to armed Russian detachments hostile to the FER along the Ussuri railroad. Therefore, the FER government would no longer consider the agreement of 29 April 1920 binding upon itself and, while pursuing the armed bands in the southern part of the Maritime province, would follow them throughout the entire territory of that province. The FER government hoped that, in view of the possibility of reaching an agreement with the Japanese government on all outstanding matters, that Japanese troops would not hinder the movement of the FER army along the Ussuri Railroad and would in fact assist the FER army in finally dispersing 'the armed bands that are disturbing the peaceful course of life in the country'.[25]

The Japanese delegates warned that if the talks were finally to fail, the plan to bring over remnants of Wrangel's army and other White forces might well be realised. Iu. Markhlevsky, the Moscow government's appointee who had been de facto head of the FER delegation since late 1921, commented that to bring over Wrangel's supporters from Constantinople was no laughing matter. However, even if Japan with the help of France decided on such an adventure, they could not carry it out before the summer, by which time the world situation would have changed. Therefore, Markhlevsky claimed, Petrov was spreading panic among the rest of the FER delegation needlessly.[26]

However, the central government was by no means completely won over by its appointee's optimism, and approached the last month of the negotiations at Dairen with some caution. From their side, the Japanese were not as peremptory in their demands towards the end of March as before, withdrawing the most odious of their '17 points', for example concerning their free right of navigation on the River Amur and the destruction of the fortifications of Vladivostok. From the FER side, on the other hand, there were several concessions which soon seemed to have gone too far. As well as appearing to accept responsibility for the 'Nikolaevsk massacre' if the Japanese committed themselves to withdrawal from Russian Sakhalin as soon as the matter was settled, the FER delegation agreed not to build any new fortresses on the coast facing Japan or on the frontiers with Korea as well as decommissioning (if not destroying) the fortifications of Vladivostok. In the economic area, the FER guaranteed Japanese citizens their property and property rights up to the date of the agreement, that is from pre-revolutionary times through to their occupation. Karakhan, deputy commissar for foreign affairs, was soon to comment that the Japanese would have been given rights that would not be extended to the citizens of any other foreign state, and would even include those activities that had been made a state monopoly in Soviet Russia. Concessions on mining, forestry and fishing in particular were looking too generous.[27]

Under pressure from Tokyo, the Japanese at Dairen said that their forces would be withdrawn from the Russian Far East only when the FER would honour its commitments in full, and only then in three months rather than the forty-five days originally envisaged. The FER attempted to reach agreement on the transfer of military property in Vladivostok in such a manner that the Merkulov régime would not acquire control over it. Suddenly, according to the Russian side, on 15 April 1922, irritated by what they saw as unnecessary delays, the Japanese delivered an ultimatum: the FER would have to accept the Japanese version of all the agreements within half an hour. The conference collapsed. Ianson believed that this sudden end to the talks would upset the Japanese bourgeoisie and isolate the Japanese militarists. Whether that was so or not, neither the FER nor the RSFSR was too upset about the collapse of Dairen. One important reason for this comparative equanimity was to be found not in the Far East but in Europe, where the international position of Soviet Russia was clearly improving with its participation in another, larger international conference at Genoa.[28]

On 20 April 1922, the US Ambassador in Japan Warren reported on a lengthy conversation with Foreign Minister Uchida the previous day giving a different version of the end of the Dairen Conference. Uchida declared that Japan was prepared to complete a military evacuation of its troops three months after an agreement about it. While this question was being discussed at Dairen, the FER delegates suddenly announced that they were leaving, Uchida concluding that they had received 'a request from the Moscow government to await the results of the conference at Genoa'. Therefore, Japan's policy was 'to await Russian developments and the outcome of the Genoa Conference'.[29]

On 26 April, Iazikov Chair of the FER Special Trade Delegation to the USA sent a note to Secretary of State Hughes asserting that the Dairen Conference was suddenly terminated on 16 April when the Japanese delegates, in addition to their demand that a general treaty be signed before the evacuation of their troops, insisted on new clauses concerning the grant to Japanese subjects of rights equal to FER citizens in commercial development and exploitation of forests and mines, the destruction of FER war materials in the Maritime Province and an agreement by the FER not to increase the size of its fleet in the port of Vladivostok. In response to the statement of the FER delegates that they were ready to consider these new proposals but that the date of the evacuation must be definitely established, their Japanese counterparts had said that they had received instructions to end the negotiations.[30]

A Soviet Russian assessment on the reasons for the breakdown of the Dairen Conference (unattributed and undated, but nevertheless official) gave first emphasis to the problem of the evacuation of the Japanese troops, which the Japanese delegation wanted to keep separate from other questions. The FER delegation insisted that it would not sign a general agreement if the Japanese did not simultaneously make a commitment to withdraw all its forces from the Maritime region not less than 45 days later. As well as rejecting this demand, the Japanese also arrogated to themselves the right to destroy all munitions in the event of an attempt at illegal seizure of them, a move which the FER delegation saw as an excuse for the destruction or the seizure of the military supplies to be averted by referring the question to a joint Russo-Japanese commission. The discussion of this point and the other about the date of the evacuation occupied the conference from 5 to 10 April. On 10 April, the Far Eastern delegation presented all of its draft agreement and demanded a definitive answer about the date of the evacuation. The Japanese would not give a firm commitment, although they agreed to most of the other points of the draft agreement. Stalemate continued for another five days, with the Japanese accusing the Far East delegation of mistrust. On 15 April, the date the Japanese ultimatum ran out, the FER delegation was given half an hour to accept or reject the Japanese version of the agreement which included some changes and unilateral reversions to earlier drafts, as well as no more than a conditional commitment to effect the evacuation of Japanese troops in three months. On 16 April, the Japanese said that in view of the FER delegation's uncompromising attitude, they were breaking off the negotiations and returning to Tokyo.[31]

Tanaka Bunichiro, a Japanese diplomat who published his history of negotiations between Japan and the Soviet Union in 1942, observed that Moscow considered that an agreement between the FER and Japan would only complicate the international situation as the chances of the recognition of the FER by the other powers declined and the chances of the recognition of Soviet Russia increased. Moreover, the FER delegates at Dairen did not sufficiently understand law and treaties or the art of compromise, and were in any case suspicious of the Japanese military and did not have faith in the latter's vague pledge of withdrawal.[32]

Diplomatic clumsiness and intransigence apart, there was a further reason for the cessation of the talks. In her consideration of another more famous meeting back in Europe, Carole Fink put it thus

> The Dairen negotiations with the Chita government had been suspended pending the outcome of the Genoa Conference; Britain and America were urging an early Japanese withdrawal and were reputedly themselves interested in the oil of Siberia and Sakhalin. The Bolsheviks, working hard for recognition, indicated that they soon intended to exert their control over the Asian province. Thus Japan had problems that the Genoa Conference might influence but not solve decisively. Being represented was merely a prestige item, which still demanded caution, prudence, and vigilance.

In fact, as Fink also points out, the Japanese delegation was uncomfortable at Genoa and excluded from private Allied talks with the Russians.[33] Nevertheless, in general, Genoa was an important part of the sequel to Washington.

The Genoa Conference: 10 April to 19 May 1922

By mid-April, the world's attention had indeed moved from the USA and Asia back to Europe. In the Thirteenth Edition of *The Encyclopaedia Britannica* published in 1926, in his contribution on 'Europe after the War', 'X' wrote that Russia's defeat followed by the Bolshevik Revolution had radically changed the position in the continent that she had developed since the time of Peter the Great at the beginning of the eighteenth century. Having lost her border territories from Finland through Poland to Bessarabia, Russia 'was now confined to the semi-Asiatic areas which had never come under the direct influence of European culture and the Western Church. She had in fact once more become not a European but an Asiatic power'. In strong disagreement, the editor appended his own footnote: 'This may appear to be so if we look at territory alone, but the vast bulk of the Russian population speaks a great European language, possesses a great European literature and belongs mainly, in every way, to the European family system.'[34]

Undoubtedly, since the Bolshevik Revolution of 1917, the frontiers of Russia had been far from fixed. Moreover, the policies of the new government were also fluid, moving from the aspiration to spread communism throughout the whole world to a readiness to compromise with capitalism. Partly in order to take rapprochement further, during the period of the Washington Conference, there was a considerable amount of discussion of a further international meeting to take place in Europe. On 24 December 1921, *The New York Times* reported the possibility of 'a European conference to deal with the European impasse on the same lines as Washington adopted so successfully about the Pacific impasse'. In the pursuit of economic and political stability, both Germany and Russia should be brought in. A source allegedly close to Lloyd George had stated that, while the USA had resolved to keep out of the European imbroglio, nevertheless, an American delegation could act as 'stakeholder for European pledges' and 'enormously increase their value without adding to her own liabilities'. On 1 January 1922, the same newspaper reported that a plan for the economic restoration of Europe was to be considered by the Allied Supreme Council at Cannes. An international industrial corporation was proposed with equal shares for Great Britain, France, Germany and the USA (if she so desired). Russia would have to be included 'as essential to the economic life of Europe as anywhere else'; any other approach would be 'just tinkering at the problem'. By 8 January 1922, *The New York Times* noted, European delegates in Washington were now turning their attention beyond Cannes to the conference projected for Genoa, and were already booking their passages home. The next day, the same journal reported that American terms had been accepted for Russian reentry into the international family of nations in the declaration of the Allied Supreme Council: that 'it is not possible to place foreign capital in order to help a country until the foreigners who provide the capital have the certitude that their property and rights will be respected, and that the fruits of their enterprise will be assured'. The reign of terror would have to be replaced by the rule of law. Responding to such concern, Chicherin wrote to Lenin on 20 and 22 January 1922 calling on him to consider amending the Constitution a little to allow some form of representation of non-working class elements in the Soviets 'if the Americans importune us too much' since 'depriving the entire bourgeoisie of political rights is shocking the Americans'. Lenin wrote the marginal comment 'Crazy' on Chicherin's memorandum, and suggested that he be sent immediately to a sanatorium.[35]

If Soviet Russia had been 'Banquo's ghost' at Versailles and the 'uninvited guest' at Washington, the spirit of the USA was to be frequently invoked at Genoa. However, we must recall that, while Soviet Russia sought representation at the earlier conferences, the USA turned down the opportunity to participate in this one. According to the British Ambassador Geddes, Secretary of State Hughes regarded the Genoa Conference as a grave error that would shore up crumbling Bolshevism, and encourage Lenin's government to persist in its mistaken policies.[36] At the same time, however, in the view of Hughes' biographer Merlo J. Pusey, 'the Secretary made it plain that any move on the part of the powers to take advantage of Russia's prostration would meet with sharp disapproval in America'.[37]

In January 1922, Lloyd George was explaining that the coming conference was not going to be organised by the League of Nations because such auspices would make it impossible to include the USA, which had excluded itself, and Soviet Russia, which had been excluded by the members. Generally, the British Prime Minister held out high hopes for the coming meeting (albeit with an unfamiliar orientation): 'As the Washington Conference is establishing peace in the great West, I am looking forward to the Genoa Conference to establish peace in the East, until they will be like the two wings of the Angel of Peace hovering over the world...'[38] In particular, he hoped that, attracted by the prospect of disarmament and reconstruction, the USA would return to Europe as 'a generous creditor...and as a guarantor of peace'.[39]

On the opening day, 10 April, Lloyd George observed that the world had become one economic unit and referred to an individual who had made an important early contribution to it becoming so, Christopher Columbus: 'A distinguished citizen of this city once upon a time discovered America and as Genoa in the past discovered America to Europe I am hopeful that Genoa once more will render another immortal service to humanity by rediscovering Europe to America.'[40]

In his speech on opening day, Chicherin held out great hopes for economic relations but also went much further in a proposal for a general limitation of armaments. The Soviet Commissar for Foreign Affairs strongly implied that Genoa should become a sequel to Washington, referring to Briand's observation at Washington that the reason why armament could not be limited was the state of armament in Russia. French and other delegates were aghast at this sudden turn in the proceedings and the Lloyd George had to pull out all his oratorical stops in order to avoid disaster, arguing for adherence to the agreed economic agenda, while conceding that if Genoa developed into a universal conference there would be plenty of time for the USA to arrive.[41]

Another difficulty arose at the first meeting of what was known as the Political Commission, when Chicherin protested against the inclusion of

Romania because it was in occupation of what he deemed to be the Russian territory of Bessarabia, and against the 'abnormal character' of the presence of Japan when it was in occupation of part of the territory of the FER allied to Russia. France and Belgium opposed the inclusion of Russia and Germany.[42]

These two powers responded to such long-held antagonism by concluding an agreement of recognition and collaboration at nearby Rapallo on 16 April. Attempting to calm even greater storms in a speech to Anglo-American journalists arguing in favour of the Genoa Conference taking its time, Lloyd George declared that there was nobody in America or Europe who would say that the Washington Conference was not worth every hour spent on it. In any future conflict, America would inevitably be brought in as the last war had brought her in. Inevitably, too, there was the possibility of 'a hungry Russia, equipped by an angry Germany'. 'If America were here', Lloyd George declared, 'she could speak with an authority, with an influence, that no other country can possibly command'. In her absence, 'Europe has got to do her best to solve her problems in her own way'. This would involve not the exclusion, but the inclusion of Russia and Germany.[43]

On the Russian question in particular, much of the discussion centred around Soviet Russia's economic system, its refusal to accept responsibility for the debts of its Tsarist and Provisional predecessors, and its insistence on state rather than individual or corporate reception of loans. On the debt question, the Russian delegation gave some pertinent historical examples. Had not the USA freed the slaves without compensation to their former owners? Was compensation given under prohibition for valuable brewing and other property left high and dry? More generally, the Russian reply on 11 May to a Memorandum of 2 May on debts and property declared

> The Russian Revolution needs no justification before an assembly of powers, many of whom count more than one revolution in their own history. Revolutions, which are violent ruptures with the past, carry with them a new juridical status in home and foreign relations. Revolutionary Governments are not bound to respect the obligations of governments which have lapsed. The French Convention proclaimed in 1792 that 'The sovereignty of peoples is not bound by the treaties of tyrants.' The United States repudiated the treaties of their predecessors, England and Spain... Russia cannot therefore be compelled to assume any responsibility towards foreign Powers and their nationals for the cancellation of public debts and the nationalization of private property.

Nevertheless, Soviet Russia would accept responsibility for the debts of its predecessors provided that any agreement was reciprocal and that 'the powers which supported counter-revolutionary movements in Russia or blockaded her are responsible for the damage done'.[44]

On political as well as economic questions, the Soviet Commissar for Foreign Affairs was not lost for words. Asked about Soviet misrule in Georgia, Chicherin responded with a denial asking the delegates to give their serious attention to what he considered to be real, not imaginary causes of bloodshed and oppression, adding a long list including the Japanese in the Far East, the Poles, Romanians, Yugoslavs, and Greeks in Europe, the French, British and Italians overseas.[45]

The impasse on economic questions at Genoa was as much repeated at the Hague Conference of June–July as it was anticipated at Cannes in January.[46] The political differences were highlighted more at the Lausanne Conference on Near Eastern Affairs meeting in December 1922, where Chicherin declared

> In former days people used to talk of 'Russian advance in Asia'... is it not now a case of 'British advance in Europe'? The best traditions of British conservatism were to establish a partition wall between the Russian and British spheres of influence, and this is what we now propose to do – laying the foundations of this wall on the freedom and sovereignty of the Turkish people.

A treaty on the Straits leading from the Mediterranean to the Black Sea would be no more than 'an expression of forces operative in the realm of fact'; an international deal would mean 'the perpetuation of disturbance instead of peace'. There would be two further consequences. One would be 'the necessity for Russia to arm, arm, arm'. The other would be 'the complete collapse of the Washington Naval Disarmament Treaty'. Chicherin continued: 'Russia welcomes the idea of the Washington Conference to which, unfortunately, she was not invited. We shall be happy to participate in any general agreement for naval disarmament, but the opening of the Straits would render general naval disarmament impossible.' The Soviet Commissar for Foreign Affairs concluded with a ringing declaration addressed to Lord Curzon in particular and, no doubt, to those whom he would see as old-style imperialists in general

> The Russian revolution has transformed the Russian people into a nation whose entire energy is concentrated in its Government to a degree hitherto unknown in history; and if war is forced upon that nation it will not capitulate. You are uneasy because our horsemen have reappeared on the heights of the Pamirs, and because you no longer have to deal with the half-witted Tsar who ceded the ridge of the Hindu

Kush to you in 1895. But it is not war that we offer you, it is peace, based on the principle of a partition wall between us and on the principle of the freedom and sovereignty of Turkey.[47]

In the same month as Lausanne, December 1922, the Soviet government hosted a disarmament conference in Moscow addressed to its immediate neighbours, Poland, Finland and the Baltic states. Although unsuccessful, this conference possibly had some little success in keeping the subject of disarmament alive.[48]

In an overall appraisal, Arnold Toynbee asserted that, although it produced no positive results, the Genoa Conference was interesting as 'the first general European conference after the War of 1914–18', for its emphasis on reconstruction, not reparation; and as 'the first attempt at a settlement between the European governments and Soviet Russia'.[49] And Stephen White observed that Genoa 'favoured the regulation of East–West differences by negotiation, in what has subsequently become known as detente'.[50] As far as the USA was concerned, Carol Fink suggested that 'Genoa's end brought relief and some satisfaction', giving the administration in Washington the freedom to give its policies on debts and reparations free rein.[51] However, as Walter LaFeber observes, the Fordney–McCumber Act of September 1922 creating a wall of tariffs around American producers made little sense: 'Europeans could not repay their debts if they could not sell their goods in the rich U.S. market.'[52] As far as Russia in particular was concerned, the idea of sending an exploratory economic mission to Russia foundered in the face of Chicherin's demands that it stay out of Soviet internal affairs and come to Russia 'only under condition of the admittance in America...of our representatives for investigation of the American market'.[53] A significant development on 25 July 1922 was the recognition of the Baltic States, but with the explanation that 'the United States has consistently maintained that the disturbed conditions of Russian affairs may not be made the occasion for the alienation of Russian territory'. The principle was not deemed to be infringed by the recognition of Estonia, Latvia and Lithuania, whose governments had been 'set up and maintained by an indigenous population'.[54]

Meanwhile, there were significant developments back in the Far East.

The Changchun Conference: 4–28 September 1922

At the end of May 1922, the puppet Merkulov régime in Vladivostok dissolved the Popular Assembly, not without some protest, and appointed yet another General, M. K. Diterikhs, formerly a member of Kolchak's entourage, who agreed to revive the early modern consultative assembly that had last met in the late seventeenth century, the *Zemskii Sobor* or Assembly of the Whole Land. Before it met, the following announcement was made in Tokyo on 24 June: 'The Japanese Government have decided to withdraw all Japanese troops from the Maritime Province of Siberia by the end of October 1922. Suitable measures will be taken for the protection of Japanese subjects.'[55] In spite of this explicit message, the *Zemskii Sobor* duly convened on 23 July 1922. The opening ceremony was decorated by imperial flags, and on 3 August, there was a landslide vote in favour of the recognition of the continued supreme power of the Romanovs. To fill the gap before the remnants of that family could be brought over from Europe, Diterikhs was elected as *pravitel'* or ruler. This last of the active White generals, like most of his predecessors, attempted to revive Holy Russia, in his case to the extent that the unit of local government was to be the parish and Orthodoxy the qualification for citizenship. As leader of the army, he gave himself the medieval title of *voevoda*, and prepared to lead units with the equally obsolete title of *druzhiny* into battle.

Before Diterikhs could draw his sword for his faith and his tsar, however, civilian negotiations were resumed on 4 September 1922 at Changchun to the south of Harbin in Japanese-controlled Manchuria. As early as 1 June 1922, about a month and a half after the collapse of Dairen, the Communist Party Politburo in Moscow considered the renewal of talks with Japan expedient provided that there was a united delegation from the RSFSR and the FER and that there would be a commitment to a specific date for the evacuation of their troops from the Japanese.[56] On 27 June, having received just such news from Poole, Chief of the Division of Russian Affairs, Department of State, Secretary of State Hughes wrote to Ambassador Warren in Tokyo welcoming the Japanese decision to withdraw from the mainland but also recalling that 'the protests which this Government made before and during the Washington Conference against Japanese occupation of Siberian territory included Sakhalin Island to an equal degree'. On 6 July, in an even-handed manner, Hughes reminded Warren that 'the generous action of the United States at the Conference on Limitation of Armament is generally understood and appreciated by Russians' and that it was 'almost unnecessary to add that any attempt of the Chita authorities to foment antagonism between the United States and other Powers or to play one Power off against another will be unsuccessful'. On 14 July, the Japanese government informed Hughes of a public statement of the same day that the occupation of the northern or Russian part of Sakhalin would be terminated as soon as satisfactory settlement had been obtained for the Nikolaevsk affair.[57] On 25 July the governments of the RSFSR and FER sent a joint note to the Japanese government acknowledging a Japanese note of 19 July promising evacuation of its troops by 1 November and offering to reopen talk at Chita or Moscow, Peking or Tokyo, or any other place mutually agreed. The Japanese government accepted the proposal on 1 August, but added the rider that the evacuation should be effected on the basis of a new general agreement drawn up from the points agreed at the Dairen Conference, and that questions which had not been decided at Dairen such as fisheries and the 'Nikolaevsk massacre' could be taken up only after the signature of the general agreement. On 6 August, the governments of the RSFSR and FER sent another note to the government of Japan agreeing that a general agreement on the basis of the Dairen talks could be signed first, and the details discussed afterwards.[58] On 24 August, the RSFSR and FER accepted Changchun from a list of meeting places proposed by Japan on 14 August. It was agreed to open talks on 4 September at Changchun at the junction of the Japanese South Manchurian Railway and the CER, equidistant from Japan and Russia (although not from Tokyo and Moscow) and well protected by Japanese guards.[59] The Soviet side was to be represented by A. A. Ioffe, a friend of Trotsky's and an experienced diplomat who had participated in negotiations from Brest–Litovsk in early 1918 to Genoa in April–May 1922. 'Mr. Yoffe' was unequivocally named 'Chief delegate' and 'Mr. Yanson' 'Second Delegate' in the joint representation of the RSFSR and FER, while their Japanese counterparts were Mr Matsudaira and Mr Matsushima respectively.[60]

Back in Moscow, by 27 July 1922, the Politburo approved Ioffe's 'Basic directives for the talks with Japan'. Ioffe made five points:

1 Categorical demand for the evacuation of all Japanese troops, without which no agreement;
2 No special political or economic privileges for the Japanese beyond those already extended to other 'bourgeois' states and citizens;
3 Talks without fear of disruption, since this would be less dangerous than action for the sake of agreement;
4 Use of the talks for agitational purposes since Japan was experiencing a pre-revolutionary period;
5 Consideration of the fact that the Soviet master trump was the mutual relationship with the USA – the attempt should be made to use it.[61]

After Ioffe left Moscow, the Politburo confirmed another, more detailed directive by L. M. Karakhan, deputy Commissar for Foreign Relations and a specialist on Asia, on 10 August 1922. In spite of the fact, he argued, that at one time the Dairen draft agreement had been generally accepted, it was necessary to deal with it now more carefully and strictly for the following reasons. Firstly, the situation had changed very much in favour of Soviet Russia. Secondly, the Dairen talks had been conducted by the FER alone, and obligations imposed upon this 'mongrel state', not upon Russia. This was not a question of prestige, rather that the FER could not be allowed to enter into an agreement with Japan that could serve as an obstacle to the ultimately inevitable Sovietisation of the FER. The Politburo also accepted Karakhan's objections to two of the points made by Ioffe. On 3 Karakhan stated that in case of the impossibility of reaching agreement the talks should be stretched out, not showing any readiness to disperse at least before the time of the evacuation of the Japanese forces. On 4 Karakhan believed that it would be too dangerous to make use of the talks for agitational purposes. All relations with Japanese communists should be severed. The Japanese communist party was unknown, except for a few members who had been in Russia. Because of the exceptional capability of the Japanese for espionage and impersonation, there were many chances of running into provocation, and during the time of the talks this could break them off.[62] While Ioffe wanted to keep the spirit of the Russian Revolution alive, then, for Karakhan it was necessary to quell it.

On the eve of the commencement of the Changchun Conference, Ioffe conceded that it might have been to some extent the fault of representatives of the FER that the Japanese had formed the impression that the Dairen draft could form the basis of a new agreement without any significant amendation. However, the Japanese had jumped the gun in believing that the Dairen draft could be signed after no more than a few changes. The delegates of the FER and RSFSR would have to insist that this was not the case.[63]

On 4 September, after opening formalities, Ioffe argued in favour of at least some open meetings, but Matsudaira objected to any of the conference being made public, and to a record being kept of all the sessions, observing that such arrangements would inhibit his desire to speak 'with absolute frankness and sincerity'. As well as echoing – wittingly or unwittingly – the language of Woodrow Wilson, Matsudaira explicitly put forward as a model 'the negotiations between Russia and England for the conclusion of the trade agreement'. The conference was to be 'not a series of debates, but an exchange of friendly and frank expressions of opinion'. If their suspicions were confirmed that the Russians were aiming at propaganda, 'there could take place a sudden reversal in the feeling of the Japanese people'. Ioffe reminded his opposite number that Soviet Russia did not recognise secret diplomacy, and that through its initiative, negotiations between states had become 'common property'. He continued: 'The chairman of the Japanese delegation surely will not claim that Lloyd George engaged in Soviet propaganda, yet he was the originator of the Genoa Conference, which was held openly, and in general there had been no secret conferences in recent years.' In the London trade talks, there had been no conference as such: the British government had negotiated with a Russian representative who was already there. Ioffe expressed greater fears about what was to ensue at Changchun. Had Matsudaira actually said, as had been reported, that the present conference was to have 'no serious import'? Moreover, the Russian delegation had before it by no means the same aim as had been reached by the Anglo-Russian Agreement. Matsudaira stated that he had given no press interviews involving 'serious import' or anything else. While the form of the negotiations in London may have differed from those now under way, however, 'the essential nature was the same – the establishment of commercial and friendly relations'. However, Ioffe insisted that the conference should aim at more than 'only the conclusion of a trade agreement'. Even the Dairen conference, he pointed out, had not been limited to trade. Matsudaira replied that there was no need to confine negotiations to trade, since the Japanese delegation had plenary powers.

Through nine further sessions, the two sides were for the most part at cross purposes on key questions such as the timing of the Japanese evacuation, the nature and extent of Russian concessions and the relationship between the FER and Soviet Russia. The eleventh and last session of the conference took place on 28 September 1922. It opened with a statement from Matsudaira based on the proceedings of the Dairen conference. Ioffe countered with the insistence that the RSFSR and FER could not accept 'that they should be treated like barbarians and that their territories should be occupied by foreign troops as a guarantee for the settlement of some conflict'. (At the tenth session, alleging that the Japanese were threatening to hold on to all of Sakhalin for ever, Ioffe had stated: 'The history of international relations knows of a case where national troops had seized the territory of savage tribes, who had murdered a missionary, as a guarantee for obtaining an adequate compensation, but the Russian delegation did not know of cases where this method had been applied to civilised people, and one cannot conceive it possible that it should be applied to Russia.') If the US Secretary of State Hughes had expressed his agreement with such an argument at the Washington Conference, 'the masses of the working people of the whole world, including the Japanese, will also side with us'. The Japanese delegation was aware that Russia was a great power. It gave too much emphasis to its own losses at Nikolaevsk, which it saw as an event unparalleled for cruelty in history. Yet Japanese troops had shot peaceful Russian inhabitants at Spassk, Nikol'sk and Vladivostok. If Russia had possessed an organised government at the time of these incidents, Ioffe declared, they would undoubtedly have led to war. The conference came to an abrupt end, with no firm agreement on any matter whatsoever.[64]

On 25 September Poole of the US State Department reported to Under Secretary of State Phillips that Skvirsky of 'the so-called Commercial

120   *After the Washington Conference*

Delegation' of the FER had called on him to communicate the Russian position on Nikolaevsk, Sakhalin and the Japanese evacuation, while expressing 'much appreciation of our attitude and especially of what Mr Hughes had done at the Armament Conference to induce the Japanese to give up the Siberian venture'. On 26 September Poole reported to Hughes himself that Saburi, the Japanese Chargé d'Affaires, had called on him to explain the reason for the final failure of the Changchun talks, making special reference to the Russian insistence on joint representation for the RSFSR and FER and Russian disappointment at not receiving immediate political recognition from Japan. Saburi also intimated that

> public opinion in Japan had been influenced by the action of Great Britain in concluding its trade agreement. Thus, the Government had felt it necessary, in order to satisfy public opinion, to go further in meeting the Russians than it would have itself been inclined to do.

On 28 September, Skvirsky wrote to Hughes complaining of continued Japanese depredations and insisting that if the Japanese had lost hundreds of people at Nikolaevsk, the Russians had lost tens of thousands from Japanese action as well as property losses amounting to hundreds of millions of gold rubles.[65]

In an undated Russian memorandum discussing the reasons for the failure of the Changchun Conference, emphasis was given to the refusal of the RSFSR and FER to accept the Japanese seizure of the territory of others on the basis of the so-called Dairen draft agreement which would also have given the Japanese great economic advantages, and to the Japanese insistence that Northern Sakhalin would be evacuated only after the problem of the 'Nikolaevsk Incident' was settled.[66]

Ioffe, the leader of the joint delegation of the RSFSR and FER made his own comments on the course and conclusion of the Changchun Conference. He described how he had tried to exploit the contradictions between the USA and Japan by maintaining close contact with American diplomatic representatives and journalists. He believed that the Sinclair Company and other US businesses were interested in Sakhalin, and that the Americans were extremely pleased with his tough line. He suggested that his phrase 'an agreement will be possible only when there is not a single Japanese soldier on Russian territory' took them into raptures. At the very least, this would appear to be something of an exaggeration.[67]

Ioffe did not have a high opinion of the Japanese negotiators, suggesting that he had never met such naively impudent diplomacy. Evidently, he suggested, both Matsudaira and his deputy Matsushima were sincerely convinced that they were gracing the Soviet side by the very fact of the talks.

On the Japanese economic demands, Ioffe said that when he responded to Matsudaira that he did not understand how negotiations could be conducted in the interest of one side only, his Japanese counterpart made the wide-eyed, childishly simple observation: 'But surely if Japanese capitalists will work in the Russian Far East, then this must be favourable to you, too.' And when Ioffe asked him the equally simple question why the former Russian government had never acceded to this Japanese demand, even though it had been sought throughout a whole decade, Matsudaira replied with a stupid smirk that the former government had been a bad one, and then became angry when Ioffe commented that, although the Tsarist government had been a bad one indeed and overthrown for that reason, the Soviet side did not consider that it had always been wrong. With the same naive impudence, Matsudaira 'ten times to the minute' observed that the Japanese people were beginning to relate better to Russians in such a manner that the latter should faint from joy, but that this mood would change in the face of stubbornness. Matsudaira took no interest in the Russian mood, Ioffe believed, and it never seemed to enter his head that the Russian side was following the Japanese press and knew full well that Japanese public opinion was sharply critical of the government precisely because of its Russian policy.[68] On this point, Ioffe himself was guilty of presumption.

While Matsudaira blamed the Russians entirely for the failure of Changchun, Foreign Minister Uchida insisted that the prime purpose of the Japanese side was to protect people, property and freedom to trade while conducting an orderly evacuation. In his later analysis, Tanaka concluded that the Russian side had formed on the basis of contacts with Japanese journalists an exaggerated view of the extent of internal opposition in Japan to the intervention. They had come to the conclusion that the Japanese government would be forced to come to more favourable terms with Soviet Russia incorporating the FER.[69]

The end of the FER: the formation of the Soviet Union – Soviet relations with Japan and China

Soon after the closure of the Changchun Conference, Chicherin observed that nothing would remain of the independence of the FER except a paper constitution if it became inundated with Japanese goods, merchants and all kinds of agents.[70] On 17 September 1922, the Politburo declared that an artificial buffer based on principles alien to the Soviet Republic was no longer necessary, and that the existence of this buffer was beginning to lose its meaning for the 'popular masses' of the FER. So the finances and administration of the two republics should be linked, while the struggle was continued against 'anti-Soviet' (that is, non-Bolshevik) parties and the 'bourgeois' order at the same time as the Whites were finally liquidated. Conveniently, the second convocation of the People's Assembly of the FER gave a mighty victory to the Bolsheviks.

The view of Ioffe in these last days was probably influential. On 17 October 1922, he wrote to Chicherin that the existence of the FER had been very harmful at the Changchun Conference: absolutely nothing justified it, and it should be liquidated without delay.[71]

Meanwhile, as the Japanese prepared for their evacuation of Vladivostok, Reds and Whites were fighting the last battles of the Russian Civil War. Assisted by partisans and strengthened by reinforcements from the Red Army, the People's Revolutionary Army of the FER won its last major victory at what became known as 'the storming of Spassk' on 9 October and went on to regain Vladivostok by 25 October, after Diterikhs and many of his followers had departed along with the Japanese. The Japanese left the local military stores virtually untouched with their keys easily accessible. But condign retribution ensued for enemies of the Soviet régime.

Now that the Japanese had finally departed, the fiction of the FER's independence was completely superfluous to Soviet requirements. Proceeding from Changchun to Peking, Ioffe noted on 9 November 1922 that Stalin had told him in the course of a telephone conversation that the Central Committee empowered him to establish the time of a possible liquidation of the FER.[72] On 13 November, possibly at Ioffe's instigation but with due regard for constitutional niceties, the FER's People's Assembly of the FER convened in Vladivostok asked for union with Soviet Russia. On 15 November, the All-Russian Central Committee (VTsIK) duly pronounced the FER an 'inseparable part' of the RSFSR. Apart from northern Sakhalin, Russia's pre-revolutionary frontiers in Asia were restored, ready for the creation of the Union of Soviet Socialist Republics just a month and a half later on 30 December 1922.[73]

According to a post-Soviet article, the formation of the Soviet Union was far from being the exclusive consequence of the acquisitive ambitions of the Communist government. In the years 1921–2, pressure came not only from the Far East but also from Central Asia and Transcaucasia for 'the creation and formation of a strictly and uniformly centralised, unitary state, succeeding in its own Bolshevik way to the [Tsarist] idea of "a unified and indivisible Russia"'.[74] As a sometime member of the former nobility, Chicherin probably understood the old concept as he worked on behalf of the new one. For example, in a memo of 31 October 1922, he wrote to Stalin objecting to a council of representatives of the constituent republics being set up as a standing body under the People's Commissariat for Foreign Affairs since it would make the PCFA 'an absolutely unwieldy institution'.[75]

As far as outstanding matters concerning Japan were concerned, for his talks with Kawakami early in 1923 as a preliminary to negotiations with Goto, Ioffe was instructed: 'The forcing of the pace of the talks and the conclusion of an agreement with Japan acquires exceptional significance in connection with Anglo-Russian conflicts and the possible further complication of our international situation in Europe. Therefore, you must take all measures to accelerate the official talks.' Moreover, one formula for the agreement could be that concluded with Germany at Rapallo in 1922.[76]

The Japanese offered to buy Sakhalin island, but the Soviet price was too high.[77] For the Japanese, as well as incurring widespread international unpopularity, the intervention had also imposed a heavy financial burden, costing 600 million yen, the equivalent of the same amount of gold rubles, according to one account.[78] And so, there was no great opposition to bringing it formally to an end without the acquisition of Sakhalin.

As a footnote to the story, let us take a glance at the 'Convention embodying the basic principles of the relations between Japan and the Union of Soviet Socialist Republics', signed on 20 January 1925 after several ups and downs in those relations in 1923 and 1924. There were seven principles as follows:

1 Japan gave full recognition to the USSR;
2 The USSR expressed its 'sincere regrets' for the Nikolaevsk massacre of 1920, Japan having withdrawn her claim for reparations and promising to withdraw her garrison from northern Sakhalin by 15 May 1925;
3 In anticipation of any future treaty of commerce and navigation, the USSR recognised the doctrine of private ownership 'to the widest possible extent and on condition of reciprocity';
4 There was to be no propaganda of an overt or covert nature by the governments themselves or their official agents;
5 Regarding natural resources, the USSR signified its willingness to grant to Japanese concessions for the exploitation of minerals, forests and other natural resources in all Soviet territories. As for oil, the USSR pledged specifically to grant 50 per cent in area of the oil fields already explored or to be explored on the east coast of northern Sakhalin during a period of five to ten years. Coal concessions were also granted on the west coast of northern Sakhalin and in the Due district;
6 Fishery rights in Soviet waters were granted to the Japanese in principle, recognition being given to a private *modus vivendi* of 1924;
7 As for debts and obligations, a settlement was reserved for further negotiations on condition that the Japanese Government and people would not be placed in any position less favourable than that which might be accorded to other governments or nationals.

Detailed agreements on the concessions were reached later in 1925 and consolidated the foundations for Japanese–Soviet economic co-operation.[79]

Just a few years after the conclusion of the Washington Conference, then, the headline in *The New York Times* of 'JAPAN GAINS MOST, RUSSIA THE LOSER' of 6 February 1922 seemed less appropriate than when first published. While Japan was to achieve most of the economic concessions that it sought, Soviet Russia made considerable political gains before the formation of the Soviet Union. With much more perspective at his disposal than *The New York Times* in 1922, the British historian E. H. Carr was to go so far as to declare in 1953 that 'Soviet Russia was in most respects the principal beneficiary of the Washington conference in the Far East'.[80] On what did Carr base his assertion? The first point to make here, which has no direct connection with the conference, is what Carr calls the 'most important' but the 'least publicized' achievement of Soviet foreign policy in the winter of 1921–2 – 'the consolidation of Soviet power in Outer Mongolia'.[81] On 5 November 1921, a treaty of mutual recognition was signed between the RSFSR and the Mongolian People's Republic on terms of strict formal equality. However, after a rearguard action by 'a conservative pro-Chinese group drawn from the old lama class', a further Soviet–Mongolian treaty of 31 May 1922 'made still more apparent the resumption by the Soviet Government of the paramount role successfully asserted in Outer Mongolia by the last Tsarist government'.[82]

While the formal recognition of the illegal Japanese Communist Party at the Fourth Comintern Congress in November 1922 did not have any great significance, the declaration then of a 'united front' of the Japanese, Chinese and Korean parties meant even less. However, although the Soviet–Mongolian treaty aroused the anger of the Chinese government in Peking, the influence of that northern government was in steep decline while that of the Kuomintang based to the south in Canton was on the rise. The Ioffe mission to the Far East in late 1922 brought about the establishment of close links with Sun Yat-sen and the Kuomintang Nationalists. The aim of the establishment of Soviet communism in China was pushed into the background while Ioffe insisted that his government had no intention of bringing about the secession from China of Outer Mongolia. There was agreement on both sides that the question of the CER could be settled only by a Soviet–Chinese conference. Ioffe went on to spend six months in Japan from February 1923 onwards. Ostensibly ignoring the suppression of communism, he helped to smooth the way towards the Soviet–Japanese agreement of January 1925.

In August 1923, a rising star of the Kuomintang in favour of collaboration with the USSR, Chiang Kai-shek, travelled to Moscow to procure arms and to study military organisation. In September, a leading Comintern activist, Mikhail Borodin, arrived in Canton at the invitation of Sun Yat-sen to act as political adviser to the Kuomintang. E. H. Carr declared: 'Within six years of the Bolshevik revolution, Soviet Russia had emerged from the penumbra of confusion and helplessness, and was intervening decisively in the policies of a major Asiatic country.'[83]

Carr's view was substantiated in 1965 by Akira Iriye in his study of the search for a New Order in the Far East, 1921-31. Beginning with 'The American Initiative' centred on the Washington Conference, Iriye moved on to 'The Soviet Initiative', consisting of a 'lost opportunity', 1922-5, followed by 'the collapse of the Washington System', 1925-6. Iriye argued that, following the lead of the USA at the Washington Conference, the great powers 'took cognizance of the passing of the old order and tried to bring about a new era of "economic foreign policy" as a basis of reconciling and promoting their interests'. However, anti-imperialist Soviet diplomacy frustrated this attempt from the beginning as it worked towards an alternative system of Sino-foreign relations. From 1922 to 1927, 'the Soviet Union was the most active agent of change in the Far East, and the Russian-inspired Nationalists successfully conquered half of China'. The USA, Great Britain and Japan were coming to realise 'the futility of basing their policies on the framework of the Washington Conference'.[84]

Conclusion

In the short run, the Washington Conference received a most positive appraisal from the British press. *The Times, The Daily Telegraph, The News Chronicle* and *The Manchester Guardian* were all enthusiastic. On the other hand, C. H. Douglas in *The English Review* ironically congratulated President Harding on having achieved 'the bloodless surrender of the world's greatest Empire, and its deletion as an effective voice at other than parochial conferences' while former First Sea Lord Admiral Sir Rosslyn Wester-Wemyss in *The Nineteenth Century* denounced 'an act of renunciation unparalleled in history'.[85]

In the Soviet Union, in a report on the world political situation to a Comintern Executive Committee meeting on 15 June 1923, Karl Radek devoted a substantial section to 'Liquidation of the Washington Treaty'. Radek quoted an article by Archibald Hurd in another British periodical *Fortnightly Review* for January 1923: 'It now looks as though even the treaty for the limitation of naval armaments, which was negotiated by the representatives of Great Britain, the United States, France, Italy and Japan, might after all prove merely a scrap of paper.'[86] Japan was greatly strengthening her strategic position through expansion of her navy as well as the secret fortification of the Bonin Isles. The USA was about to spend nearly

$300 million on the maintenance and increase of its navy, while Great Britain was committed to an outlay of £9 million for the construction of the naval base of Singapore. Emphasis on Singapore meant that Great Britain intended to concentrate its main fleet near the Pacific, thus circumventing the Washington Treaty which forbade fortification in that ocean itself. Hurd asserted that these developments made Japan more dependent on Soviet Russia, with which it wished to make peace.[87]

Radek drew four conclusions from Hurd's argument:

1   Europe's decline was about to accelerate as that old continent moved not towards peace, but towards more and bigger war. Armies and military budgets there were larger than before 1914, and the risk of conflict correspondingly greater.
2   Soviet Russia, the only revolutionary power, was in danger because it was becoming stronger, and, depending on the inaction or action of the international proletariat, would have to fend off attack by itself or be part of a more general counter offensive.
3   The German working class and the German revolution were in the greatest peril, caught between the disintegrating bourgeoisie and French expansionism – between fascism and imperialism.
4   The revolution in the East was in danger from British imperialism in Persia, Turkey, Egypt and India.[88]

Nearly eighty years on, now that both the British Empire and the Comintern have been no more for about half a century, we have a longer perspective on the Washington Conference that may allow us to make a more objective assessment.

Let us consider a number of counterfactual questions:

1   What if Soviet Russia had been invited to the Washington Conference? This would not necessarily have been a positive step. Had the rhetoric of Comintern, or even the language used by Chicherin at Genoa, been brought into the discussions on disarmament or the Far East, the cause of recognition of Soviet Russia could have been harmed rather than helped. In any case, Hughes remained dead set against recognition of Soviet Russia, and the new diplomacy foundered.
2   Had the FER and its Special Delegation been accorded a greater degree of recognition, would this have helped or hindered the cause of world stability? As it was, as we have seen, the Special Delegation played the part of a 'Trojan Horse' within the citadel of capitalism, exerting some influence on Borah and other Senators, for example, although more study would be needed to ascertain the degree of success in this and

other endeavours. Without any mention of the Special Delegation, a post-Soviet historian Iu. N. Tsipkin considers that the FER was indeed 'a democratic state, where the revolutionary dictatorship of the people predominated'. He suggests that, although the Soviet government exploited the FER for its own purposes of avoiding direct confrontation with Japan and maintaining the territorial integrity of the Russian Far East, the experiment in democracy was nevertheless of definite interest and potential value to the new Russian Republic evolving since 1991.[89] Yet there was no possibility of its survival as a beacon of democracy with its incorporation into the Soviet Union back in 1922.

3   What would have been the consequences if the other powers, in particular the USA, had exercised more restraint on Japanese imperialist ambitions in the Far East, exerting more pressure for an earlier end to intervention? Might this have led to more rather than less violence? Did the USA and its associates act according to the outmoded principle of the 'balance of power', not wanting to rein in Japan too hard lest Soviet Russia attempt to exert its revolutionary influence in China in a more unbridled fashion. Could it be that Japan was seen as a necessary counterweight to revolutionary disturbance in the Far East? In his memoirs, Herbert Hoover recalled that he had advised Hughes at the time of the Washington Conference that there was a threat to China from Communism as well as from banditry and warlordism. Moreover, 'unless order was restored by the Chinese themselves or by the united action of all the other nations or both, then Japan was likely to act'. While Japan had no claim to acquire more territory, she certainly had legitimate need for Chinese raw materials and Chinese markets for her own manufactures. Hoover 'doubted the capacity of any of the then Chinese leaders to re-establish central power and order without foreign help and suggested that this conference should face the question positively instead of just a negative hands-off policy'.[90] He therefore implied that Japan had a key role to play in the maintenance of stability in China.

4   What if the Washington Conference had dovetailed with the process begun by the Paris Conference to produce an 'association of nations' which the USA could have joined? If the USA had attended the Genoa Conference, could world stability as well as the interests of the USA been advanced? If, by whatever route, Soviet Russia followed by the USSR had been more integrated with the 'association of nations', might some of the negative features of Soviet development been reduced in such a manner that the policy of Socialism in one country would not have led to the excesses of Stalinism? Certainly, the neglect of international relations by investigators of the phenomenon has led to explanations that are less than fully satisfactory.

5   Had the USA been less concerned to maintain the territorial integrity of Tsarist Russia even under Soviet power, albeit with important exceptions such as Finland, Poland, and later Bessarabia and the Baltic states, might a process of fragmentation set in? As it was, in many respects the period we have been studying promoted rather than undermined the process of the formation of the Soviet Union. Was there a tacit acknowledgement of this American contribution to Soviet consolidation?

Generally speaking, by considering what did happen rather than what might have happened before, during and after the Washington Conference, this study has illustrated aspects of the interrelationship between the powers in the period following the First World War and the Russian Revolution. The study has demonstrated how the USA was already achieving preponderance over older empires and how Asia was assuming an importance comparable to that of Europe in an increasingly global US policy. Some of this reality shone through the vaporous rhetoric of the 'new diplomacy' both American and Soviet, which also threw light on the gestation of the superpowers. On a minor scale, the creation, activity and demise of the FER served as a reflection of Soviet policy towards the Washington Conference as well as in the Far East itself. Memories of the Washington Conference were strong at the time of the Genoa Conference back in Europe, when Britain and France attempted to regain some of their lost initiative and Germany and Russia began their revival. Thus, as some observers detected at the time, the Versailles–Washington system was being undermined almost as soon as it had been created. Further evidence for such evanescence was to be found in the Far East where Soviet influence was making itself strongly felt at other conferences during the same period. Less apparently then, but clearly enough now, US policies at the Washington Conference had contributed to the growth of that influence in the making of the Soviet Union.

Notes

1 Introduction: before the Washington Conference

1 *Congressional Record*, 4 March 1921, pp. 4–6. Norman Angell's *America and the New World-State: A Plea for American Leadership in International Organization*, New York, 1915 was among the works arguing for the USA's leadership before the entry into war.
2 Geddes to Curzon, 15 April 1921, enclosed in Curzon to Lloyd George, 20 April 1921, Lloyd George Papers, F/13/2/19, as cited in Lloyd C. Gardner, *Safe for Democracy: The Anglo-American Response to Revolution*, New York, 1987, p. 307. Earlier, Geddes had already written to Lloyd George's secretary of a group in Harding's entourage aiming 'to transfer the centre of English speaking power to North America... They regard England as crippled and this as their opportunity and they propose to grasp it – not in hatred but in fulfilment of their country's destiny'. Geddes to Kerr, 3 January 1921, Lloyd George Papers, F/60/4/11 as cited by Erik Goldstein, 'The Evolution of British Diplomatic Strategy for the Washington Conference', in Erik Goldstein and John Maurer, eds, *The Washington Conference 1921–22: Naval Rivalry, East Asian Stability and the Road to Pearl Harbor*, Ilford, 1994, p. 13.
3 Minutes of the Imperial Conference, CAB 32/2, First and Second Meetings, as cited by Erik Goldstein, 'The Evolution', pp. 6, 11, 15.
4 John St Loe Strachey, 'English-speaking Peoples, Relations of', *Encyclopaedia Britannica*, Thirteenth Edition, vol. I, London and New York, 1926, pp. 1011–12; Denna Frank Fleming, *The United States and World Organization, 1920–1933*, New York, 1938, p. 79.
5 John Chalmers Vinson, *The Parchment Peace: The United States Senate and the Washington Conference, 1921–1922*, Athens, Georgia, 1955, pp. 57, 90, 95–6; Thomas H. Buckley, *The United States and the Washington Conference, 1921–1922*, Knoxville, 1970, pp. 17–18, 32–3.
6 Harold J. Goldberg (ed.) *Documents of Soviet–American Relations*: vol. 1, *Intervention, Famine Relief, International Affairs, 1917–1933*, Gulf Breeze, Florida, 1993, pp. 262–3. The Far Eastern Republic (1920–2) will be discussed in Chapter 4.
7 Belgium was to be included among the nine powers represented at the Conference, along with the USA, the British Empire and its dominions, France, Italy, the Netherlands, Portugal, Japan and China.
8 Quoted in Goldstein, 'The Evolution', p. 6.

9 *The New York Times*, 20 September 1921.
10 Paul N. Miliukov, *Russia: To-Day and To-Morrow*, London, 1922, p. 303.
11 Quoted by Linda Killen, 'The Search for a Democratic Russia: Bakhmetev in the United States', *Diplomatic History*, 2, 1978, 255.
12 *The New York Times*, 28 October 1921.
13 Root quoted by Philip C. Jessup, *Elihu Root*, New York, 1964, vol. 2, p. 353. Root recalled in 1930 that he had recommended that the leader of the Bolshevik Revolution, Lenin, should be arrested, tried, imprisoned and executed. Ibid., p. 369.
14 Quoted in E. H. Carr, *The Bolshevik Revolution, 1917–1923*, vol. 3, Harmondsworth, 1966, p. 28, note 2, with the additional explanation given by Trotsky as quoted by one of his associates: 'I wanted to have more leisure for party affairs.'
15 Goldberg, *Documents*, vol. 1, pp. 36–9.
16 This paragraph from Goldberg, *Documents*, vol. 1, pp. 68–71.
17 David R. Francis, formerly mayor of St Louis and Governor of Missouri, was a political appointee rather than a career diplomat, and therefore less concerned than others with the niceties of protocol.
18 Ibid., pp. 71–91. Since Czechoslovakia was not officially created before 28 October, I have adopted the term 'Czecho-Slovak' widely employed before (and even after) then.
19 Ibid., pp. 91–5.
20 A career diplomat, Poole became chief of the Division of Russian Affairs for the Department of State early in 1920.
21 Ibid., pp. 112–22.
22 Arno J. Mayer, *Politics and Diplomacy of Peacemaking: Containment and Counter-Revolution at Versailles, 1918–1919*, London, 1968, pp. 329–30.
23 Goldberg, *Documents*, vol. 1, pp. 122–8; David S. Foglesong, *America's Secret War against Bolshevism: U.S. Intervention in the Russian Civil War, 1917–1920*, Chapel Hill NC, 1995, pp. 179–87.
24 Goldberg, *Documents*, vol. 1, pp. 132–7; Foglesong, *America's Secret War*, p. 280.
25 Goldberg, *Documents*, vol. 1, pp. 137–40.
26 Ibid., pp. 153–4.
27 Ibid., pp. 150, 154–6. For a thorough and judicious appraisal, see J. D. Smele, *Civil War in Siberia: The Anti-Bolshevik Government of Admiral Kolchak, 1918–1920*, Cambridge, 1996.
28 Quoted by Gardner, *Safe for Democracy*, p. 246. Gardner goes on to say that Wilson wrote to Hoover that he was 'very much impressed with this letter… and am ready to say at once that I agree with you'.
29 John M. Thompson, *Russia, Bolshevism, and the Versailles Peace*, Princeton, 1966, pp. 400–2.
30 Goldberg, *Documents*, vol. 1, pp. 158–60.
31 Ibid., pp. 166–9, 173–7. In fact, of course, Ukraine and 'Caucasus' were soon to be incorporated in the Soviet Union. The union of Bessarabia with Romania remained a matter of dispute.
32 Ibid., pp. 169–73.
33 Foglesong, *America's Secret War*, pp. 235, 295–8, supplemented by personal communication; V. I. Goldin, *Rossiia v grazhdanskoi voine: Ocherki noveishei istoriografii (vtoraia polovina 1980-kh–90-e gody)*, Arkhangel'sk, 2000.
34 Walter LaFeber, *The American Age: United States Foreign Policy at Home and Abroad since 1750*, New York, 1989, pp. 81–5, 206–9.

35 Raymond Leslie Buell, *The Washington Conference*, A Dissertation presented to the Faculty of Princeton University for the Degree of Doctor of Philosophy, New York and London, 1922, p. 40.
36 Ibid., pp. 62–3. For similar views, see Miliukov, *Russia To-Day and To-Morrow*, pp. 305–9. Miliukov names extensive use of a book entitled *What Japan Wants* by Mr Yoshi S. Kuno, assistant professor at the University of California.
37 Buell, *The Washington Conference*, pp. 359–60. The Fordney–McCumber Tariff of 1922 erected the barriers that Buell feared.
38 Sadao Asada, 'Japan's "Special Interests" and the Washington Conference, 1921–22', *American Historical Review*, 1961–2, vol. 67, 62–3.
39 Walter LaFeber, *The Clash*, p. 114.
40 Buell, *The Washington Conference*, pp. 41–4, 50. For general if not specific support of Buell's assertions concerning Finland, see Michael Futrell, 'Colonel Akashi and Japanese contacts with Russian revolutionaries in 1904–5', *St. Anthony's Papers*, 1967, vol. 20, 4. I have not been able to substantiate the allegations about Japanese activities in Abyssinia and India. On intervention in Korea and China, see for example Ki-baik Lee *A New History of Korea*, trans. Edward W. Wanger with Edward J. Shultz, Seoul, 1984, pp. 306–27; Arnold Xiangze Jiang *The United States and China*, Chicago, 1988, pp. 51–6. For reference to the secret Russo-Japanese treaty of 1916, see *Japanese Intervention in the Russian Far East*, Special Delegation of the Far Eastern Republic to the United States of America, Washington, DC, 1922, p. 2.
41 Buell, *The Washington Conference*, pp. 51–2, 56.
42 *The New York Times*, 14 January 1921.
43 'In signing the concessions which we have granted to the Americans', Lenin was alleged to have said, 'we make acute the relations between America and Japan. We profit by this, as by other similar conflicts between our enemies. Our concessions to foreign capitalists are in reality a moral and material victory for us'. This reflects, but does not reproduce exactly, the sentiments expressed by Lenin in a speech of 21 November. See *PSS*, vol. 42, p. 23.
44 Buell, *The Washington Conference*, p. 68. In any case, *The New York Times* of 23 November 1920 had thrown doubt upon the completion of the Vanderlip concession contract, citing a Soviet newspaper source provided by the State Department to the effect. Moreover, the State Department had pointed out that the Soviet Russian government had demanded recognition by the US government before any such contract became valid. For its part, the US government would not look upon contracts made by US citizens or British citizens as valid unless they were confirmed by a regularly constituted and recognized representative government in Russia. In a speech of 8 December 1920, without mentioning Vanderlip by name, Lenin observed: 'It is most profitable to us to lease Kamchatka and receive part of the products, the more so that we are really unable to avail ourselves of it or utilize it. The treaty has not yet been signed, and it has been met by a frenzy of rage in Japan. By means of this treaty we have still more aggravated the differences between our enemies.' See Harold J. Goldberg, *Documents of Soviet–American Relations: Propaganda, Economic Affairs, Recognition*, Gulf Breeze, FL, 1995, 2, p. 219. For an interesting account of the whole imbroglio, see Albert Parry, 'Washington B. Vanderlip, the "Khan of Kamchatka"', *Pacific Historical Review*, vol. 17, no. 3, 1948.
45 Buell, *The Washington Conference*, p. 97.
46 Ibid., pp. 364–5.

132 *Notes*

47 Buell, *The Washington Conference*, p. 364.
48 Ibid., p. 98.
49 Ibid., p. 101.
50 Ibid., pp. 108–9.
51 Ibid., pp. 104–5.
52 Quoted in ibid., p. 113.
53 Quoted in ibid., p. 119.
54 Ibid., pp. 132–4.
55 *Washington Conference on the Limitation of Armaments* [henceforth WCLA], 2 vols., printed for the Foreign Office, London, [1922], vol. 1, p. 1. Curzon received the proposed agenda on 13 September.
56 Buckley, *The United States*, pp. 40–1.
57 Goldberg, *Documents*, vol. 1, pp. 268–9. Sèvres was a treaty with Turkey in 1920 superseded by Lausanne in 1923.
58 Mayer, *Politics and Diplomacy*, pp. 329–30.
59 Ernest R. May, 'Foreword', Erik Goldstein and John Maurer, *The Washington Conference, 1921–22: Naval Rivalry, East Asian Stability and the Road to Pearl Harbor*, Ilford, 1994, [pp. iv–viii].
60 May himself is not exempt from such a charge, for example in his observation that the Treaty of Riga of 1921 'allowed the new, revolutionized Russia to isolate itself temporarily from the great power system in which Tsarist Russia had been an integral force'. Ibid., [pp. vi–vii]: 'obliged' would be a better word than 'allowed'.
61 E. I. Popova, 'Vashingtonskaia konferentsiia 1921–1922gg. v otsenke sovetskikh istorikov', G. N. Sevost'ianov and others (eds) *Amerikanskii ezhegodnik 1971*, Moscow, 1971, pp. 166–90.
62 A. Iu. Sidorov, *Vneshniaia politika Sovetskoi Rossii na Dal'nem Vostoke, 1917–1922*, Moscow, 1997, pp. 8–10.

2 The Washington Conference: armaments and the Far East

1 Dr Hans Wehberg, *The Limitation of Armaments: A Collection of the Projects Proposed for the Solution of the Problem, Preceded by an Historical Introduction*, Washington, DC, 1921, pp. vi, 5, 8–9.
2 Ibid., pp. 43, 65, 70.
3 Ibid., p. 76.
4 This paragraph from John Chalmers Vinson, *The Parchment Peace: The United States Senate and the Washington Conference, 1921–1922*, Athens, GA, 1955, pp. 133–5.
5 Ibid., pp. 136–7.
6 Quoted by Erik Goldstein, 'The Evolution of British Diplomatic Strategy for the Washington Conference', in Erik Goldstein and John H. Maurer (eds), *The Washington Conference, 1921–22: Naval Rivalry, East Asian Stability and the Road to Pearl Harbor*, London, 1994, p. 27. It is worth noting that Arthur Lee had been a friend of Theodore Roosevelt Sr.
7 Mark Sullivan, *Our Times: The United States, 1900–1925*, vol. 6, *The Twenties*, New York, 1935, p. 193.
8 Goldstein, 'The Evolution', p. 28.
9 Lenin, *PSS*, vol. 51, p. 320 (to Rykov); vol. 53, p. 83 (to Trotsky); and vol. 45 (to Stalin as dictated by telephone). See also A. K. Selianichev, *V. I. Lenin i*

stanovlenie sovetsko-morskogo flota, Moscow, 1979, pp. 199, 201–2. Selianichev points out that plans drawn up at the Tenth Party Congress in March 1921 for the restoration of the Red fleet by 1926 were completed by 1929. Ibid., pp. 204–11. And see Jürgen Rohwer and Mikhail S. Monakov, *Stalin's Ocean-Going Fleet: Soviet Naval Strategy and Shipbuilding Programmes, 1935–1953*, London, 2001, p. 7, which quotes People's Commissar for the Army and Navy describing in 1925 the situation as it was in 1921: '... we had no Navy'. In ibid., p. 8, the authors observe on the same situation: 'The continued fighting in the Far East had no effect on the Navy, because no ships were left there.'

10 L. E. Berlin, intro., *Vashingtonskaia konferentsiia po ogranicheniiu vooruzhenii i tikhookeanskim i dal'nevostochnym voprosam, 1921–1922gg.*, Moscow, 1924, p. 14.
11 Ibid., p. 15.
12 WCLA, 2 vols., printed for the Foreign Office, London [1922], vol. 1, pp. 252–3.
13 *Conference on the Limitation of Armaments, Washington, November 12, 1921–February 6, 1922*, [henceforth CLA] Government Printing Office, Washington, DC, 1922, pp. 134, 138, 140, 142, 144.
14 Berlin, *Vashingtonskaia konferentsiia*, p. 17. In *The Times* of 25 November 1921, Lord Curzon was quoted as saying 'It is no use reducing our armaments at sea if we are still to contemplate the piling up of vast armaments in land'. He went on to say that all nations must make proportionate sacrifices, and that 'if we are willing to reduce our naval protection let no other Power be allowed to build up any other engine of attack, either in the air or under the sea (cheers), which might render our sacrifice nugatory and which might leave us in the paralysing position of having incurred undue risk'. In general, he did not think that anybody would deny that the steps taken at Washington 'marked a great and notable stride forward in the moral progress of mankind'.
15 Committee on Program and Procedure with respect to Limitation of Armament, 23 November 1921, CLA, p. 440.
16 CLA, 1921–22. (Treaties, Resolutions, and *c*.) Miscellaneous No. 1, London, 1922. Command Paper 1627 [henceforth Cmd.] 1627, pp. 3–19.
17 CLA, pp. 526, 536, 540, 542.
18 Berlin, *Vashingtonskaia konferentsiia*, pp. 20–1. Joel Blatt, 'France and the Washington Conference' in Goldstein and Maurer (eds), *The Washington Conference, 1921–22*, p. 211 writes: 'The British and Americans pursued their own self-interest (as did the French), and largely left France to wander its own path.'
19 Cmd. 1627, pp. 19–22.
20 Ibid., pp. 23, 24, 37.
21 Berlin, *Vashingtonskaia konferentsiia*, pp. 22–3.
22 'Five-Power Treaty', Cmd. 2029, p. 7.
23 Michael Graham Fry, 'The Pacific Dominions and the Washington Conference, 1921–22', in Goldstein and Maurer (eds), *The Washington Conference*, pp. 60–101.
24 Cmd. 1627, pp. 38–40.
25 Putnam Weale, *An Indiscreet Chronicle from the Pacific*, New York, 1922, pp. 186–7 (as quoted by Wm. Roger Louis, *British Strategy in the Far East, 1919–1939*, Oxford, pp. 107–8).
26 Berlin, *Vashingtonskaia konferentsiia*, pp. 27–8.
27 Cmd. 1627, pp. 70–3.
28 Ibid., pp. 73–6.
29 FRUS, 1922, vol. 1, p. 876. The original Russian version in DVP, IV, No. 323.

30 Cmd. 1627, pp. 61–3.
31 Berlin, *Vashingtonskaia konferentsiia*, pp. 31–2.
32 Westel W. Willoughby, *China at the Conference: A Report*, Westport, Conn., 1922, p. iii.
33 Berlin, *Vashingtonskaia konferentsiia*, p. 33.
34 CLA, pp. 866–8.
35 See Wang Li, 'Sovereignty, *Status Quo* and Diplomacy: A Case Study of China's Interaction with the Great Powers 1912–22', Unpublished PhD Thesis, Politics and International Relations, University of Aberdeen, 2003, especially Chapter 8, 'The Washington Conference and China's Destiny'.
36 CLA, p. 890. Philip C. Jessup, *Elihu Root*, vol. 2, New York, 1964, p. 466. wrote: 'Had the United States followed Root's idea of cultivating friendship with Japan while insisting on respect for Chinese sovereignty, we might now find ourselves in a position of helpful friendliness with both those Asiatic powers, much to our own benefit and to theirs.' The idea had been expressed in the Root-Takihara agreement of 1908.
37 Walter LaFeber, *The Clash: US–Japanese Relations throughout History*, New York, 1997, p. 143.
38 Shidehara, Wang and Hughes in Cmd. 1627, pp. 64–70.
39 Ibid., pp. 76–7.
40 Berlin, *Vashingtonskaia konferentsiia*, p. 37.
41 Cmd. 1627, pp. 87–8. CLA, p. 226, records that this remark of Balfour's was followed by laughter.
42 WCLA, vol. 1, p. 745.
43 Cmd. 1627, pp. 42–6.
44 Ibid., pp. 47–51.
45 Ibid., pp. 55–6, 58–60.
46 Ibid., pp. 54–8.
47 Berlin, *Vashingtonskaia konferentsiia*, p. 42.
48 Ibid., p. 43; E. I. Popova, 'Vashingtonskaia konferentsiia 1921–1922gg. v otsenke sovteskikh istorikov', in G. N. Sevost'ianov and others, *Amerikanskii ezhegodnik 1971*, Moscow, 1971, pp. 176–8.
49 Thomas H. Buckley, *The United States and the Washington Conference, 1921–1922*, Knoxville, Tennessee, 1970, p. 195. Jessup, *Elihu Root*, vol. 2, p. 466 wrote: Buell 'covers the ground thoroughly'.
50 Raymond Leslie Buell, *The Washington Conference*, New York, 1922, pp. 326–7. Similarly, in *Isolated America*, New York, 1940, p. 52. Buell wrote: 'The only sanction of the Washington treaties, therefore, was the word of Japan, and in 1931 Japan violated its word.' However, he went on to concede: 'Seven years earlier, however, the American Congress destroyed the spirit created at Washington when it unilaterally terminated the Gentleman's Agreement and in the Immigration Act of 1924 excluded Japanese from entering the United States, since they were ineligible for citizenship.' Secretary of State Hughes warned that the act 'would largely undo the work of the Washington Conference.' Walter LaFeber, *The Clash: US–Japanese Relations throughout History*, New York, 1997, p. 145.
51 See the verdict of Root's biographer in note 35.
52 Buckley, *The United States*, p. vii.
53 Yamato Ichihashi, *The Washington Conference and After: A Historical Survey*, New York, 1928.
54 See note 1.

55 Asada, Sadao, 'Japan's "Special Interests" and the Washington Conference, 1921–1922', *American Historical Review*, vol. 66, no. 1, 1961.
56 See note 3.
57 See note 4.
58 On the other hand, publications on the US and Japanese intervention, and on US–Soviet relations in general tend to say little about the Washington Conference.
59 E. I. Popova, 'Vashingtonskaia konferentsiia', pp. 167–74.
60 A. Iu. Sidorov, *Vneshniaia politika sovetskoi Rossii na Dal'nem Vostoke, 1917–1922*, Moscow, 1997.
61 Ibid., pp. 127–33. And see the evaluation of E. H. Carr in the conclusion to Chapter 5.
62 M. B. Fuks, 'Rol' regional'nykh vlastnykh struktur vo vneshnei politike Sovetskoi Rossii na Dal'nem Vostoke v pervoi polovine 1920-kh godov', *Russkii istoricheskii zhurnal*, tom 1, no. 2, 1998; 'Osobennosti razvitiia sovetsko-amerikanskikh otnoshenii v kontekste usileniia voenno-politicheskogo sopernichestva na Dal'nem Vostoke mezhdu SSHA i Iaponiei, 1917–1923', *Russkii istoricheskii zhurnal*, tom 1, no. 3, 1998.

3 Soviet Russia and the USA: the new diplomacy

1 Alexander Hamilton, 'The Value of Union to Commerce and the Advantages of a Navy', and the similar views of James Madison in Benjamin F. Wright, intro. and ed., *The Federalist*, Cambridge, MA, 1966, pp. 141–2, 296–7.
2 For attempts to set out aspects of this comparison and its context, see Paul Dukes *World Order in History: Russia and the West*, London, 1996; *The Superpowers: A Short History*, London, 2000.
3 For the most complete overview, see Norman E. Saul's three-volume work, *The United States and Russia: Distant Friends...1763–1867*; *Concord and Conflict... 1867–1914*; and *War and Revolution...1914–1921*, all published by University Press of Kansas in 1991, 1996 and 2001 respectively.
4 See for example Saul, *Concord and Conflict*, Chapter 6, 'Disharmony and War'.
5 Walter Alison Phillips, Lecky Professor of Modern History at the University of Dublin, 'Diplomacy', *Encyclopaedia Britannica*, Twelfth Edition, New Volume 30, London and New York, 1922, p. 840. This and two other new volumes were dedicated by permission to His Majesty King George the Fifth and Warren Gamaliel Harding, President of the United States of America. The quotation, from J. A. Hobson's *Towards International Government*, London, 1915, p. 68. continues 'even using bluff frankness as a choice method of deception'.
6 Dukes, *The Superpowers*, pp. 36–40.
7 Betty Glad, *Charles Evans Hughes and the Illusions of Innocence: A Study of American Diplomacy*, Urbana, 1966, pp. 180, 322–3.
8 Edward Rhodes, 'Charles Evans Hughes Reconsidered, or Liberal Isolationism in the New Millennium', Anthony Lake and David Ochmanek (eds), *The Real and the Ideal: Essays on International Relations in Honor of Richard H. Ullmann*, New York, 2001.
9 Hughes to Samuel Gompers, president of the American Federation of Labor, 19 July 1923, as quoted in Glad, *Charles Evans Hughes*, pp. 312–13.
10 'Response to the Delegation of "The Women's Committee for Recognition of Russia" which was received by Mr. Hughes on March 21, 1923', Charles E. Hughes, *The Pathway of Peace*, New York, 1925, p. 60. At the end of his

speech, a member of the delegation asked: 'Mr. Hughes, what would happen if the United States did recognize Russia?' The Secretary of State declined to answer. The Soviet journal *Izvestiia* commented: 'In 1918 Hughes' speech would not surprise anybody. In 1923 it is very much out of tune and is an anchronism.' See Katherine A. S. Siegel, *Loans and Legitimacy: The Evolution of Soviet–American Relations, 1919–1933*, Lexington, KY, 1996, p. 91.
11 Merlo J. Pusey, *Charles Evans Hughes*, 2 vols, New York, vol. 2, 1963, p. 523.
12 J. Riddell (ed.), *Founding the Communist International: Proceedings and Documents of the First Congress, March 1919*, New York, 1987, pp. 31–3, with Lenin's own italics.
13 R. A. Archer, trans., *Second Congress of the Communist International: Minutes of the Proceedings*, 2 vols, London, 1977, vol. 1, pp. 115–20, 303–9.
14 Brian Pearce, trans. and ed., *Congress of the Peoples of the East, Baku, September 1920: Stenographic Report*, London, 1977, pp. 90, 104–5.
15 Douglass C. North, *Growth and Welfare in the American Past: A New Economic History*, Englewood Cliffs, NJ, 1966, p. 166 observes: 'The first postwar cloud was the sharp, brief recession of 1921.'
16 This is rhetorical exaggeration. The Supreme Council no longer existed as such, but the USA was indeed involved in an informal manner in international discussions on the reparations and famine questions.
17 Harold J. Goldberg (ed.), *Documents of Soviet–American Relations*: vol. 1, *Intervention, Famine Relief, International Affairs, 1917–1933*, Gulf Breeze, 1993, pp. 264–8.
18 *The First Congress of the Toilers of the Far East*, reprint, London, 1970, pp. 4, 5–6, 7, 10–11, 13, 15.
19 Ibid., pp. 22, 24, 25, 32–3, 36, 37, 39. Korea and Mongolia were indeed mentioned at the Conference, if not discussed. This is one of several examples of Zinoviev's rhetorical exaggeration.
20 Ibid., pp. 141, 142–3, 144, 145.
21 Ibid., pp. 148, 155, 210, 214, 221, 229.
22 J. H. Brimmell, *Communism in South East Asia*, Oxford, 1959, p. 48.
23 Chicherin to Lenin, 21 December 1921, quoted by A. Iu. Sidorov, *Vneshniaia politika sovetskoi Rossii na Dal'nem Vostoke (1917–1922gg.)*, Moskva, 1997, p. 93.
24 E. H. Carr, *The Bolshevik Revolution, 1917–1923*, London, 1966, vol. 3, p. 68. Richard K. Debo, *Revolution and Survival: The Foreign Policy of Soviet Russia, 1917–18*, Liverpool, 1979, pp. 86, 148. The American diplomat was DeWitt Clinton Poole, the American consul-general in Moscow, from 1920 chief of the Division of Russian Affairs of the Department of State.
25 In December 1923, when the German Ambassador asked the Soviet government to dissociate itself officially from the policy of the Third International, Chicherin replied: 'That the Third International has its headquarters in Moscow is just a matter of chance. After all, it won't occur to anybody to hold the Belgian king responsible for the activities of the Second International just because it has its headquarters in Brussels.' Yelena Belevich and Vladimir Sokolov, 'Foreign Affairs Commissar Georgy Chicherin', *International Affairs*, 3, 1991, 95.
26 Goldberg, *Documents*, vol. 1, pp. 270–1.
27 V. I. Lenin, *Polnoe sobranie sochinenii*, fifth edition, Moscow, 1977, vol. 44, pp. 304–5.
28 Brian Pearce, trans. and ed., *The Military Writings and Speeches of Leon Trotsky: How the Revolution Armed*, 4 vols, London, , 1981, vol. 4, pp. 410–13.
29 Carr, *The Bolshevik Revolution*.

30 A former socialist of British origin who had left the US Socialist Party after it had denounced the US entry into the First World War at its Congress in St Louis in April 1917, John Spargo was the author of a number of books including *Bolshevism: The Enemy of Political and Industrial Democracy*, New York, 1919; *The Psychology of Bolshevism*, New York, 1919; *The Greatest Failure in All History: A Critical Examination of the Actual Workings of Bolshevism in Russia*, New York, 1920; and *Russia as an American Problem*, New York, 1920. He also wrote most of the 'Colby Note' of August 1920 denouncing Soviet Russia 'as the negation of American political principles and moral values' as described by David S. Foglesong, *America's Secret War against Bolshevism: U.S. Intervention in the Russian Civil War, 1917–1920*, Chapel Hill, NC, 1995, p. 291. Spargo's reputation reached Lenin, who denounced him as a former member of the Second International, now 'an American social-chauvinist' arguing that Soviet trade agreements with capitalist trade agreements were a sign of weakness. In fact, Lenin asserted, the concessions and other agreements showed the necessity for the capitalists to come to terms with Soviet Russia, which had never claimed to bring about world revolution single-handed but always recognised that the final victory would depend on the workers of all countries. V. I. Lenin, 'Our External and Internal Position and the Tasks of the Party', Speech to the Moscow Province Conference of the RCP(b)', 21 November 1920, *PSS*, vol. 42, pp. 24–5. See also D. G. Nadzharov, 'Istoki istoricheskogo sovetovedeniia v SSHA: amerikanskaia literatura o V. I. Lenine i sovetskoi vneshnei politike, 1917–1920', G. N. Sevost'ianov and others (eds), *Amerikanskii ezhegodnik*, 1971, pp. 159–60.

31 RDS, 316.71.0858–0870 (861.01/401). State Department stamp 13 February 1922, but probably composed about March 1921.

32 A vast amount of information gathered by the State Department is located in RDS. The role of the State Department is discussed further in Chapters Four and Five. And see Natalie Grant, 'The Russian Section: A Window on the Soviet Union', *Diplomatic History*, vol. 2, no. 1, 1978.

33 Katherine A. S. Siegel, *Loans and Legitimacy: The Evolution of Soviet–American Relations, 1919–1933*, Lexington, KY, 1996, p. 49.

34 Walter LaFeber, *The Clash: U.S. – Japanese Relations throughout History*, New York, 1997, pp. 129–30. *The American Age: United States Foreign Policy at Home and Abroad since 1750*, New York, 1989, pp. 318–9.

35 Siegel, *Loans*, pp. 53, 62, 63, 66; Lloyd C. Gardner, *Safe for Democracy: The Anglo-American Response to Revolution, 1913–1923*, 1987, pp. 181–2.

36 Bertrand M. Patenaude, *The Big Show in Bololand: The American Relief Expedition to Soviet Russia in the Famine of 1921*, Stanford, CA, 2002, pp. 32–4.

37 Goldberg, *Documents*, vol. 1, pp. 190–8. Benjamin M. Weissman, *Herbert Hoover and Famine Relief to Soviet Russia, 1921–23*, Stanford, CA, p. 36.

38 Goldberg, *Documents*, vol. 1, 198–200.

39 Weissman, *Herbert Hoover*, p. 15.

40 Lenin, *PSS*, vol. 44, pp. 75–6, published in *Pravda*, 6 August 1921. Goldberg, *Documents*, vol. 1, p. 218, gives 'September 1921' as the date of Lenin's appeal. Although it is not our purpose here to examine the responses to the appeal, one of them might well have been the agreement of 22 November 1921 between the Soviet of Labour and Defence and a group of American workers led by Bill Heywood and others. See *DVP*, IV, p. 513.

41 C. J. C. Quinn, assistant director of the Russian unit of the ARA, Warsaw, 29 August 1921, in *Documents of the ARA, Russian Operations*, Stanford, CA, 1931, vol. 1, pp. 66–8, quoted in ibid., pp. 215–16.

42 PSS, vol. 53, p. 134.
43 Carr, *The Bolshevik Revolution*, vol. 3, pp. 178–9.
44 Lenin to Stalin and all members of the Politburo, *PSS*, vol. 53, pp. 140–2.
45 *PSS*, vol. 54, pp. 312, 316.
46 All from Goldberg, *Documents*, vol. 1, pp. 222–8.
47 All from ibid., pp. 229–35.
48 Ibid., p. 255.
49 Carr, Williams and Filene cited by Weissman, *Herbert Hoover*, p. 188.
50 Foglesong, *America's Secret War*, pp. 243–4, 265–6.
51 Patenaude, *The Big Show*, p. 279.

4 The Far Eastern Republic: a Trojan Horse?

1 *Far Eastern Tribune*, Vladivostok, 8 March 1921, as translated and sent from Vladivostok by MacGowan to the State Department, 'Records of the Department of State relating to the Internal Affairs of Russia and the Soviet Union, 1910–29', RDS, 316.169.0049–50.
2 *Far Eastern Tribune*, Vladivostok, 9 March 1921, as translated and sent from Vladivostok by MacGowan to the State Department, RDS, 316.169.0051–2.
3 Raymond Leslie Buell, *The Washington Conference*, Princeton, NJ, 1922, p. 5.
4 Frederick R. Dickinson, *Japan in the Great War, 1914–1919*, Cambridge, MA, 1999, p. 252. Dr Uesugi Shinkichi, who had studied in pre-war Germany, wrote: 'Subjects have no mind apart from the Emperor. If they act according to the mind of the Emperor, they can realize their true nature and attain the moral ideal.' Quoted by D. C. Holton, *Modern Japan and Shinto Nationalism*, Chicago, 1943, p. 10.
5 See Hasegawa, Tsuyoshi, *The Northern Territories Dispute and Russo-Japanese Relations*, 2 vols, *Between War and Peace, 1697–1985*, Berkeley, CA, 1998, vol. 1, pp. 27–9.
6 *Japanese Intervention in the Russian Far East*. Published by the Special Delegation of the FER to the USA, Washington, DC, 1922, p. 1; G. A. Lensen, *Japanese Recognition of the USSR: Soviet-Japanese Relations, 1921–1930*, Tokyo, p. 5; Hasegawa, *The Northern Territories*, 1970, vol. 1, pp. 31–2.
7 Walter LaFeber, *The Clash: U.S.–Japanese Relations throughout History*, New York, 1997, pp. 115–16.
8 *Japanese Intervention*, p. 3.
9 LaFeber, *The Clash*, p. 118.
10 The *zemstvo* was a form of limited local self-government first set up in the reign of Alexander II.
11 *Japanese Intervention*, pp. 6–7.
12 Ibid., pp. 10–11.
13 Ibid., pp. 12–13.
14 Ibid., p. 16.
15 A. Iu. Sidorov, *Vneshniaia politika sovetskoi Rossii na Dal'nem Vostoke, 1917–1922*, Moscow, pp. 37–44. Lenin's telegram on the taking of Novonikolaevsk, *PSS*, 1997, vol. 51, p. 92.
16 Buell, *The Washington Conference*, p. 31.
17 V. S. Poznanskii (ed.), *Dal'nevostochnaia politika Sovetskoi Rossii (1920–1922gg.): Sbornik dokumentov Sibirskogo biuro TsK RKP(b) i Sibirskogo revoliutsionnogo komiteta*, Novosibirsk, 1995, pp. 17–18.
18 Lenin, *PSS*, vol. 51, p. 334.

19 Poznanskii, *Dal'nevostochnaia respublika*, p. 18.
20 Lenin, *PSS*, vol. 51, p. 137. On 9 March 1920, Lenin wired Smirnov that the Mensheviks and SRs must subordinate themselves to the Bolsheviks. Ibid., p. 156. While the context is not clear, it seems that Lenin's instruction concerned the attitude of the Mensheviks and SRs towards the new republic rather than their participation in it.
21 *A Short Outline History of the Far Eastern Republic*. Published by The Special Delegation of the FER to the USA, Washington, DC, 1922, p. 7.
22 Ibid., p. 9.
23 Ibid., pp. 9–16.
24 Canfield F. Smith, *Vladivostok under Red and White Rule: Revolution and Counterrevolution in the Russian Far East, 1920–1922*, Seattle, WA, 1975, pp. 35–6.
25 Hara Teruyiki, 'Japan Moves North: The Japanese Occupation of Northern Sakhalin (1920s)', Stephen Kotkin and David Wolff, *Rediscovering Russia in Asia: Siberia and the Russian Far East*, London, 1995, p. 62.
26 *A Short Outline*, p. 23.
27 Ibid., p. 27.
28 These were described at length in *The Far Eastern Republic: Its Natural Resources, Trade and Industries*. Published by The Special Delegation of the FER to the USA, Washington, DC, 1922.
29 *A Short Outline*, pp. 28–31.
30 *A Short Outline*, p. 34.
31 *FRUS*, II, 1921, pp. 702–5.
32 *DVP*, IV, no. 111, pp. 111–65.
33 Ibid., no. 131, p. 198; Lensen, *Japanese Recognition*, pp. 14–15.
34 *A Short Outline*, pp. 34–5.
35 *FRUS*, 1921, II, pp. 705–12.
36 *A Short Outline*, pp. 36–7.
37 Ibid., p. 38.
38 RDS, 316.169.0175–7.
39 Ibid., 316.174. 0507–21.
40 *FRUS*, II, 1921, pp. 736–41.
41 Ibid., pp. 735–6, 741–2, 744–6.
42 Henry Kittredge Norton, *The Far Eastern Republic of Siberia*, London, 1923, p. 188. Norton is described on the frontispiece as 'Author of "The Story of California", etc.'
43 B. I. Mukhachev, *Aleksandr Krasnoshchekov: istoriko-biograficheskii ocherk*, Vladivostok, p. 153, 1999. E. H. Carr, *The Bolshevik Revolution*, vol. 1, London, 1978, p. 361. suggests that the recall 'may have been due to tardy realization that a government which included former American revolutionary agitators [e.g. Krasnoshchekov] was unlikely to enjoy much favour at Washington'. On 30 March 1922, Lenin wrote to Molotov that it had been a great mistake to dismiss Krasnoshchekov, whom he had discovered in the course of conversation to be 'intelligent, energetic, knowledgeable and experienced'. *PSS*, vol. 54, p. 219.
44 Sidorov, *Vneshniaia politika*, pp. 47, 79.
45 Lensen, *Japanese Intervention*, p. 18.
46 *FRUS*, II, 1921, pp. 715–16.
47 Lensen, *Japanese Intervention*, pp. 26–30; John A. White, *The Siberian Intervention*, New York, 1969, pp. 430–3.

48 *DVP*, IV, no. 242, pp. 381–2.
49 Sidorov, *Vneshniaia politika*, pp. 82–5.
50 Carr, *The Bolshevik Revolution*, vol. 3, p. 509.
51 Sidorov, *Vneshniaia politika*, p. 85. See also AVPRF, fond 147, opis 2, papka 11, delo 30, list 10.
52 AVPRF, fond 146, opis 4, papka 3, delo 8, listy 1–4.
53 *FRUS*, II, 1921, pp. 716–17.
54 Ibid., pp. 719–20, 732.
55 *DVP*, V, nos. 4 and 5, pp. 17–19.
56 Lensen, *Japanese Recognition*, p. 33.
57 Sevost'ianov, G. N. and others, *Rossiia XX vek: dokumenty. Sovetsko-Amerikanskie otnosheniia: gody nepriznaniia, 1918–1926*, Moscow, 2002, pp. 195–7.
58 *FRUS*, II, 1921, pp. 747–8.
59 James K. Libbey, *Alexander Gumberg and Soviet-American Relations, 1917–1933*, Lexington, KY, 1977, p. 92.
60 See RDS, 861A01/216 for State Department accounts of these meetings, including criticism of FER policies on Mongolia.
61 In the FER delegation's own account, Reinsch is written 'Rerich' and Branham 'Brenkh', but the context makes their identity clear.
62 Katherine A. S. Siegel, *Loans and Legitimacy: The Evolution of Soviet–American Relations, 1919–1933*, Lexington, KY, 1996, pp. 90–1. Armand Hammer with Neil Lyndon, *Hammer*, New York, 1987, p. 107 describes Lucy Branum [*sic*] as 'a plucky little social worker and former suffragist who was also much taken with the ideals of the Revolution'.
63 On 7 February 1922, Iazikov was to send a communication about the FER's economic resources and possible concessions to Hoover, who replied that he was very interested and did not doubt that American businessmen would be too. However, he was sending the note on to the State Department for its consideration of the FER's suggestions. *DVP*, V, no. 45, pp. 86–9.
64 AVPRF, fond 490, opis 4, papka 21, delo 22, listy 45–48. See also *FRUS*, II, pp. 717–9, 1921. *DVP*, IV, no. 324, pp. 568–70.
65 AVPRF, fond 490, opis 4, papka 21, delo 22, list 2.
66 We have been unable to establish the authenticity of these documents. Buell, *The Washington Conference*, p. 36 writes that up to November 1921, 'consuls in Harbin confirmed the report that the British and French governments had agreed to transport 10,000 Wrangel troops to Vladivostok'. He cites as source 'Kokusai dispatch, Japan *Weekly Chronicle*' 1 December 1921, adding that according to a Dalta dispatch of 24 December 1921, '768 soldiers of Wrangel's and Denikin's former armies had just arrived at Vladivostok'. On 5 January 1922, after consulting with Kolesnikov, Foreign Minister of the Provisional Government in Vladivostok, Poole wrote to Hughes that no more than 200 sailors and 100 Cossacks were among a group of about 900 refugees arriving in Vladivostok in October 1921, and that this information tended 'very strongly to dispose finally of the alleged Franco-Japanese agreement as a fabrication'. *FRUS*, II, 1922, pp. 840–1. However, Anne Hogenhuis-Seliverstoff, *Les relations Franco-Soviétiques, 1917–1924*, Paris, 1981, makes no mention of the alleged agreement.
67 It is interesting to note aspects of the Far Eastern version of the story, as reported by *Russkii Krai*, the official newspaper of the Vladivostok government, 25,

26 January 1922

ACTIVE FIGHTING OF THE GREAT POWERS AGAINST THE BOLSHE-VIKS. We are informed from a reliable source that in the American Governmental circles are being discussed problems of the intended active military operations against Soviet Russia in the spring of this year. Animated discussions are taking place between Washington, Paris and Tokio. Field Marshal Joffre has instructions to conclude negotiations with the Japanese Government.
IMPORTANT STATEMENT BY JOFFRE...
From an authoritative source we are informed that declaration made by Field Marshall Joffre regarding Europe's desire to fight militant communism not only by an economic blockade but by force of arms was received with great satisfaction by the Japanese military circles.

AVPRF, fond 129, opis 6, delo 12, list 15. For more newspaper views on this question, see G. S. Saradzhan, 'Burzhuaznaia pressa o deiatel'nosti delegatsii DVR v Vashingtone (1921–1922 gg.)', *Voprosy istochnikovedeniia i istoriografii*, vol. 3, Vladivostok, 1974.
68 Henry W. Nevinson, *Last Changes, Last Chances*, London, 1928, p. 246.
69 Quoted by Libbey, *Gumberg*, p. 93.
70 *To the Washington Conference on Limitation of Armaments. Memorandum of the Special Delegation of the Far Eastern Republic*, Washington, DC, 1922 as translated in *DVP*, V, no. 9, pp. 21–44.
71 John Chalmers Vinson, *The Parchment Peace: The United States Senate and the Washington Conference, 1921–1922*, Athens GA, 1955, pp. 130–1.
72 AVPRF, fond 490, opis 4, papka 21, delo 22, list 53.
73 AVPRF, fond 490, opis 4, papka 21, delo 22, listy 50–1. See *DVP*, V, no. 50, pp. 92–4; *FRUS*, II, 1922, pp. 844–6, copy sent to Hughes by Iazikov.

5 After the Washington Conference: conclusion

1 CR, vol. 62, part 3, p. 2391.
2 CR, vol. 62, part 3, p. 3146.
3 CR, vol. 62, part 3, p. 3187. Mr Borah went even further back to consider Rameses and the Hittites. CR, vol. 62, part 4, p. 3787.
4 CR, vol. 62, part 3, pp. 2882, 2926; part 4, p. 3557.
5 CR, vol. 62, part 5, pp. 4339, 4600.
6 In the FER delegation's account, Newton was written as 'Naiman', Kirchwey as 'Kerchnei' and Bliven as 'Blivei'. From the context, however, their identities seem certain.
7 AVPRF, fond 129, opis 6, delo 4, listy 12, 20.
8 CR, vol. 62, part 4, pp. 4068, 4072–3.
9 Iazikov and Ianson to Hughes both from AVPRF, fond 490, opis 4, papka 21, delo 22, listy 35–40. Iazikov sent a copy of the Ianson note to the Japanese at Dairen. Ibid., list 41. See also *DVP*, V, no. 94, pp. 169–70.
10 I have been unable to confirm the name of this fur firm.
11 In an undated letter to Iakov Davidovich Ianson, the FER's Foreign Minister, Iazikov, the head of the FER delegation, wrote that the US Senate records contained details of the 'loans' given to Kolchak, Iudenich and Wrangel, with the

142 Notes

remaining credits being at the disposal of Bakhmetev. AVPRF, fond 490, opis 4, papka 21, delo 22, list 31.
12 Boris Brazol or Brasol was 'Member of the Russian Monarchical Delegation to the Washington Conference'. K-O was probably Joseph K. Okulitch, 'Representative in United States of the Urals, Orenburg, Siberian, Semirechensk, Yenissei, Amur and Ussuri Cossack Troops'. See 'Records of the Department of State', 316.46.0220, 316.71.0587.
13 AVPRF, fond 490, opis 4, papka 21, delo 22, list 33.
14 Linda Killen, 'The Search for a Democratic Russia: Bakhmetev and the United States', *Diplomatic History*, 2, 1978, 256.
15 FRUS, 1922, II, pp. 875–84.
16 AVPRF, fond 490, opis 5, papka 34, delo 35, listy 5–50. See also AVPRF, fond 129, opis 6, delo 12, listy 1–7 for information on such businesses as Marion Steam Shovel Co., Railway Steel-Spring Co., Huber[?] Manufacturing Co., General American Tank Co. [i.e. railroad tank cars], Electric Bond and Share Co. (controlled by General Electric Co.) and Consolidated Steel.
17 I have been unable to confirm the name of this fur firm.
18 AVPRF, fond 490, opis 4, papka 21, delo 22, list 32.
19 James K. Libbey, *Alexander Gumberg and Soviet–American Relations, 1917–1933*, Lexington, KY, 1977, p. 96. In following pages, Libbey gives details of some of Skvirsky's later activities as well as of Gumberg's.
20 F. E. Dzerzhinsky to L. P. Serebriakov, the Central Committee Secretary, with a copy to Trotsky, 1 February 1922, quoted by A. Iu. Sidorov, *Vneshniaia politika sovetskoi Rossii na Dal'nem Vostoke, 1917–1922*, Moskva, p. 98, 1997.
21 Quoted in ibid., p. 152.
22 Karakhan to the Politburo, no date, but appended to protocol of meeting 10–13 March 1922, quoted in ibid., p. 97.
23 George A. Lensen, *Japanese Recognition of the USSR: Soviet–Japanese Relations, 1921–1930*, Tokyo and Tallahasee, FL, p. 34, 1970.
24 AVPRF, fond 490, opis 4, papka 21, delo 23, listy 20–21. The FER government looked after Thomas. For example, early in 1922, 34 boxes of provisions including strong drinks were imported by him without duty or tax. Ibid., list 26.
25 AVPRF, fond 490, opis 4, papka 21, delo 22, listy 42–43, in English. The date 14 March is indicated in *DVP*, V, no. 91, pp. 166–8.
26 Markhlevsky to Chicherin, no date, but about the same, that is 20 March 1922, as his letter to the People's Commissariat of Foreign Affairs demanding Petrov's recall. Sidorov, *Vneshniaia politika*, pp. 98, 152.
27 Ibid., pp. 99–100, including Karakhan to the Politburo, 26 July 1922.
28 Ibid., pp. 101–3.
29 FRUS, II, 1922, pp. 850–1.
30 FRUS, II, 1922, pp. 851–2.
31 AVPRF, fond 146, opis 4, papka 102, delo 6, listy 89–90.
32 Lensen, *Japanese Recognition*, pp. 47–8.
33 Carole Fink, *The Genoa Conference: European Diplomacy, 1921–1922*, Chapel Hill, NC, 1984, pp. 205–6.
34 *Encyclopaedia Britannica*, Thirteenth Edition, vol. I, p. 1061. 'X' appears to have been in sympathy with the Eurasians who argued that Russia had a special destiny bestriding both continents.
35 Yelena Belevich and Vladimir Sokolov, 'Foreign Affairs Commissar Georgy Chicherin', *International Affairs*, 3, March 1991, 95.
36 Michael J. Fry, *Illusions of Security: North Atlantic Diplomacy, 1918–1922*, Toronto, ON, 1972, pp. 193–4.

37 Merlo J. Pusey, *Charles Evans Hughes*, 2 vols, New York, 1951, vol. 2, p. 525.
38 J. Saxon Mills, *The Genoa Conference*, London, [1922], pp. 20–1.
39 Katherine A. S. Siegel, *Loans and Legitimacy: The Evolution of Soviet–American Relations, 1919–1933*, Lexington, KY, 1996, p. 68.
40 Mills, *The Genoa Conference*, pp. 56–7.
41 Ibid., pp. 66–9.
42 Ibid., pp. 75–6.
43 Ibid., pp. 117–21, 137. According to J. Saxon Mills, Lloyd George later joined the same journalists for informal afternoon conversation and answered all questions 'in both the English and American languages, with much patience and humour', insisting in buoyant mood that he was open to all ideas.
44 Ibid., p. 214. In the Reply, Chicherin also stated 'The principle of nationalization without indemnities is a slogan dear to all Russian hearts. Our people believe that private property is a form of privilege analogous to the feudal rights which obtained before the French Revolution or to the serfdom in Russia before the time of the Tsar Alexander II. These ancient privileges having been abolished, we wish the same to be done with private property. Upon this point we cannot give way'. Stephen White, *The Origins of Detente: The Genoa Conference and Soviet–Western Relations, 1921–1922*, Cambridge, 1985, pp. 180–2, points out that the memorandum's uncompromising nature could have been influenced by Lenin's objections to earlier vacillations.
45 Ibid., pp. 184, 191. White, *The Origins*, p. 190, observes that Chicherin at Genoa had 'a vigorous exchange of views with Viscount Ishii on the subject of Japanese troops in Siberia and the status of the Soviet Far Eastern Republic'.
46 See Cmd. 1621, Cmd. 1724.
47 Cmd. 1814, *Lausanne Conference on Near Eastern Affairs, 1922–1923: Records of Proceedings and Draft Terms of Peace*, London, 1923, pp. 148–9.
48 Zinovy Sheinis, *Maxim Litvinov*, Moscow, 1988, p. 178; E. H. Carr, *The Bolshevik Revolution, 1917–1923*, London, 1966, vol. 3, pp. 440–1.
49 *Encyclopaedia Britannica*, Thirteenth Edition, vol. II, p. 166.
50 White, *The Origins*, p. 210.
51 Fink, *The Genoa Conference*, p. 306.
52 Walter LaFeber, *The American Age: United States Foreign Policy at Home and Abroad since 1750*, New York, 1989, p. 325.
53 Siegel, *Loans and Legitimacy*, pp. 71–2.
54 FRUS, 1922, II, p. 873.
55 FRUS, 1922, II, p. 853.
56 AVPRF, fond 146, opis 4, papka 102, delo 6, list 103.
57 FRUS, 1922, II, pp. 854–5.
58 *DVP*, V, nos. 220, 224.
59 Lensen, *Japanese Recognition*, pp. 55–6.
60 AVPRF, fond 146, opis 1, papka 1, delo 1, list 23.
61 Quoted by A. Iu. Sidorov, *Vneshniaia politika*, p. 104.
62 Ibid., pp. 104–5.
63 Quoted in ibid., pp. 105–6.
64 All the foregoing on the Changchun Conference from an English-language transcript of the Russian record of it located at AVPRF, fond 146, opis 1, papka 1, delo 1, listy 23–182. The newspaper *Izvestiia* published two articles on 28 September supporting Ioffe's arguments at Changchun and quoting from them extensively. See *DVP*, V, Nos. 268, 269, pp. 600–4.
65 This paragraph from FRUS, 1922, II, pp. 856–61.

66 AVPRF, fond 146, opis 4, papka 102, delo 6, list 103 – *Chan'-Tsunskaia Konferentsiia i prichiny ee razryva*.
67 Ioffe to Chicherin and Stalin, 20 September 1922 and quoted by Sidorov, *Vneshniaia politika*, p. 107.
68 Ioffe to the leaders of the Bolshevik party and Comintern, 2 October 1922, ibid., pp. 107–8.
69 Lensen, *Japanese Recognition*, pp. 76–7. For further description of Ioffe's views, see ibid., pp. 78–81.
70 Chicherin, *Stat'i*, p. 203, quoted in ibid., p. 108.
71 Ibid., p. 110.
72 Ioffe to Stalin and Chicherin, ibid., p. 108.
73 Ibid., p. 110; Smith, *Vladivostok*, pp. 141–65.
74 L. N. Nezhinskii, 'U istokov bol'shevistsko-unitarnoi vneshnei politiki (1921–1923gg.)', *Otechestvennaia istoriia*, no. 1, 1994, p. 89.
75 Belevich and Sokolov, 'Foreign Affairs Commissar', 97.
76 AVPRF, fond 146, opis 4, papka 102, delo 6, listy 109–10.
77 Hara Teruyuki, 'Japan Moves North: The Japanese Occupation of Northern Sakhalin (1920s)', Stephen Kotkin and David Wolff (eds), *Rediscovering Russia in Asia: Siberia and the Russian Far East*, London, 1995, p. 65.
78 Sidorov, *Vneshniaia politika*, p. 111.
79 Hirosi Saito, 'Japan', *Encyclopaedia Britannica*, Thirteenth Edition, vol. II, pp. 590–1.
80 E. H. Carr, *The Bolshevik Revolution, 1917–1923*, London, 1978, vol. 3, p. 536.
81 Ibid., p. 519.
82 Ibid., pp. 515–16.
83 Ibid., p. 540.
84 Akira Iriye, *After Imperialism: The Search for a New Order in the Far East 1921–1931*, Cambridge, MA, 1965, pp. 2–3.
85 Harold and Margaret Sprout, *Towards a New Order of Sea Power: American Naval Policy and the World Scene*, Princeton, NJ, 1940, pp. 259–60.
86 Archibald Hurd, 'Is the Washington Treaty Doomed?', *Fortnightly Review*, 1 January 1923, p. 1.
87 Wittingly or unwittingly, Radek attributes to Archibald Hurd observations that he did not make in the article cited, where there is no mention of the Bonin Isles nor of Singapore, nor any reference to rapprochement between Japan and Russia. The only reference to Russia in Hurd's article is on p. 25 as follows

> *Le Temps* has suggested that the Naval Treaty should be annulled and a New Treaty negotiated in view of the admission of the Russian delegates to the discussion at Lausanne on the freedom of the Straits. It is contended that the reappearance of Russia as a naval Power presents unforeseen difficulties. On the other side of the Channel in recent years a curious conception of the meaning of naval power has constantly found expression. The raising of the bogey of Russia merely illustrates it once more. To all intents and purposes the Russian fleet does not exist... Russia may appear to some French eyes as a possible danger, but as a naval Power she is dead to the limit of vision.

88 Goldberg, *Documents*, vol. 1, pp. 297–300.
89 Iu. N. Tsipkin, 'Dal'nevostochnaya respublika: byla li al'ternativa?', *Otechestvennaia istoriia*, no. 3, 1993, 170, 173.
90 *The Memoirs of Herbert Hoover: The Cabinet and the Presidency, 1920–1933*, London, 1952, pp. 180–1.

Bibliography

Abbreviations (guide to full titles)

AVPRF	Arkhiv
Cmd. 1627	Conference on Limitation
CLA	Conference on the Limitation
CR	Congressional Record
PSS	Lenin, V. I.
RDS	Records of the Department of State
WCLA	Washington Conference on the Limitation

Primary sources

Arkhiv vneshnei politiki rossiiskoi federatsii, Fond 129, 146, 147, 490. [AVPRF]
Congress of the Peoples of the East, Baku, September 1920: Stenographic Report, trans. and ed., Pearce, Brian, London, 1977.
Conference on Limitation of Armament. Washington, 1921–22. (Treaties, Resolutions, &c), Miscellaneous no. 1, London, 1922. Command Paper 1627. [Cmd. 1627]
Conference on the Limitation of Armaments, Washington, November 12, 1921–February 6, 1922, Washington, DC, Government Printing Office, 1922. [CLA]
Congressional Record, Washington, DC, 1921–2. [CR]
Dal'nevostochnaia politika Sovetskoi Rossii (1920–1922gg): Sbornik dokumentov Sibirskogo biuro TsK RKP(b) i Sibirskogo revoliutsionnogo komiteta, ed. Poznanskii, V. S., Novosibirsk, 1995.
Documents of Soviet–American Relations, 3 vols: vol. 1, Intervention, Famine Relief, International Affairs, 1917–1933; vol. 2, Propaganda, Economic Affairs, Recognition, 1917–1933; vol. 3, Diplomatic Relations, Economic Relations, Propaganda, International Affairs, Neutrality, 1933–1941, ed. Goldberg, Harold J., Gulf Breeze, FL, 1993, 1995, 1998.
Documents of the American Relief Administration: Russian Operations, 1921–1923, vol. 1, Stanford, CA, 1931.
Dokumenty vneshnei politiki, Moscow, 1959–67, especially vols 3, 4, 5.
Encyclopaedia Britannica, Thirteenth Edition, London and New York, 1926.

146 *Bibliography*

The Far Eastern Republic: Its Natural Resources, Trade and Industries, Special Delegation of the Far Eastern Republic to the United States of America, Washington, DC, 1922.
The Federalist, ed. and intro. Wright, Benjamin F., Cambridge, MA, 1966.
The First Congress of the Toilers of the Far East, reprint, London, 1970.
Foreign Relations of the United States, 2 vols 1921, 2 vols 1922, Washington, DC, 1936, 1938.
Founding the Communist International: Proceedings and Documents of the First Congress, March 1919, ed. Riddell, J., New York, 1987.
Hoover, Herbert, *The Memoirs of Herbert Hoover: The Cabinet and the Presidency, 1920–1933*, London, 1952.
Hughes, Charles Evans, *The Pathway of Peace*, New York, 1925.
Japanese Intervention in the Russian Far East, Special Delegation of the Far Eastern Republic to the United States of America, Washington, DC, 1922.
Lausanne Conference on Near Eastern Affairs, 1922–1923: Records of Proceedings and Draft Terms of Peace, Cmd. 1814, London, 1923.
Lenin, V. I., *Polnoe sobranie sochinenii*, izdanie piatoe, Moscow, 1975–9. [*PSS*]
The Limitation of Armaments: A Collection of the Projects Proposed for the Solution of the Problem, Preceded by an Historical Introduction, ed. and intro. Wehberg, Dr Hans, Washington, DC, 1921.
Mezhdunarodnye otnosheniia na dal'nem vostoke, 1870–1945, Zhukov, E. M. and others, Moscow, 1951.
The Military Writings and Speeches of Leon Trotsky: How the Revolution Armed, trans. and ed. Pearce, Brian, 4 vols, London, 1979–81.
The New York Times, different dates.
'Records of the Department of State relating to the Internal Affairs of Russia and the Soviet Union, 1910–29', National Archives Microcopy no. 316, Washington, DC, 1966. [RDS]
Rossiia XX vek: dokumenty. Rossiia i SSHA: diplomaticheskie otnosheniia 1900–1917, ed. Sevost'ianov, G. N. and others, Moscow, 1999.
Rossiia XX vek: dokumenty. Sovetsko–Amerikanskie otnosheniia: gody nepriznaniia, 1918–1926, ed. Sevost'ianov, G. N. and others, Moscow, 2002.
Second Congress of the Communist International: Minutes of the Proceedings, trans. and ed. Archer, R. A., 2 vols, London, 1977.
A Short Outline History of the Far Eastern Republic, Special Delegation of the Far Eastern Republic to the United States of America, Washington, DC, 1922.
Soviet Russia and the Far East, 1920–1927, eds Eudin, Xenia J. and North, Robert C., Stanford, CA, 1957.
The Times, different dates.
Washington Conference on the Limitation of Armaments, Foreign Office, 2 vols, London, [1922] [WCLA].

Secondary sources

Angell, Norman, *America and the New World-State: A Plea for American Leadership in International Organization*, New York, 1915.

Asada, Sadao, 'Japan's "Special Interests" and the Washington Conference, 1921–1922', *American Historical Review*, vol. 67, 1961–2.

Belevich, Yelena and Sokolov, Vladimir, 'Foreign Affairs Commissar Georgy Chicherin', *International Affairs*, 3, 1991.

Berlin, L. E., intro., *Vashingtonskaia konferentsiia po ogranicheniiu vooruzhenii i tikhookeanskim i dal'nevostochnym voprosam, 1921–1922gg.*, Moscow, 1924.

Brimmell, J. H., *Communism in South East Asia*, Oxford, 1959.

Buckley, Thomas H., *The Washington Conference, 1921–1922*, Knoxville, TN, 1970.

Buell, Raymond Leslie, *The Washington Conference*, A Dissertation presented to the Faculty of Princeton University in Candidacy for the Degree of Doctor of Philosophy: Accepted by the Department of History and Politics, May, 1922, New York, 1922.

Buell, Raymond Leslie, *Isolated America*, New York, 1940.

Carr, E. H., *The Bolshevik Revolution, 1917–1923*, 3 vols, reprint, London, 1978.

Debo, Richard K., *Revolution and Survival: The Foreign Policy of Soviet Russia, 1917–18*, Liverpool, 1979.

Debo, Richard K., *Survival and Consolidation: The Foreign Policy of Soviet Russia, 1918–1921*, Montreal, QC, 1992.

Dickinson, Frederick R., *Japan in the Great War, 1914–1919*, Cambridge, MA, 1999.

Dukes, Paul, *World Order in History: Russia and the West*, London, 1996.

Dukes, Paul, *The Superpowers: A Short History*, London, 2000.

Dukes, Paul and Brennan Cathryn, 'The uninvited guest: Soviet Russia, the Far Eastern Republic and the Washington Conference, November 1921 to February 1922', *Sibirica*, vol. 2, no. 2, 2002.

Dukes, Paul, 'The Changchun Conference: 4–28 September 1922', Litvin, A. L., ed, *Russian Historical Mosaic, For John Keep*, Kazan, 2003.

Fink, Carole, *The Genoa Conference: European Diplomacy, 1921–1922*, Chapel Hill, NC, 1984.

Fleming, Denna Frank, *The United States and World Organization, 1920–1933*, New York, 1938.

Fletcher, Florence A., 'The Far Eastern Republic', Unpublished MA thesis, Columbia University, 1923.

Foglesong, David S., *America's Secret War against Bolshevism: US Intervention in the Russian Civil War, 1917–1920*, Chapel Hill, NC, 1995.

Fry, Michael J., *Illusions of Security: North Atlantic Diplomacy, 1918–1922*, Toronto, ON, 1972.

Fuks, M. B., 'Rol' regionalnykh vlastnykh struktur vo vneshnei politiki Sovetskoi Rossii na Dal'nem Vostoke v pervoi polovine 1920-kh godov', *Russkii istoricheskii zhurnal*, tom 1, no. 2, 1998.

Fuks, M. B., 'Osobennosti razvitiia sovetsko–amerikanskikh otnoshenii v kontekste usileniia voenno-politicheskogo sopernichestva na Dal'nem Vostoke mezhdu SSHA i Iaponiei, 1917–1923', *Russkii istoricheskii zhurnal*, tom 1, no. 3, 1998.

Futrell, Michael, 'Colonel Akashi and Japanese contacts with Russian revolutionaries in 1904–5', *St. Antony's Papers*, vol. 20, 1967.

Bibliography

Gardner, Lloyd C., *Safe for Democracy: The Anglo-American Response to Revolution*, New York, 1987.
Glad, Betty, *Charles Evans Hughes and the Illusions of Innocence: A Study of American Diplomacy*, Urbana, IL, 1966.
Goldin, V. I., *Rossiia v grazhdanskoi voine: Ocherki noveishei istoriografii (vtoraia polovina 1980-kh – 90e gody)*, Arkhangel'sk, 2000.
Goldstein, Eric and Maurer, John, eds., *The Washington Conference, 1921–22: Naval Rivalry, East Asian Stability and the Road to Pearl Harbor*, Ilford, 1994.
Grant, Natalie, 'The Russian Section: A Window on the Soviet Union', *Diplomatic History*, 2, 1, 1978.
Hammer, Armand, with Lyndon, Neil, *Hammer*, New York, 1987.
Hasegawa, Tsuyoshi, *The Northern Territories Dispute and Russo-Japanese Relations*, 2 vols, vol. 1, *Between War and Peace, 1697–1985*, vol. 2, *Neither War nor Peace, 1985–1998*, Berkeley, CA, 1998.
Hobson, J. A., *Towards International Government*, London, 1915.
Hogenhuis-Seliverstoff, Anne, *Les relations Franco-Soviétiques, 1917–1924*, Paris, 1981.
Holton, D. C., *Modern Japan and Shinto Nationalism*, Chicago, IL, 1943.
Hurd, Archibald, 'Is the Washington Treaty Doomed?', *Fortnightly Review*, 1 January 1923.
Ichihashi, Yamato, *The Washington Conference and After: A Historical Survey*, New York, 1928.
Iriye, Akira, *After Imperialism: The Search for a New Order in the Far East, 1921–1931*, Cambridge, MA, 1965.
Jessup, Philip C., *Elihu Root*, 2 vols, New York, 1964.
Jiang, Arnold Xiangze, *The United States and China*, Chicago, 1988.
Kolodkin, Milton A., 'Russian Interests at the Washington Conference on the Limitation of Armament, 1921–1922, with Special Reference to United States' Policy', Unpublished MA thesis, Columbia University, 1955.
Killen, Linda, 'The Search for a Democratic Russia: Bakhmetev in the United States', *Diplomatic History*, 2, 1978.
Kotkin, Stephen and Wolff, David, *Rediscovering Russia in Asia: Siberia and the Russian Far East*, London, 1995.
LaFeber, Walter, *The American Age: United States Foreign Policy at Home and Abroad since 1750*, New York, 1989.
LaFeber, Walter, *The Clash: US–Japanese Relations throughout History*, New York, 1997.
Lee, Ki-baik, *A New History of Korea*, trans. Wagner, Edward W. with Shultz, Edward J., Seoul, 1984.
Lensen, G. A., *Japanese Recognition of the USSR: Soviet–Japanese Relations, 1921–1930*, Tokyo, 1970.
Libbey, James K., *Alexander Gumberg and Soviet–American Relations, 1917–1933*, Lexington, KY, 1977.
Louis, William Roger, *British Strategy in the Far East, 1919–1939*, Oxford, 1971.
McKercher, B. J. C., ed., *Anglo-American Relations in the 1920s: The Struggle for Supremacy*, London, 1991.

Maddox, R. J., *William E. Borah and American foreign policy*, Baton Rouge, LA, 1970.
May, Ernest, *The Washington Conference*, Cambridge, MA, 1973.
Mayer, Arno J., *Politics and Peacemaking: Containment and Counter-Revolution at Versailles, 1918–1919*, London, 1968.
Mills, J. Saxon, *The Geneva Conference*, London, [1922].
Mukhachev, B. I., *Aleksandr Krasnoshchekov: Istoriko-biograficheskii ocherk*, Vladivostok, 1999.
Nadzharov, D. G., 'Istoki istoricheskogo sovetovedeniia v SSHA: amerikanskaia literatura o V. I. Lenine i sovetskoi vneshnei politike, 1917–1920', *Amerikanskii ezhegodnik, 1971*, ed. Sevost'ianov, G. N. and others.
Nevinson, Henry W., *Last Changes, Last Chances*, London, 1928.
Nezhinskii, L. N., 'U istokov bol'shevistsko-unitarnoi vneshnei politiki (1921–1923gg)', *Otechestvennaia istoriia*, no. 1, 1994.
Nish, Ian, *Alliance in Decline: A Study in Anglo-Japanese Relations, 1908–23*, London, 1972.
North, Douglass C., *Growth and Welfare in the American Past: A New Economic History*, Englewood Cliffs, NJ, 1966.
Norton, Henry K., *The Far Eastern Republic of Siberia*, London, 1923.
Parry, Albert, 'Washington B. Vanderlip, the "Khan of Kamchatka"', *Pacific Historical Review*, vol 17, no. 3, 1948.
Popova, E. I., *Politika SSHA na Dal'nem Vostoke, 1918–1922*, Moscow, 1967.
Popova, E. I., 'Vashingtonskaia konferentsiia 1921–1922gg v otsenke sovetskikh istorikov', *Amerikanskii ezhegodnik 1971*, ed Sevost'ianov, G. N. and others, Moscow, 1971.
Pugach, Noel H., *Paul S. Reinsch: Open Door Diplomat in Action*, Millwood, NY, 1979.
Pusey, Merlo J., *Charles Evans Hughes*, 2 vols, New York, 1963.
Radosh, Ronald, 'John Spargo and Wilson's Russian Policy 1920', *Journal of American History*, vol. 52, 1965.
Rhodes, Edward, 'Charles Evans Hughes Reconsidered, or Liberal Isolationism in the New Millennium', Lake, Anthony and Ochmanek, David, eds, *The Real and the Ideal: Essays on International Relations in Honor of Richard H. Ullmann*, New York, 2001.
Rohwer, Jürgen and Monakov, Mikhail S., *Stalin's Ocean-Going Fleet: Soviet Naval Strategy and Shipbuilding Programmes, 1935–53*, London, 2001.
Rupen, Robert, *How Mongolia is Really Ruled: A Political History of the Mongolian People's Republic, 1900–1978*, Stanford, CA, 1979.
Salzman, Neil V., *Reform and Revolution: The Life and Times of Raymond Robins*, London, 1991.
Saradzhan, G. S., 'Burzhuaznaia pressa o deiatel'nosti delegatsii DVR v Vashingtone, 1921–1922', *Voprosy istochnikovedeniia i istoriografii*, no. 3, DVGU, Vladivostok, 1974.
Saul, Norman E., *Distant Friends: The United States and Russia, 1763–1867*, Lawrence, KS, 1991.
Saul, Norman E., *Concord and Conflict: The United States and Russia, 1867–1914*, Lawrence, KS, 1996.

Saul, Norman E., *War and Revolution: The United States and Russia, 1914–1921*, Lawrence, KS, 2001.
Scott, James B., *President Wilson's Foreign Policy*, New York, 1918.
Selianichev, A. K., *V. I. Lenin i stanovlenie sovetsko-morskogo flota*, Moscow, 1979.
Sheinis, Zinovy, *Maxim Litvinov*, Moscow, 1988.
Sidorov, A. Iu., *Vneshniaia politiki Sovetskoi Rossii na Dal'nem Vostoke, 1917–1922*, Moscow, 1997.
Siegel, Katherine A. S., *Loans and Legitimacy: The Evolution of Soviet–American Relations, 1919–1933*, Lexington, KY, 1996.
Smele, Jon D., *Civil War in Siberia: The Anti-Bolshevik Government, 1918–1920*, Cambridge, 1996.
Smith, Canfield F., *Vladivostok under Red and White Rule: Revolution and Counterrevolution in the Russian Far East, 1920–1922*, Seattle, WA, 1975.
Sprout, Harold and Margaret, *Towards a New Order of Sea Power: American Naval Policy and the World Scene*, Princeton, NJ, 1940.
Stephan, John, *The Russian Far East: A History*, Stanford, CA, 1994.
Sullivan, Mark, *Our Times: The United States, 1920–1925*, 6, *The Twenties*, New York, 1935.
Thompson, John M., *Russia, Bolshevism, and the Versailles Peace*, Princeton, 1966.
Tsipkin, Iu. N., 'Dal'nevostochnaya respublika: byla li al'ternativa?', *Otechestvennaia istoriia*, no. 3, 1993.
Uldricks, Teddy J., *Diplomacy and Ideology: the Origins of Soviet Foreign Relations, 1917–1930*, London, 1979.
Vinson, John Chalmers, *The Parchment Peace: The United States Senate and the Washington Conference, 1921–1922*, Athens, GA, 1955.
Wang, Li, 'Sovereignty, *Status Quo* and Diplomacy: A Case Study of China's Interaction with the Great Powers, 1912–1922', Unpublished PhD Thesis, Politics and International Relations, University of Aberdeen, 2003.
Weissman, Benjamin M., *Herbert Hoover and Famine Relief to Soviet Russia, 1921–1923*, Stanford, CA, 1974.
White, John A., *The Siberian Intervention*, New York, 1969.
White, Stephen, *The Origins of Detente: The Genoa Conference and Soviet–Western Relations, 1921–1922*, Cambridge, 1985.
Whiting, Allen S., *Soviet Policies in China, 1917–1924*, New York, 1954.
Willoughby, Westel W., *China at the Conference: A Report*, Westport, CT, 1922.
Zhukov, E. M., *Mezhdunarodnye otnosheniia na dal'nem vostoke, 1870–1945*, Moscow, 1951.

Index

The index is to be used in conjunction with the list of contents on pp. v–vi. Since Great Britain, Japan, Soviet Russia and the USA occur *passim*, their inclusion would have been superfluous. The spelling of names and places has not been modernised, but is given as in the sources.

Abbot, J.F., US commercial attaché 89
Abyssinia 16, 131n40
Aircraft 20, 28, 31, 32
Aircraft carriers 22, 30
Alaska 33, 43
Aleutian islands 33
Allied Supreme Council 111, 136n16
All-Russian Committee for Aid to the Hungry 70, 71
Amami-Oshima 33
American Relief Administration 6, 69–72
Amur river 14, 76, 80, 90, 92, 96, 108
Anglo-French *Entente Cordiale* 19
Anglo-Japanese alliance 2, 18–20, 33, 34, 55, 59, 76
Anglo-Russian trade agreement 118–19
ARA *see* American Relief Administration
Archangel 52, 67
Armenia 11, 53
Asada, Sadao, historian 15, 45
Australia 33, 55
Austria 1, 10, 11, 56
Avksent'ev N., Russian politician 5, 6
Azerbaijan 11

Baikal, Lake 74, 79
Baker, N.D., US Secretary of War 9
Bakhmetev, B.A., Russian Provisional Government diplomat 6, 94, 95, 104, 105
Baku 53
Baldwin Locomotive 105
Balfour, A., British statesman 27, 29, 31, 34, 42
Baltic Sea 66

Baltic states 11, 52, 67, 115, 128; *see* Estonia, Latvia, Lithuania
Beatty, D., British admiral 27
Belgium 4, 7, 39, 68, 113, 129n7
Bell, E., US diplomat 89, 90
Berlin, L.E., historian 28, 29, 31, 32, 34, 38, 39, 41, 43, 44
Bessarabia 11, 52, 110, 113, 128, 130n31
Billard, journalist 103
Bliukher, V.K., FER Minister of Military Affairs 89, 91
Bliven, B., journalist 103
Bonin islands 33, 125, 144n87
Borah, W.E., US senator 3, 98, 102, 104, 126
Borden, Sir R., Canadian statesman 41
Borodin, M., Soviet diplomat 125
'Boxer Rebellion' 13, 75
Branham, L., historian 96, 105, 140n62
Brazil 4
Brazol, B., White leader 104, 142n12
Brest-Litovsk treaty 7, 11, 60, 61, 117
Briand, A., French statesman 29, 31, 112
Brimmell, J.H., historian 60
British Imperial Conference 3
Buckley, T.H., historian 45
Buell, R.L., historian 14, 15, 16, 17, 18, 19, 44, 75, 134n50
Bull, H., political scientist 22
Bullitt, W.C., US emissary 10, 11, 12
Buriats 78, 87

Caine, US admiral 103
Caldwell, J.K., US diplomat 89, 92

Index

California 18, 98–9
Canada 15, 33, 55
Canals *see* Panama, Suez
Cannes Conference 111
Canton 39, 124, 125
Capital ships 27, 28, 30, 31, 32
Carnegie Endowment for International Peace 25
Caroline islands 16
Carr, E.H., historian 61, 72, 124, 125
Carr, US delegate to Comintern 58
Caspian Sea 66, 105
CER *see* Chinese Eastern Railway
Chatfield, A.J., British admiral 27
Cheka, secret police 89, 106
Chiang Kai-shek, Chinese official 124
Chicherin, G.V., Soviet Commissar for Foreign Affairs 3, 4, 5, 8, 9, 10, 12, 20, 21, 28, 46, 54, 61, 62, 63, 69, 71, 72, 73, 78, 81, 85, 86, 89, 91, 92, 93, 106, 111, 112, 114, 115, 121, 122, 126, 136n25, 143n44, 143n45
Chientao 36
China 1, 2, 3, 4, 7, 13, 14, 15, 16, 17, 20, 22, 23, 26, 29, 34, 36, 37, 38–43, 44, 46, 52, 55–60, 75, 76, 85, 91, 94, 96, 100, 101, 124–5, 127, 129n7
Chinese Eastern Railway 5, 6, 12, 20, 37, 38, 75, 117
Chita 5, 74, 79, 81, 82, 88, 89, 90
Clark, C., Speaker of US House of Representatives 26
Clemenceau, G., French Prime Minister 10, 53, 66
Clifford, US official 95
Coal *see* Mining
Comintern 52–7, 61, 62, 70–1, 73
Congress of the Peoples of the East 53
Constantinople 107
Crane, US diplomat 88
Crimea 85
Cuba 15, 58
Curzon, Lord, UK Foreign Secretary 5, 30, 42, 85, 104, 133n14
Czecho-Slovaks 8, 9, 10, 130n18

Dairen 14, 36, 88
Dalny [Dairen] 4
Davies, J.W., Major, US military attaché 89
Davis, E., journalist 95, 101
Davis, M., journalist 95
Davis, N.H., US official 102
Dearing, F., US official 95
Debo, R.K., historian 61

Debts, European 54–5, 63, 115; pre-Soviet 10, 63, 113–14
Declaration of Independence 48
Dickinson, F.R., historian 75
Diterikhs, M.K., White general 115, 116, 122
Douglas, C.H., journalist 125
Due 123
Dzerzhinsky, F.E., Soviet secret police chief 106

Earthquake 43
East Indies 43, 58, 60
Egypt 9, 100, 126
Eiduk, A., ARA Russian representative 71
English-speaking union 2
Estonia 12, 67, 115
Evans, journalist 95

Far Eastern Republic vii, 5, 13
Filene, P.J., historian 72
Fink, C., historian 110, 115
Finland 10, 11, 12, 52, 65, 66, 110, 115, 128, 131n40
First International 53
Fishery 17, 76, 90, 92, 96, 108, 117, 123
Fleming, D.F., historian 2
Fletcher, F.A., US official 95
Foglesong, D.S., historian 13
Fordney–McCumber tariff 115; *see also* Tariffs
Forestry 17, 91, 96, 108, 123
Formosa 33
France 1, 3, 7, 8, 9, 14, 19, 20, 21, 22, 28, 29, 30, 32, 33, 34, 35, 37, 39, 55, 56, 57, 59, 66, 68, 75, 78, 84, 97–8, 101, 112–13, 125, 129n7
France, J.I., US senator 96, 102, 103, 105
Francis, D.R., US diplomat 8, 9, 130n17
Fuchs [Fuks], M.B., historian 46

Gardner, L.C., historian 45
Gary, E.H., Judge, industrialist 26
Gas 20, 31, 32
Geddes, Sir A., British diplomat 1, 2, 112, 129n2
Genoa Conference 58, 105, 108, 109, 110–15, 118, 126, 127, 128
Georgia 11, 114
Germany 1, 9, 10, 11, 14, 19, 25, 29, 41, 42, 54, 55, 56, 63, 66, 68, 69, 75, 97, 111, 113, 123, 128

Index   153

Goldin, V.I., historian 13
Goldstein, E., historian 27
Gompers, S., AF of L leader 105
Goodrich, J.P., Indiana governor, US senator 68, 96
Gorky, M., Russian writer 51, 69
Goto, Baron, Japanese diplomat 123
Graves, US Major 95, 104
Graves, W.S., US General 9, 11, 95, 104, 105
Great Lakes 25
Greenberg, US businessman 88
Grodekovo 83
Guam 28
Gumberg, A., FER delegation secretary 94, 97

Hague Peace Conferences 25, 26
Haiti 100
Hamilton, A., US statesman 48
Hammer, A., businessman 96
Hangkow 39
Harbin 14, 37, 89, 116
Hard, W., journalist 95
Harding, journalist 103
Harding, W.G., US President 1, 3, 26, 56, 74, 94, 99, 101, 125
Harrison, Miss, journalist 103
Haskell, Colonel W.N., US ARA chief 71
Hawaiian islands 33, 43
Hay, J., US Secretary of State 13, 49
Hitchcock, US senator 98
Hobson, J.A., British publicist 49, 50
Hong Kong 33
Hoover, H., US Secretary of Commerce 6, 11, 68, 69, 70, 71, 95, 96, 105, 127, 140n63
Horvath, White general 6
Hughes, C.E., US Secretary of State 1, 2, 3, 5, 20, 26, 27, 29, 31, 34, 35, 36, 37, 41, 51-2, 69, 89, 92, 93, 94, 95, 96, 97, 98, 99, 103, 104, 105, 109, 112, 116, 119, 120, 126, 127, 134n50, 136-7n10
Hughes, US official 95
Hunchun 36
Huntington, S.P., political scientist 23
Hurd, A., journalist 125, 126, 144n87

Ianson, Ia. D., FER diplomat 89, 91, 92, 93, 103, 104, 106, 107, 108, 117, 141n11
Iazikov, A.A., second FER Foreign Minister 34, 94, 97, 99, 103, 109, 140n63
Ichihashi, Y., historian 45
India 9, 16, 19, 56, 57, 58, 126, 131n40
Indochina 57, 60
International Financial Consortium 40

Ioffe, A.A., Soviet diplomat 117, 118, 119, 120, 121, 122, 123, 124, 140-1n67
Ireland 9
Iriye, Akira, historian 125
Irkutsk 57
Ishii, K., Japanese Foreign Minister 76, 143n45
Italy 3, 7, 8, 21, 28, 29, 30, 32, 33, 37, 125, 129n7
Iurin, I.L., first FER Foreign Minister 86, 88, 89, 93

Jameson, US official 95
Japanese Colonial Conference 18
Java 58
Joffre, Marshal 103, 140-1n67
Johnson, H., US senator 98

Kalmykov, I, White ataman 80
Kamchatka 14, 16, 131n44
Kappel, V., White general 18, 83
Karakhan, L.M., Soviet diplomat 86, 91, 92, 106, 107, 108, 117, 118
Karavaev, P.N., FER official 94
Katayama Sen, Japanese member of Comintern 57, 59, 60
Kato, Baron T., Japanese admiral 29
Kawakami, Japanese diplomat 123
Kerensky, A.F., Russian Provisional Government Prime Minister 92
Khabarovsk 80, 92, 106
Kiaochow 41
Kirchwey, Miss F., journalist 103
K-O see Okulitch
Kobe 89
Kolchak, A.V., White 'Supreme Ruler' 9, 11, 12, 13, 18, 36, 69, 72, 79, 80, 92, 95, 115, 141-2n11
Korea 14, 16, 19, 36, 56, 57, 58, 59, 60, 75, 76, 78, 102, 124, 136n19
Kozhevnikov, I.L., FER diplomat 90
Krasnoshchekov, A.M., FER President 74, 89, 92, 139n43
Kuno, Y.S., historian 131n36
Kuomintang 124
Kurile islands 33

LaFeber, W., historian vii, ix, 15, 40, 68, 77, 115
Langdon, W.H., US naval officer 16
Lansing, R., US Secretary of State 8, 9, 68, 76
Lansing-Ishi agreement 76
Latin America 13, 15, 26
Latvia 12, 67, 94, 115
Lausanne Conference 114-15

154 Index

League of Nations 1, 3, 9, 11, 20, 44, 50, 54, 63, 112
Lee, A., Lord, British admiral 27
Lenin, V.I., Chairman of Sovnarkom 7, 12, 17, 28, 49, 50, 52, 53, 61, 63, 69, 70, 71, 78, 79, 111, 131n43, n44, 137n30, 139n20
Lensen, G.A., historian 75, 90
Leonardi, US official 95
Liaotung peninsula 75
Libbey, J.K., historian 94
Lithuania 12, 67, 94, 115
Little, journalist 103
Litvinov, M., Soviet diplomat 10, 105
Lively, D.O., American Red Cross official 88
Lloyd George, D., British Prime Minister 2, 10, 53, 59, 111, 112, 113, 118, 143n43
Lodge, H.C., US senator 96
Loo Choo islands 33
Lozovsky, A., Secretary of Profintern (Trade Union International) 57

McKinley, W.B., US senator 98, 99
Macmurray, US official 95
Manchuria 14, 37, 38, 39, 40, 75, 76, 82, 87, 98, 100, 116
Mariana islands 32
Markhlevsky, Iu., Soviet diplomat 91, 93, 107
Marshall islands 16
Martens, L.C.A.K., Soviet diplomat 6, 12
Matsudaira, Japanese diplomat 117, 118, 119, 120, 121
Matsushima, Japanese diplomat 90, 91, 117, 120
May, E.R., historian 22, 23, 45, 132n60
Mayer, A.J., historian vii, 21
Merkulov, S., White leader 87, 91, 92, 97, 103, 108, 115
Micronesia 33
Miles, B., US official 94
Miliukov, P.N., Russian historian and politician 5, 6, 98
Mining 17, 108, 123
Mongolia 38, 39, 40, 46, 58, 59, 60, 75, 78, 86, 87, 100, 124, 136n19, 140n60
Mongolian invasion 17
Monroe, J., US President 14
Morgan, J.P., financier 94
Morits, C., journalist 95
Morrow, colonel 104
Moscow 57
Moses, G.H., US senator 99
Murmansk 8

Nansen, Dr F., Norwegian Foreign Minister 69
Navies 28, 29, 30, 32, 125, 132–3n9; *see also* Aircraft carriers, Capital ships, Submarines
Netherlands 34, 39, 43, 129n7
Nevinson, H.W., journalist 95, 97, 98
New Economic Policy 53–4, 64, 91
Newton, W.T., journalist 103
New Zealand 33
Nicaragua 28, 100
Nicholas I, tsar 49
Nicholas II, tsar 25, 26
Nicolson, H., British diplomat 51
Nikolaeva, member of Comintern 60
Nikolaevsk 36, 81, 82, 86, 90, 91, 92, 93, 96, 108, 116, 117, 119, 120, 123
Nikol'sk 18, 119
Norris, G.W., US senator 104
Novonikolaevsk [Novosibirsk] 78

OGPU, secret police 106
Oil 17, 110, 123
Oka river 79
Okulitch, J.K., White leader 104, 142n12
Okuma, Count S., Japanese Prime Minister 18

Pacific Isles 60
Pacific Steamship Company 105
Pak-Kieng, Korean delegate to Comintern 58
Palmerston, Lord, British statesman 66
Panama Canal 28, 33
Pan-Germanism 19
Pan-Slavism 19
Paris Peace Conference vii, 10, 20, 52, 53, 69, 127
Patenaude, B.M., historian 72
Pavlovich, V.M., Soviet orientalist 53
Peffer, N., journalist 94
Peking 39, 94, 124
Persia 53, 126
Persius, L., German naval captain 25
Pescadores 33
Peter the Great 110
Petrograd 57
Petrov, Dr F.N., FER official 90, 92, 107, 142n26
Philippines 9, 32, 57, 58
Phillips, US official 119
Phillips, W.A., historian 49
Pitkin, professor 103
Pokrovsky, M.N., historian 23
Poland 12, 52, 53, 60, 65, 66, 110, 115, 128

Index   155

Polk, F.L., US acting Secretary of State 7
Poole, D.C., US official 9, 10, 95, 116, 119, 120, 130n20, 136n24, 140n66
Popova, E.I., historian 23, 24, 43, 44, 45
Port Arthur 4, 14, 75
Porto Rico 58
Portugal 39
Prinkipo, 10, 12
Pusey, M.J., historian 52, 112

Rabinov, businessman 96
Race, racism 2, 18, 98–9, 102, 134n50
Radek, K., Comintern official 125, 126
Railways 20, 40, 43; *see also* Chinese Eastern, South Manchurian, Trans-Siberian, Ussuri
Rapallo treaty 113, 123
Red Cross 9, 88, 94
Red Scare 13
Reed, J.A., US senator 102
Reinsch, Dr P.S., US diplomat 96, 103
Riga 70
Riga treaty 132n60
Robins, R., social reformer, diplomat 63, 94, 103, 105
Robinson, J.T., US senator 102, 103
Romania 60, 113
Roosevelt, T., Jr, US Assistant Secretary of Navy 27
Root, E., US statesman 6, 40, 130n13, 134n36
Rosen, Baron, Russian publicist 19
Roy, Indian member of Young Communist International 58
Rozanov, White general 80
Rush–Bagot Agreement 25
Russia, Provisional governmment 6, 67, 94, 104–5
Russia, Tsarist 1, 5, 49, 52, 66, 67, 75–6, 112; *see* Debts, European
Russian Civil War 9, 13, 52, 122, 130n23, 137n30
Russian Constituent Assembly 5
Russo-Japanese war 17, 18, 19, 66, 76

Saburi, Japanese diplomat 120
Saforov, G., Chairman of Comintern 60
Sakhalin 14, 36, 37, 76, 81, 82, 90, 92, 93, 96, 100, 101, 108, 110, 116, 119, 120, 123
San Domingo 15, 100
Sao-ke Sze, Chinese official 39
Sarraut, A., French official 31, 35
Sato, Japanese general 17
Schanzer, C., Italian statesman 29
Schiller, spokesman for Young Communist International 58

Schurman, J.G., US diplomat 93, 94
Schwab, C.M., industrialist 26
Second International 53
Semenov, G.M., White ataman 35, 36, 80, 81, 82, 86, 87, 89, 97, 104, 105
Sèvres Treaty 21
Shantung 14, 41, 42, 76, 98, 101
Shidehara, Baron K., Japanese diplomat 12, 35, 36, 37, 40, 41, 99
Shimada, Japanese diplomat 90
Shortridge, S.M., US senator 98
Siberia 75, 77, 78, 80, 85, 86, 88, 89, 90, 97, 98, 100–1
Sidorov, A.Iu., historian 23, 24, 46
Siegel, K.A.S., historian 96
Simpson, Dutch delegate to Comintern 58
Sinclair Company 105, 120
Singapore 33, 43, 126, 144n87
Skvirsky, B.E., FER official 94, 98, 102, 103, 104, 106, 119, 120
Smirnov, N.N., Chairman of Sibrevkom 79
Smith, C.H., engineer 95, 98, 104
Smuts, General J.G., South African Prime Minister 2
South Africa 55
South Manchurian Railway 117
Soviet Information Bureau 106
Spain 14, 113
Spargo, J., US publicist 64–8, 69, 137n30
Spassk 119, 122
Stalin, J.V., General Secretary of the CPSU 49, 72, 122
Submarines 20, 22, 28, 31, 32, 97
Suez Canal 56
Sullivan, M., journalist 27
Sun Yat-sen, Chinese President 16, 124, 125
Sungari River 90
Sutherland, G., ex-US senator 98, 99

Tachibana, Japanese general 17
Tanaka Bunichiro, Japanese diplomat 110, 121
Tao, Chinese delegate to Comintern 58
Tariffs 15, 20, 42, 115; *see also* Fordney–McCumber tariff
Thomas, E.B., US diplomat 89, 142n24
Thompson, J.M., historian vii
Thompson, W.B., US official 94
Tibet 19
Timber *see* Forestry
Toinet, French publicist 26
Toynbee, A., historian 115
Transcaucasia 11, 12, 122, 130n31

156 *Index*

Trans-Siberian Railway 7, 8, 9, 12, 37, 38, 78
Trianon treaty 60
Trotsky, L.D., Soviet commissar 7, 8, 46, 54, 61, 63, 69, 79, 106, 130n14
Tsipkin, Iu. N., historian 127
Turkey 1, 10, 53, 126
Twenty-One Demands 39, 40, 76

Uchida, Yasuya, Japanese Foreign Minister 107, 108, 109, 121
Uesugi, Dr Shinkichi 138n4
Ukraine 11, 12, 60, 130n31
Umfrid, O., pastor 25
Ungern Sternberg, Baron, White general 86, 87
Union of Democratic Control 50
Urga [Ulan-Bator] 86
Ussuri Railway 78, 83
Uvarov, Count, Russian statesman 49

Vanderlip, W.B., US businessman 16, 17, 131n44
Verkhne-Udinsk [Ulan-Ude] 80, 81, 86
Versailles treaty 1, 2, 21, 22, 26, 33, 44, 50, 54, 57, 59, 60
Vinson, J.C., historian 27, 45
Vladivostok 4, 8, 9, 12, 14, 16, 18, 35, 37, 58, 67, 76, 77, 79, 80, 81, 82, 85, 90, 91, 92, 100, 103, 108, 109, 115–16, 119, 122, 140n66
Volga river 9, 70
Vologda 8

Wang Chonghui, Chief Justice, Chinese official 40
Warren, US diplomat 92, 108, 116
Watson, T.E., US senator 102
Wehberg, Dr H., historian 25, 26
Wei-hai-Wei 39, 41, 42
Wester-Wemyss, Sir R., British admiral 125
White, S., historian 115
Williams, W.A., historian 72
Willis, F.B., US senator 98, 99
Willoughby, W.W., adviser to China 38, 39
Wilson, W., US President 1, 3, 5, 7, 8, 9, 10, 11, 12, 13, 26, 44, 49, 50, 53, 67, 94, 95, 118, 130n28; Fourteen Points 7, 10, 11, 50, 67, 84, 95
Wong, Chinese delegate to Comintern 58
Wood, J., journalist 95
Wrangel, Baron P.N., White general 85, 97, 98, 107, 140n66, 141–2n11

Yap 2, 59, 102
Yen, Chinese official 96
YMCA 9
Yodoshu, Chinese delegate to Comintern 59
Yoodzu, Japanese delegate to Comintern 57
Yourin *see* Iurin

Zinoviev, G.E., President of Comintern 57, 58, 59, 60, 62, 70